THE UNEXPECTED
JOURNEY OF CARING

THE UNEXPECTED
JOURNEY OF CARING

The Transformation from
Loved One to Caregiver

DONNA THOMSON
ZACHARY WHITE, PHD

Foreword by Judy Woodruff

ROWMAN & LITTLEFIELD
Lanham • Boulder • New York • London

Published by Rowman & Littlefield
An imprint of The Rowman & Littlefield Publishing Group, Inc.
4501 Forbes Boulevard, Suite 200, Lanham, Maryland 20706
www.rowman.com

6 Tinworth Street, London SE11 5AL, United Kingdom

British Library Cataloguing in Publication Information Available

Library of Congress Cataloging-in-Publication Data

Names: Thomson, Donna, 1955– author. | White, Zachary, author.
Title: The unexpected journey of caring : the transformation from loved one
    to caregiver / Donna Thomson and Zachary White.
Description: Lanham : Rowman & Littlefield, [2019] | Includes bibliographical
    references and index. |
Identifiers: LCCN 2018048801 (print) | LCCN 2018049535 (ebook) | ISBN
    9781538122242 (Electronic) | ISBN 9781538122235 (cloth : alk. paper)
Subjects: | MESH: Caregivers—psychology | Home Nursing—methods |
    Social Support
Classification: LCC RA645.3 (ebook) | LCC RA645.3 (print) | NLM WY
    200 | DDC 362.0425—dc23
LC record available at https://lccn.loc.gov/2018048801

♾™ The paper used in this publication meets the minimum requirements of
American National Standard for Information Sciences—Permanence of Paper
for Printed Library Materials, ANSI/NISO Z39.48-1992.

Printed in the United States of America

CONTENTS

FOREWORD
BY JUDY WOODRUFF

In my public life, I'm a news hound, asking questions every day, trying to get to the bottom of developments in Washington, around the country, and the world, that affect all of our lives.[1] In my personal life, when we're lucky enough to have extended visits with our older son, I'm a caregiver. Jeffrey has an array of disabilities that mean he needs help with almost all activities of daily living. We talk nonstop, laugh together, get angry and impatient at times, but our bond is unbreakable. Caring for him has enriched my life in ways I never dreamed possible. That care, now part-time, on the heels of more regular care when he was younger and lived with us, has ingrained in me the value of those who do this work, unheralded and mostly invisible.

They are this country's silent army. Approximately forty-five million Americans have provided unpaid care to an adult or child in the past year:[2] mothers and sometimes fathers of young children, daughters and sons of aging parents, wives and husbands of ailing spouses, and parents of children with medical problems or chronic conditions. They are saints in our midst. The work they do every day, and often through the night, unappealing and often physically hard, is vital to the survival of their loved ones. The care they provide makes it possible for their family members to carry on, to function in as normal a manner as possible, to "fit in" to the demands society places on all of us.

This book is meant for those caregivers, aimed at helping them understand they're not alone, providing them with reminders that the range of emotions they feel is entirely normal, and giving them valuable tools to put their experiences in perspective. Donna Thomson and Zachary White draw from their own decades of studying and writing about caregiving to help those mothers, daughters, sons, husbands, and others who end up in these roles with little or no warning or preparation. Perhaps one day they woke up and realized this was an invitation they couldn't refuse. Or maybe they've been living the caregiver role for years and are just now ready to think about what it means.

Wherever you are in your own caregiving experience, there is something to learn here to help you: to relate to other caregivers, to accept both the ups and downs of the daily routine, to search for support in your community, and, when you're ready, to advocate successfully for the needs of caregivers with no voice of their own. In other words, it's an opportunity for caregivers to reach out and help one another. And it's a welcome basket of ideas, perspectives and advice to get you through tonight, tomorrow, and beyond.

INTRODUCTION

A new caregiver is like a driver in a foreign land. The vehicle is a stick shift, the terrain is mountainous with many switchbacks, and there are no maps, timetables, or rest stops. A catastrophic event or diagnosis catapults a caregiver into a territory that is poorly lit and offers up no familiar landmarks. The roads in this new world are all one-way, careening toward a new normal. There is no going back.

Fear, confusion, self-doubt, and almost unendurable worry swirl to make the first days of sudden-onset caregiving a blur. At this stage, it's difficult to retain information or to make important decisions. A future that was once so sure and so carefully planned is suddenly random, chaotic, and completely unknowable.

There are a few basic truths that reveal themselves in almost every story of the early days of giving care to someone with a serious illness, disability, or life-threatening effects of aging. The first is that love remains intact. Looking into the eyes of a loved one and touching her hand is the beginning of resolve to harness love as the fuel for building a new kind of future together.[1] When it melds with need, the power of love cannot be overestimated in healing the hearts and minds of families. It is the single most important ingredient in locating the path forward and the strength to walk it.

The second truth is that in caregiving, time slows down. As matters of a *before-caregiving* life cease to be important, a sensation of powerlessness will likely invade the caregiver psyche. Survivors of automobile accidents often describe the sensation of time slowing down when recounting their experience of a traumatic and life-changing event. This is a deeply human response to extreme fear and anxiety, and it's a helpful one for caregiver self-preservation.

A new caregiver will have many, many questions. But there are a few that are vital to ask in the early days: "Can I do this alone?" "Who will help me?" At first, identifying one friend or key ally who will promise to make personal support a priority will be a big first step toward positive action and healing in the caregiving family. Building a coordinated team of support will come later, but at first, securing a commitment of abiding friendship from a single support person is enough.

As days, weeks, and years pass, the caregiver is slowly transformed. If the need for care grows incrementally, it may seem that at first, each helping task is perfectly doable. But taken together and over time, the burden of care may become overwhelming. This is especially true in the case of degenerative disease combined with the caregiver's own aging and life or work responsibilities.

To survive long-term caring, a rearrangement of priorities is required, a coming to grips, a reconciliation of personal goals, a "settling in" to care. But sometimes there are natural barriers to making peace with caregiving. Caregivers may engage in a battle of priorities, culminating in making enemies of both work and home. They may crave multiple social connections and the consoling "noise" of an independent and bustling working life.

Does being "settled in" to a caring role represent liberation or captivity? Being in the right place, doing the right thing is natural for young parents caring for their children. But what of an older parent caring for an adult child with disabilities? What about the kind of parental care that feels like a role reversal in the case of Alzheimer's? At the start of a care journey, a caregiver might strive to finish caring tasks quickly in order to return to "normal" life. But with the passing of weeks and months spent in an intimate relationship with a loved one who is ill or infirm, time shifts, and the disorientation of the caregiver role is injected with routine that temporarily silences the chaos. Yet, amid the routine, ongoing tensions emerge that mark the caregiver role as infused with contradictory needs and desires.

On the one hand, a caregiver may stop wishing to be somewhere else. Being alone with a loved one can morph into a natural way to be. Then, a caregiver notices that the slowness and quiet of caring is in itself a presence, not an absence. Settling *for* the reduced ambitions of caring for a loved one opens a door to a life rich with humanity and meaning, but also a life that is difficult to explain to others—a life others say they admire but stop short of walking toward out of fear and misunderstanding.

Of course not everyone falls into a taxing but intimate rhythm of caring. If a loved one is suffering, the call to care can be a call to battle against pain and exhaustion. But in the absence of anguish, caring can become a quiet truce in a land that is foreign to most other people. Here, there is the possibility of intimacy, of reflecting on hopes, dreams, and mortality. Here, there is the chance to be grateful for small joys and tender mercies. And with this enhanced connection, there is an unprecedented proximity to suffering, fear, grief, and doubt that few others know (or want to know). The true wisdom of caregiving lies in realizing that the meaning of care cannot be delayed until "it" is over because care changes us and our loved ones throughout the process. Caregivers can't help but realize that their control of *what* happens is limited, but what they can affect is how they make sense of their experiences and how they use these stories to connect to others along the way. And even if these insights and wisdom are not present because home is too chaotic to experience stillness, caregivers will learn the meaning of forbearance—the essential ingredient in being able to proclaim with certainty, "I'm glad I stayed and did the right thing."

Our goal isn't to tell caregivers what they should feel or think about their care experiences. Rather than present clichés or top tips, we wrote this book to provide readers with tools for self-understanding and glimpses of possibility that do not deny the breadth, scope, and uniqueness of anyone's particular caregiver realities. Caregivers are experts about their own particular situations. What follows is an exploration of the common and recurring ways in which anyone who cares for another is transformed over time by the role they have taken.

Caregivers will no doubt insert themselves into the transformation stories in the following chapters, but allied health professionals may find new understanding of their caregiving clients there, too. Conversations between caring families, friends, and health professionals may be enriched and informed by the truths revealed in this book so that they may share stories and experiences that have existed in the shadows far too long.

This book is an exploration of what happens to us when we stay, when we care, when we turn toward—not away—from our loved ones, and how deep care for another transforms us and our relationships.

Donna Thomson and Zachary White, PhD

1

I'M (NOT) A CAREGIVER

You have a choice before you. In one room, you can listen to someone speak about how to develop executive leadership and presence. In another room, you can listen to someone talk about caregiving. Which room do you think most people will walk into? Which speaker do you think most people want to hear from?

Who doesn't want to be a leader? Contacts can be made. Tips can be gleaned. Business cards can be exchanged. Ladders of success can be climbed. Leadership is aspirational—it provides a clear direction toward something better in the future. Growing. Learning. Evolving. In this room, promotion, advancement, and opportunity are possible and seemingly within reach.

Who wants to learn about caregiving? The reality is that few people will volunteer to come into this room. Caregiving doesn't get you close to people you want to meet. And there's no ladder to advancement anywhere to be seen. Growing? Learning? Evolving? Really?

The label "caregiver" is charged with all kinds of meaning because it signifies so many different things to people. Whatever you call it—informal caregiving, unpaid caregiving, intense caregiving, total caregiving, extreme caregiving, caretaker, carer, chronic caregiver, care partner—few want to give themselves over to this identity and all that it implies.[1] And it's not because they don't want to care for someone they love or because they're not caring. The term *caregiver* is considered stifling and suffocating because few of us want to find ourselves trapped within the confines of this constrictive label. It doesn't breathe. It's too hot. It doesn't allow you to be who you want to be. It doesn't appear to look good on you, nor does it have the look you expected. Although caregiving is becoming an increasingly common

1

and necessary part of life,[2] why are so many people reluctant to self-identify as caregivers?

"No, not me. I'm not a caregiver."

Most caregivers are loved ones who provide, on average, twenty-four hours a week of unpaid care.[3] Yet the one role most of us will assume at some point in our lives—whether we want to or not—has no deliberate onboarding or socialization process, making it difficult to prepare for caregiving or to even know when the role begins.

Unlike most other roles in life, people don't dream about caregiving. They—we—don't preemptively think about what this experience will look like, how it will change us, what it will ask of us, or how it will impact our existing relationships. In the quiet moments of life, there is little motive to collectively talk about care at the dinner table or with family and friends. Discussions only seem to make it into our everyday conversations when accompanied by caregiving's silent partner: urgency. We anticipate and talk about all kinds of relationships—romantic, friendship, parent-child, spousal—but caregiving seems to come at us unexpectedly, leaving us perpetually off balance. Typically, one person is designated (or drafted) to attend to all things care related—personal, emotional, financial, legal, and medical, as well as issues of companionship, transportation, food, shelter, and safety—even though the idea of *a* caregiver mistakenly reinforces the belief that care is an individual task rather than a collective enterprise.[4]

"I'm not really a caregiver; that's for professionals."

Too often, we tell ourselves and others that we aren't caregivers because the title "caregiver" means you must have special training and fancy titles after your name. Formal roles have acronyms—MD, RN, LPN, PhD, JD, LCN, LCSW, PSW—constantly informing people of their legitimacy, purpose, and usefulness. Informal, family-based, and nonpaid roles like caregiving, however, are often invisible because there are no performance reviews or accreditations reminding others that what is happening is real and important. Without the legitimacy of role formality, caregivers are left without needed guidance and direction along their journey.

Medical professionals, like doctors and nurses, have an inherent advantage over caregivers when it comes to role legitimacy. Through years of exhaustive dedication, they have earned two magical letters that follow their names—MD or RN. The credentials that accompany their names give patients and family members permission to know that, amid the uncertainty of physical pain or suffering, someone is different enough from them—in education, training, expertise, experience—to possess the possibility of answers and relief.

Informal caregivers are rarely, if ever, considered experts by family and friends. They may be thought of as caring and loving, yet because caregivers are familiar, they aren't considered and treated as experts. Consequently, what caregivers say is typically interpreted as a hint or a suggestion, not something that should be written down. Since most caregivers don't have formal credentials following their names, no matter how much time and effort is dedicated to the caregiver role, others may feel empowered to critique, question, and sometimes oppose what caregivers say because it is performed by people who are intimately known by family and friends, not experts. Medical professionals have medical opinions. Because they are family, caregivers' concerns and support needs are often discounted simply because they share a common history.[5]

But there's something more that separates professional caregivers from informal caregivers. When someone walks into the waiting room in a doctor's office, they have already accepted the physician's and nurse's credibility. People make appointments, in advance, to see a doctor or nurse. They dress up, in advance, knowing they will be seen in public. They typically drive to see a doctor. They patiently wait, in a waiting room, because these efforts (and hassles) are believed to be worth the benefit of finding answers. Appreciation and respect almost always follow such sacrifices.

For caregivers, their turf is in the private context of the home. Everyone is welcome in the private space of caregiving. There is no waiting time. No appointments have to be made to see you. Accessibility and familiarity shape how caregivers are received by others. Too often, caregiving is undervalued because care occurs beyond other's awareness and appreciation: before and after "official" spaces of care, before and after diagnoses, when others aren't looking, when others are sleeping, when cures and answers are elusive and impossible, when others don't know what's going on, and when it appears that others don't care what's happening.

"I'm just doing what I can. I'm not doing anything special."

Although there are caregivers next door, down the street, and in the next cubicle, caregiver experiences often go unnoticed because there are no public ways of acknowledging their efforts. Days, months, or even years may pass without anyone paying any special attention. Few will recognize their years of service, effort, impact, performance, or capacity because there is no special hierarchy differentiating one caregiver from the next. Unlike almost any other relationship, there are ostensibly no discernible stages or turning points in a caregiver relationship. And unlike almost any other type of formal role, there are no promotions, annual reviews, accolades, or opportunities for feedback.

Parents, relatives, and friends won't be able to brag about your experiences. There are no "schools" of informal caregiving—no Harvard or Stanford to use as a guiding goal from which others can respect and admire. Others may speak highly of you and your efforts, but it begins and ends there. There is nothing for outsiders to use to show their support of your value—no jerseys to buy that bind you to another through shared identification, no bumper sticker that highlights your efforts, no stock market of care that would legitimate your endeavors, and no alumni network that focuses people's attention to your ongoing caregiver challenges.

"I'm different from other caregivers."

Because the label "caregiver" is so vague and broad, it becomes a way in which people can assert uniqueness in articulating why they're *not* caregivers. The label is so deceptive because it makes everyone it approaches feel as if they are different from others, thereby excluding any benefits of being a part of such a group of people who may share similar needs, challenges, and experiences. Resisting the label of caregiver is a way of refusing an identity that they don't want, don't feel they would fit into, or don't believe relates to their situation; or they are uncertain what calling themselves a "caregiver" might mean to them and those closest to them.[6] This resistance has many forms.

"I'm too young to be a caregiver."

The need for care, or caregiving, doesn't concern itself with where you are in life,[7] what you are doing, what you had planned on doing, what you thought you would become, or what others thought you should be doing. It will never respect that you may not feel ready for such responsibilities. Caregiving is never timely. It's always intrusive, finding you when it's most inconvenient. The needs of care call out to you when you least expect your life to be upended. A parent's cancer diagnosis doesn't care that you are a freshman in college. A child's disability has no interest in the fact that your parenting role will be different than you ever imagined. A spouse's diagnosis pays little attention to the ways you envisioned your partnership. A mother-in-law's dementia doesn't consider the fact that you did not budget for both her ongoing care needs and your children's college tuition. Simply put, caregiving is an equal-opportunity life changer as young, old, and older are finding themselves being called upon in ways that they may not have expected, even though the need for care is growing at an ever-increasing pace.[8] No generation is unaffected, as it doesn't matter if you are a baby boomer, Gen Xer, or millennial. Care needs come at you when you least want them, expect them, or think you can handle them.

"I work, I don't have the luxury of calling myself a caregiver."

Too many people believe someone is *either* a caregiver *or* not a caregiver. In the twenty-first century, either-or labels don't reflect the changing landscape that requires us to be simultaneously employees *and* caregivers, working *and* caring. Caregiving isn't a women's problem or a men's problem, as men and women are equally likely to be caregivers.[9] Rather, it's an ongoing challenge that requires constantly negotiating the various parts of our selves, relationships, and responsibilities. When a majority of working caregivers experience work-related impacts as a result of their dual working-caregiver roles,[10] declaring *"I am a caregiver"* is neither a comprehensive nor accurate statement. You are a caregiver *and* you are also something else. No one has the luxury of being *only* a caregiver. For some of us, that *something else* is a formal job we go to every day that often takes us far away from the person we want to care for. But we have to go regardless. For some of us, that *something else* is an informal set of obligations and duties that never stop piling up. For all of us, caregiving exists within already existing relationships and obligations. In a world with bills, contracts, expectations, mortgage payments, passions, desires, and ongoing relationships, no one can specialize only in caregiving.

"It's not like what I'm experiencing as a caregiver is an emergency."

We unquestionably pull over for emergency vehicles as they race by, sirens blaring, lights flashing to rescue and help someone in need. Yet, at the same time, the ritualized appreciation of acute emergencies has also desensitized us to challenges that too often remain in the shadows, discarded not by intention but because chronic challenges of care don't fit in a culture that recognizes acute emergencies but little else.

Physical emergencies call for immediate action. People plan for and respond to emergencies in unison. There are drills. Response teams strategize about who might be called and where they will meet. Emergencies call us all into action—out of our everyday routine and into a response mode that is singularly focused. Chronic care and relational needs, on the other hand, just don't work that way. Everyday needs are messy and ambiguous.

Caregivers don't have sirens. But if they did, they would probably be told to turn them off because caregiver concerns don't have clear beginning and ending points. Instead, they linger, taking their own time, disrupting lives in ways that defy speed and closure and containment. Most of us respect the nature of emergencies by *getting out of the way* so that professionals can do their thing. Flashing lights and screaming sirens don't accompany chronic needs. No one pulls over for them. Between what others call emergencies and the ongoing challenges of caregiving, titles such as "caregiver" may only be hinted at.

THE MOMENT YOU REALIZE SOMETHING HAS CHANGED

Despite what you call yourself, or whether you acknowledge you are a caregiver, there is a moment. The moment when you can't escape the realization that life as it once was will never be the same. The moment the permanence of a loved one's diagnosis becomes real. The moment a loved one can no longer remember your name. The moment you realize that no matter what you do, a cure won't be possible. The moment you are reminded that it is you, and you alone, who are responsible for complete and ongoing care. Even before others notice, you may begin mourning for what can never be, as others around you keep going and moving while your world no longer makes sense. Even though you may look and sound the same to others, you are not. You can't be.

The safety net of habit and routine is replaced by a heightened sense that life is fragile and unpredictable. It's as if you find yourself walking on a tightrope without a net. And the scariest part is that you may have been living all this time without a net but had never noticed until now. But now that you do notice, you can't unlearn what you know and return to life as it once was. Every caregiving experience is different, but behind every caregiver story is a moment—a moment when you realize that the care and love you are called to provide can't help but change you in every way possible.

A NEW WAY OF SEEING AND BEING

Personal transformation is usually an experience we actively seek out—not one that hunts us down. In the twenty-first century, becoming a caregiver is a transformation that comes at us, requiring us to rethink everything we once knew. When a loved one becomes a caregiver, everything changes—responsibilities, beliefs, hopes, expectations, and relationships. "Being" a caregiver is not something most people think about or dream about, let alone prepare for, because this role and relationship seemingly defies understanding. Rarely, if ever, will you hear caregivers speak of themselves as a class or group. Caregivers don't allow themselves the privilege and comfort of the "we" because there is no union of caregivers, simply a legion of "I's" doing and being and serving. Not seeing ourselves as part of something larger than our own individual experiences comes at a cost.

Making It Personal

My mother is feisty and intensely proud. She has no time for institutions or rules and never turned down an invitation for dinner or a party. When she began to show signs of memory loss and severe anxiety in the early evenings, I asked Mom's family physician for a referral to a geriatric psychiatrist.

On the day of the appointment, we introduced ourselves to the doctor. "Are you the caregiver?" he asked me. "Oh no! Oh no, no, no. I'm the daughter," I laughed nervously. I glanced at Mom. She was staring at me, stone-faced. Then she put her hand on mine.

Over the years since that day, I've learned about that word—caregiver. I've discovered that even though I don't like it, sometimes I have to use it to get the services that our family needs. But I feel like a bad daughter when I do. What really annoys me is reading that services for caregivers exist but very few people have used them because not enough of us "identify as caregivers." Of course we don't! If I told my mom that I was her caregiver, it would be like a betrayal of our mother-daughter relationship and all of our family history of love and loyalty. I don't want to publicly declare my mother's incapacity by calling myself a caregiver. Alzheimer's has stolen enough of my mom's dignity—I don't want to take away even more. She flatly refuses to accept paid help because she says it's "for old people." But of course, she calls me when she needs anything.

I don't think I should be blamed for not accepting services that force me to declare myself a caregiver. We should think of a new word for caregiver, and I shouldn't have to sell out my mom to get the help we need. —Patsy S. (who cares for her mother but does not call herself a "caregiver.")

PREFACE TO CHAPTERS 2–6

Disorientation:
From Loved One to Caregiver

Everyone seeks transformation. To be changed and catapulted into something other than who you are—the better, stronger, fiercer version of yourself. Transformations are always impressive and awe inspiring. But before anyone is transformed, something else has to happen. This isn't the part of the transformational process that most people pay attention to because it's all about what happens *before* others begin noticing how you are different. This is about what happens to you in private—precisely when you are alone in your thoughts while the rest of the world moves on and forward as if nothing is changing.

What is it that happens before anyone can experience transformation?

Disorientation. Look up the word "disorient,"[1] and you'll find that it's the opposite of "enlighten." Who would want to spend time trying to figure out the very aspects of their experiences that are so confusing and messy? Somewhere along our care journey, we will experience disorientation. Like an unexpected attack of vertigo—the world around us is turned upside down, transforming everything we once saw, believed, and expected into something that throws us off balance. Caregiver disorientation is not like a one-time vertigo attack but one that we experience at different times with differing degrees of intensity. Bouts of disorientation can knock us off our feet. They can make us question ourselves and everything we've taken for granted. They can keep us from wanting to get out of bed. And they can make us nauseous—not the kind of nausea most other people think about, though. This kind of nausea can bring us to our knees and can make us feel out of sorts when we close our eyes. It can find us while we are doing what used to bring us great joy and pleasure. And it can even hunt us down when we are with people who used to bring us so much comfort.

If we ignore our inevitable feelings of being overwhelmed, confused, angry, defiant, helpless, and deeply alone, then we are denying vital parts of our experiences that are transforming us. Since caregiving is always different from what we imagined it to be (not that any of us imagined our caregiver role in advance), our disorientation can be deep, intense, and lonely. This book is written to help you begin making sense of the very experiences that transform you throughout your caregiver role. There is no logical progression to these experiences of disorientation because each of our care roles is distinct, based on the type of care we are providing; the circumstances; the quality of our relationship with our loved one; the kind of condition, illness, or life interruption our loved one is enduring; our own care expectations; and the support we feel (or don't feel) from others in our care roles.

Despite these differences, it's important to remember that the reasons for our disorientation aren't just about us. No, disorientation is an inevitable by-product of what happens when care meets love, especially when we can't be prepared for what this role asks us to do and become. Some of us are in the midst of experiencing these transformational moments of disorientation. Others may be trying to make sense of what happened when they provided care for a loved one days, months, and years ago. And some may be anticipating a care role they see coming at them.

Each of the next five chapters explores the reasons *why* the care role can be so disorienting. Each chapter also highlights how these uncomfortable and challenging experiences of disorientation also invite new ways of understanding ourselves and our evolving values and purpose. Perhaps most importantly, the following chapters might just remind us of what connects us as caregivers, because whoever we are and wherever we are in the caregiver process, the road to transformation begins with an understanding of how the caregiver role both takes from us and gives to us in ways we could never have imagined.

2

LIVING IN BETWEEN SCRIPTS

Everyone understands brain cancer. Or, scratch that, everyone understands the kinds of responses that brain cancer requires. Surgery. Chemotherapy. Radiation. Rehabilitation. In the midst of the fight, everyone knows their parts as if each of them has a script instructing them on what to say and how to act. *"We can beat this." "She has so much to live for." "Never, ever give up." "Stand up to the cancer." "Know that you're not alone." "We can beat this—together." "We're praying for your mom. For your entire family."*

But then, something happens in the caregiver journey that turns everything upside down and inside out. Suddenly, your life narrative, or script, no longer makes sense as your story goes in a direction no one thought possible.[1] The story, your loved one's story, your story, the "cure" story you have mapped out in your head, betrays you exactly when what happens isn't what you thought would—or should—happen. When a loved one becomes ill, when a condition is chronic not temporary, when surgery does not work, when an illness isn't diagnosed and suffering continues, when someone you love becomes disabled, when an illness means living with unwelcomed realities rather than overcoming them—everything changes.[2]

It's as if someone steals the script you had been working off your whole life, crosses out all of your lines, your loved one's lines, your friend's lines, and your coworker's lines.[3] You aren't just staring at a blank page—you're staring at a blank page knowing exactly how your story was supposed to unfold. Your script lines weren't just written on a page. You feel as though they were written in you. Even if you wanted to let go of what was lost, you can't forget the lines that felt like reality.

Caregivers don't get to start over with a new script. Whatever our ages, wherever we are in life, we have to rewrite our scripts without any preparation or practice and when we are exhausted and vulnerable. Life and relationship scripts are important because they tell us how we should act, what and who is (un)important, and how we (should) talk to ourselves and respond to others.[4] Whether we know it or not, most of us walk around with a story in our head dependent on structures of meaning that provide coherence.[5] Individual dreams. Accomplishments. Goals. Relationships thought about, dreamed about, and planned. We only realize we have a story with a clear beginning, middle, and end when the story we used to tell and retell no longer works because the very script we so depended on for our story to make sense is taken from us.

Caregiving doesn't just change what you do and how you spend your time; it changes how you think about the very elements that provide your story meaning: your relationship to your future, past, and present.[6] Some people talk about losing their voice. Caregivers often feel as though their voices are taken from them—edited without their control and in ways they never dreamed possible. In the transformation from loved one to caregiver, caregivers can't help but feel disoriented and confused because the script that once made so much sense and seemed so natural now feels inauthentic, unworkable, misleading, and counterproductive in response to the challenges of newfound experiences.

WAVING GOODBYE TO THE FUTURE

The more you deeply care for another person, the more your future disappears. It's not that your future actually disappears, but how you think about the future is irrevocably altered when you become a caregiver (even if you don't call yourself a caregiver yet). Talking about the future is a preoccupation for most people. Think about how much time the people around you devote to thinking, talking, planning, and dreaming about what they plan on doing in an hour, tomorrow, next week, next month, next year, and next decade. On Thursday, we begin thinking about the weekend, and on the weekend, we begin planning for the summer, and in the summer, we begin planning for the holidays.

In the shift from loved one to caregiver, the role of the future in your caregiver script completely changes.[7] For caregivers, thoughts about the future can begin to feel like a kind of betrayal because the future can no longer be assumed to be a desired destination when it is submerged in uncertainty, fear, and anxiety. Caregivers are constantly reminded that the future can't be predicted. Most other people live life as if the future is connected to the present through an unchanging, straight, and permanent line because, it is assumed, tomorrow will be exactly like today. And, if tomorrow is exactly like today, prediction is possible and expected. Caring for a loved one, however, is remarkably humbling because our care constantly reminds us that a loved one's physical condition doesn't care about what we think will (or should) happen in the future. One hour to the next, let alone one day to the next, is filled with uncertainties and anxieties reminding us that prediction can be perilous and wildly inaccurate. For others, what is happening now is almost always viewed a sign of what will happen in the future. For caregivers, what is happening now may not indicate anything other than what is happening now—it is a sign that may signify nothing, despite our deepest desires.

As the ability to predict what will happen next evaporates into the everyday realities of our loved one's physical (in)capacities, how we think about the future can't help but change us. No longer is the future a place where we can project goals, aspirations, and fantasies. No longer is the future simply a means to escape the unpleasantness of the present and to use as motivation to get through the moment. No longer can we bond with friends and coworkers over what is going to happen next, or what we hope will happen tomorrow, or what we plan to do this weekend, or what we will do once we retire. In other people's scripts, the future is the unquestioned protagonist. In the caregiver script, the future is a character that is mysterious and duplicitous, a source of ongoing stress, and a constant reminder that your growing distrust of the future distinguishes you from those whose life scripts are drastically different.

Most people's dreams of the future almost never account for the fragility of life, love, care, illness, disappointment, and rejection. Too often, dreams can't keep up with who we've become. Dreams can be incredibly deceptive because they often omit the messiness and tensions and responsibilities that characterize our everyday relationships. Most people don't dream of loving someone when it's not easy. Who dreams of what life will be like when we love someone who becomes ill? Who dreams of managing the challenges of work and caregiving and children?

Who dreams of being depressed? Who dreams of struggle? Who dreams of bodily interruptions?

The unqualified faith others have in what will happen (often conflating what *will* happen with what they *want* to happen) begins to sound odd, strange, and inauthentic to caregivers whose projections about what will happen are grounded in the realities of their caregiving situation. Caregivers, in particular, are vulnerable to specific script patterns that once made so much sense (pre-caregiving) but now can misguide because of the splintering relationship with the future your care experiences inspire.

"Once this is over, then . . . "   This orientation to the future is based on linear thinking that presupposes complete control of what is to come. This future-based script pattern is a cultural habit stipulating that the present is worthy of enduring because of what it might lead to—graduation, a better job, a salary increase, marriage, and so on. Planned expectations about the future can sometimes be enriching sources of motivation, but this type of belief about the future often belies situations that don't fit with others' beliefs that they can control what happens next. For caregivers, the future may seem so ambiguous or dire that it can become a constant source of distress, an ongoing reminder of expanding powerlessness. Although a control mind-set may "work" for others, it is hazardous for caregivers because it presumes the present situation is worthless except for what it might lead to, thereby exacerbating perceptions of the value of everyday care experiences as meaningless.

"You're next diagnostic will be in . . ."   Schedules are often determined for caregivers—from one test to the next, from one doctor's visit to the next, and from one rehabilitation visit to the next. Next appointments, as guides to the future, are worthy and necessary. Yet providers' appointments for us and our loved ones can also make it more difficult to cope with the never-ending, always-something-more, out-of-control feeling that frequently accompanies prognostic thoroughness. In the process, hopes and expectations can't help but be dragged from one appointment to the next—days, weeks, and months into the future—leaving caregivers with a feeling that peace of mind cannot be achieved until the next appointment, the next confirmation, the next blood test, the next screening, the next second opinion, the next treatment, and the next surgery. Amid a seemingly never-ending waiting game, this future-based script can be deceptive because it implies that peace of mind must be constantly deferred to some future date determined by others.

"We are going to . . ."   Relationships depend on creating a shared future. Relationship participants enhance closeness when they willingly conjure a shared future by communicating shared truths of what they expect and hope will come. *"I will love you today and forever." "I can't wait until we are able to renew our vows." "I like us best when we are able to slow down and enjoy a cup of coffee together." "When we retire, we will travel and see the world together." "We will be such great parents—we will be there for our children when they need us."* Sharing expectations about the future of your relationship is a vital ingredient to closeness and intimacy. For caregivers, however, talking about the future of a relationship may not be possible when illness or incapacity inhibits communicating the "we-ness" that so many others take for granted. Without being able to count on these conversations that project a relationship into the future, the very feelings we have about our relationships (spouse, parent-child, child-parent, sibling, etc.) may be injected with increasing doubt, fear, and separation.

A DIFFERENT KIND OF MEMORY

The more you care for another—the more the past disappears. Once again, the past does not literally disappear, but how caregivers think about the past changes.[8] With the intensive and ongoing focus the caregiver role requires, the meaning of the past changes; it becomes increasingly difficult to find comfort in a past that seems completely divorced from current realities. When caregivers perceive a disconnect between their current situation and what they remember to be "normal," they are more likely to be dissatisfied with the authenticity of their current script. A growing awareness that your current script is becoming incompatible with your pre-caregiver script can make you feel "off" and perpetually unsettled.[9] You may not feel like reading or watching television. You may not feel comfortable with the lights on. But you aren't satisfied when the lights are off. You may not feel like talking but desperately want to feel connected to someone. You are exhausted but can't sleep at night. Feeling "off" may be an unavoidable sign that the script you are living in now no longer fits, and even worse, may be corrosive to your ability to provide quality care for your loved one and yourself.

Part of what makes us human is the capacity to magically transport ourselves into a time and place that makes us feel peaceful and authentic.

Look up any definition of nostalgia,[10] and it will talk about a longing for the past—a kind of eternal homesickness that allows for a return to a time, place, and role that was seemingly simpler. But not all people experience nostalgia in the same way. For most non-caregivers, the past has nostalgia and is meaningful because it can be leaned on for comfort and guidance. This nostalgic script of the past, however, can become a source of newfound angst and disorientation for caregivers, reminding them of everything that is different in their current experiences. Everything that once was, but that is no longer. Everything that once was, but that may not be possible again. Everything that seemingly made so much sense but is now so complicated.

Caregivers don't simply have memories of what has happened—they have memories of what was expected to happen—but can't now—with the person they love and care for. Most people's memories are unidirectional—they flow only in the direction of present to past through the rivers of experience that have already occurred. Caregivers, on the other hand, have a much more expansive view of memories. They don't simply have memories of what has happened because caregiver memories can defy the gravitational laws of memory.[11]

They have ongoing "memories" of what will not or cannot happen. These memories, contrary to what others might believe, are just as vivid, detailed, and poignant as any memory of what has already occurred. They are seen and felt and heard. The difference is that these memories can't be recorded by photographs or appreciated by an audience of others. These memories—future memories—live only in the mind and heart of the individual caregiver. Consequently, caregivers are prone to experiencing not only a homesickness for the past but also "nostalgia" for what can no longer be possible. Grieving over what can no longer happen is a critical challenge of the caregiver script that becomes more flagrant when the memories of what once was and what (should) have been makes you feel like a stranger to yourself.

OVERWHELMED BY THE PRESENT

Most people talk about a desire to "live in the moment." The "now" moment that everyone else talks about wanting to be "in" can overwhelm caregivers.[12] When the typical scripts associated with avoiding, escaping, and enduring the present moment—the future and past—have been irrevocably altered, caregivers can feel overwhelmed by being in the moment in a different way than others.

Common action verbs such as to do, to make, to become, to move, to provide, to change, to lead, to stop, to expect, to decide, and so on, all highlight an unrestricted capacity to act in the world. Non-caregivers unquestionably use verbs to describe how they shape their everyday because they haven't (yet) had to doubt the usefulness of their ability to bring about change. For caregivers, a wavering confidence in their ability to bring about action is a side effect of trying to reconcile a future that seems to come at them unexpectedly—contorting them into feelings of powerlessness. Caregivers act in their world(s), too, but their day-to-day care experiences necessitate a much more nuanced association between themselves as individual subjects—caregivers—and their loved ones. Whereas most people think sickness is only about what happens to one person's body, caregivers' ongoing and repeated exposure to the illness experience reminds them they aren't always in control.

First, only when you spend time with and near those who are sick can you fully appreciate that the body's voice—aches, pains, discomfort, suffering—can't always be ignored. Illness is an ongoing reminder that the body works on its own schedule—not yours. Calendars are typically full of appointments, meetings, and to-do lists based purely on future availability and preference. But a loved one's illness or condition doesn't care what was planned. A loved one's needs can't be postponed. Whether brief or permanent, near-illness experiences invite caregivers to look in the social mirror and see themselves and their capacities differently than they might have ever before. When other people see themselves in the world, their script only allows them to notice the inseparable mirror images of desire *and* change, positive thinking *and* result, cause *and* effect. Spending time near illness means never being able to forget that there are forces at play beyond mere will and desire. Love alone cannot cure bodies—despite our deepest desires to the contrary. Care, up close, inhibits caregivers from believing they can do whatever they want, whenever they want, fracturing trust in their ability to bring about a desired result (e.g., change) regardless of how much they want or need it to happen. When caregivers see themselves in the world, they can't help but begin to notice what others don't see: the desire for something to happen may exist completely apart from a capacity to change a loved one's situation. Positive thinking can exist while also surrounded by suffering. And cause and effect may be a fiction that, in retrospect, seems like a cruel joke.

Second, caregivers are constantly humbled because their experiences teach them that sickness eventually finds us all—regardless of size, strength, income, ethnicity, or background. Humility is not a space most others inhabit on a daily basis. Unlike others, caregivers can't help but witness what most others overlook. Near illness, life appears fragile. Vacations can be canceled. Dreams can be interrupted. Schedules turned upside down. Habits broken. When near the sights and sounds of a loved one's discomforts, caregivers are affected, too—often finding themselves in a state of perpetual unease that inspires a growing unwillingness to declare unqualified verbs of action. While most people talk about the future using the language of unlimited possibility, caregivers may begin to experience a growing distrust in their pre-caregiver script because the future that had once been so precious may now feel like shards of glass, ready to cut if not handled with intricate care and ongoing caution.

Third, caregivers recognize their profound interdependence. Because of caregivers' near-illness experiences, something drastic and disruptive occurs in how they conceive of themselves as subjects. The power of the "I" begins to be revealed for what it camouflages—caregivers are inescapably linked to the people they care about and for. Caregivers comfort their loved ones by providing reassurance that they can close their eyes and know they will not wake up alone. In the process of caring for another in such a profound way, caregivers also need reassurance because they often feel unprotected from the doubts and fears associated with the realization that their "I" can't be neatly separated from the person they care for and about. Their worries can't help but become yours. The "I" and "you" of caregiving can become so interwoven that to untangle one from the other would render both meaningless. People are frequently thought of as sick *or* well, caregiver *or* cared for—exaggerating the differences between our loved ones and us. Over time, caregivers know that illness can't be quarantined in bodies alone because they can't help but see parts of themselves in those they care for, just as your loved ones see themselves in you. Talking about the "I" as if it existed in isolation and distinctly independent—from the influences of others—can't help but begin to seem strange, inauthentic, betraying the taken-for-granted belief that independence is not only possible, but a good to be strived for and celebrated as a sign of empowerment.

The transformation from loved one to caregiver inevitably fractures the scripts that shaped your pre-caregiver understandings of future, past, and present. And once your faith in a script is disrupted, you can't help but change—whether you want to or not.

A NEW WAY OF SEEING AND BEING

When life scripts require rewriting, uncertainty and anxiety can become the new normal.[13] Yet there is also something else that can emerge. In the transformation from loved one to caregiver, shock, anger, disappointment, and disorientation are signs that the script you have depended on for so long will no longer suffice. Amid this disorientation, a new way of seeing and being is possible. Authenticity is a side effect of being open when others have their eyes closed. The irony is that most people think their eyes are wide open, but they can't be when they only have had one script in front of them. Unlike you, they can't know what they don't see. Unlike you, they are only as good as the lines that have been handed to them—the clichéd patterns of thinking and being that they didn't even know were possible to edit and rewrite.

You are in between[14] the scripts of your previous non-caregiver life and the emerging caregiver script. This in-between moment is dizzying and overwhelming. At the same time, you are more aware of yourself, the people around you, and your role in the world than you may have ever been before. It's like moving to a new city. In those first six weeks or so, you are most open to recognizing what locals might miss because they no longer see what is around them. You don't have a set pattern. You are at that rare moment when old habits are passing away, and new ones will soon emerge. Just as in a new city, you are more willing to venture forth without leaning on habit as the sole guide. Because you don't know where you should be or where others expect you to be, at this moment—in between scripts—you are simultaneously the most lost and the most open you may ever be.

The present is where most people *think* they want to be. They constantly talk about wanting to "live in the moment." "Carpe diem!" "Live like every moment is your last." These sayings are inspiring to those who have to constantly remind themselves that life is fleeting. For caregivers, reminders are not necessary. Your care experiences aren't simply reshaping your expectations of the future; they are also reshaping how you live, without depending on the crutch of the future. When you don't dare dream about the future, the present is your only refuge.

Outsiders describe their world as hectic—driving from one event to another, endless work obligations, running errands, getting food on the table, child care responsibilities, vacations, hobbies, and so on. The pace of this script is the same—always fast. Slowing down is considered a weakness. Caregivers, however, must not only operate in a world defined by speed and movement, they must also adjust to the nuanced pace of care. When caring for someone we love, fast is out of tune. Care requires calmness, softness, lowered voices, and intimate spaces. Care's pace isn't defined by how fast something can be done, but by a need to slow the world down. To remember a smile on our loved one's face. To appreciate the rhythm of a loved one's breathing pattern or freeze-frame a moment of shared laughter.

Living in between scripts means that you can reintroduce yourself to the present moment in ways others simply cannot. When someone expects something to happen again, something is lost in translation. The moment is inevitably experienced, only in part, because the expectation that it will happen again inhibits an all-in approach that requires absolute mental, physical, and spiritual attention. In between scripts, your attention has been freed from knowing what it should notice. It is radically open because it is drawn to focus not on what something might mean in the future, but on what exists in that particular, ephemeral, never-to-be replicated moment. When the pre-caregiver future script is punctured by care experiences, there is a unique opportunity to begin rethinking and rewriting how you seek to experience the world. Reintroducing yourself to the moment is a radical shift in orientation that will not translate well to those who are more loyal to a script that positions the present simply as a means to the future.

In the fleeting state of living without a script to guide you, radical openness is possible, and seeing anew is available in ways not previously accessed. When you orient yourself to your everyday as if it will never happen again, what does a sip of coffee taste and smell like? What does a sunrise look like? What does shared laughter between you and your loved one feel like when it deeply reverberates, as if that moment of shared laughter so consumes your attention that nothing else matters?

Others preoccupy themselves with changing the person in front of them—"More of this," "Less of that," You need to do this," "You can't do that." This is called "care" and "love" in most other relationships. But this way of engaging another is built on the belief that care means focusing on who we want (and need) the people we care about to become. In other words, it's almost always dependent on a future-based script that denies the possibility of being with another—fully. In between scripts, you are more open to noticing the person in front of you without the distorted lens of what *could be*. This is an opportunity to realize that when we drop our obsession with seeing what isn't—rather than what is—something emerges that is completely missed by most others. Most people use the word *love* to describe how they feel about another person and how being with that person makes them feel about themselves. This kind of experience with another requires a rethinking of what it means to think about ourselves when we can't necessarily make the person we care for better. Living fully in between scripts means allowing your attention to be directed to the actual realities before you, rather than the endless possibilities of what might be, what could be, and what should be. This radical change in attention doesn't just change how we look at our loved one, it also shapes how we can see ourselves.

If the story of our life in our minds were mapped, we would most intimately know our becoming, future self because the future is where success is found and life is lived and ladders are climbed. Progress is where we are going. It is what we lead with when interacting with others. Our future self is believed to take us places. And it's the part of the self we know most impresses others. It is the featured protagonist of the pre-caregiver script that receives most of the attention and accolades. In the process, what is left unknown and unexplored is the sacred space of the present, which caregivers can approach like few others. Perhaps for the first time, and perhaps for the only time, you can begin to know your current self. Perhaps for the first time, and perhaps for the only time, you can begin to experience the spontaneity and deep intensity of life that others cannot access because they (unknowingly) are so reliant on a future script as the sole guide for being in the world.

Making It Personal

Last year, I started caring for my mom, and it has been hard. Really hard. I had to quit my job and leave my husband and daughter to move in with Mom in Milwaukee—I live in Madison. Dad passed five years ago, and he had been Mom's main caregiver since her diagnosis of early-onset Alzheimer's. So after his passing, there was no one else to look after Mom. I felt that I had no choice but to come and live here.

I know now how hard it must have been for my dad. Some nights if Mom is calm, I sit looking at our family photos and I just cry. I wish that I would have helped Dad more when he was still alive. Mom's needs are slowly becoming more than I can handle. It's hard for her to swallow now, which scares me, and of course she doesn't know who I am. Sometimes she becomes very agitated, and that's the worst.

Mom's apartment is on the fifth floor of a nice brownstone in downtown Milwaukee. There's a large picture window above the kitchen sink, and one of my pleasures is looking at the sun sparkling on the dew there in the morning. What I want to tell you about is what I see through the window in the evenings. There's an apartment below us, and I have a view into their kitchen. Not into their kitchen really, but into their sink. I can see a woman's hands peeling avocados or potatoes there. The thing is, she's really good at peeling. She's not very fast, but she is so deliberate and so . . . skillful. Her hands can peel an avocado without breaking the peel—it falls in a spiral into the sink, and then her knife goes whoosh, whoosh, cutting slices to the pit.

A few months ago, I began to wait and watch for those hands. They comforted me. I looked at my own hands. I thought how strange it was that my hands are here, not in my own home, or shuffling papers on my old desk at work. I take a potato, turning it over under the warm water and rubbing it with my thumbs. With the peeler, I begin to slowly remove a single, snaking peel that falls into the sink. I think, I am feeding my mom and myself with this potato. This is right now, and I am preparing food without which we will not live. Since that night, peeling vegetables has become a form of prayer for me—a prayer to be okay with being in the present with my mom.

3

A HYPER-INTOLERANCE
OF OTHERS

As your life narrative, or script, changes, so do you. One way to understand how caregivers change in the transformation from loved one to caregiver is to examine what happens to your relationships with other people. This second transformation explores the sources of caregiver disconnection with people and their beliefs. This transformation is a prelude to perceptions of hyper-aloneness, initiated by a growing intolerance for other people's habits, expectations, and taken-for-granted assumptions that seem to defy, contradict, and torment your daily caregiver experiences and evolving beliefs.[1]

When you are a lifeline for another person's needs, connections with people beyond your specific care situation are transformed beyond what anyone can point to or see happening. Too often, this change is overlooked because the emerging differences between you and the world you used to live in and take for granted are camouflaged as questions—*"Why do I feel so alone?"* *"Why is it that the more time, energy, and attention I provide to my loved one in need, the less comfortable I feel interacting with family and close friends?"* *"Why do I feel so frustrated and out of place in the company of people I used to enjoy?"*

Wherever you are in the caregiver process, life revolves around another person. You must anticipate his needs. You must account for her challenges. You can't help but feel the responsibility that you, alone, are the difference between life and death, needless pain and comfort, or chronic management and an ever-growing list of health complications. This deep care requires a complete focus on another's needs. As a caregiver, your everyday, minute-to-minute tasks and choices matter. If you don't feed your loved one, who will? If you don't change your loved one, who will? If you don't attend to their financial needs, who will? If you don't order and pick up medications, who will? The acute awareness of the one-sided nature of the caregiver relationship is not an indictment of the caregiver role as much as it is a description of the inescapable recognition that you, and you alone, are responsible for the ongoing care of your loved one. If something goes wrong with the nebulizer or oxygen generator, there are consequences. Life and death consequences.

Caregiving focuses your attention so much that it also blurs the people and conversations and expectations of those that situate themselves just on the edge of your focus—relationships with family and friends and coworkers. This form of caregiver myopia irrevocably changes how you think about the people around you as you are reminded of the widening schism between your new world and the world you once inhabited.

A GROWING INTOLERANCE

As a caregiver, you see what others don't or can't, or more accurately, you can't help but notice what your care experiences awaken—a stinging awareness of the misalignment between what you once believed and your current caregiver realities. Throughout your care experiences, other people's beliefs and expectations can become intolerable because they defy your everyday realities. Below are a set of interrelated beliefs that begin to differentiate you from others, and also serve to remind you that the people and beliefs you once surrounded yourself with may no longer fit.

(Im)Patience

While others get caught in the rut of boredom born from the expectation that life is continuous from one day to the next, unremarkable in its constancy, the everyday realities of caregiving remind you that life is not constant, but constantly interrupted and interruptible. Always changing. Fragile. Unpredictable.

It is not other people's belief in constancy that eventually becomes intolerable; rather, it is the set of beliefs related to constancy that shape how people experience life, including boredom, meaninglessness, and an unwillingness to experience life with emotion and intensity. Over time, caregivers' tolerance for triviality—the latest celebrity news and gossip, the rise and fall of sports teams, and so on—becomes tiring for them. Spending time with people who suffer, or who are struggling, means it is more difficult to digest others' fascination with the passing fads of popular culture. Incessant chatter about faraway scandals can become exhausting and overwhelming when others seem more interested in noticing what is happening far away, or on television, but not in the lives and homes of caregivers. Caregiver challenges are not abstract—but, instead, struggles of life and death. Yet so much of other people's thoughts and discussions about the trivial, the ephemeral, or the just plain silly suddenly becomes senseless when contrasted with a life characterized by life-and-death responsibilities and decisions.

Caregivers' daily experiences remind them of what they cannot escape—nothing about life can or should be postponed. Restful and uninterrupted sleep is not something one can expect, but a privilege that may seem like an impossibility. Planning for vacations is omitted in favor of constantly adjusting and readjusting schedules to others' needs— doctors' availability and a loved one's ever-changing and unpredictable physical state. The luxury of delaying conversations until you and your partner are both "ready" is no longer possible amid a growing realization that your everyday is defined by an unrelenting urgency of the now that defies others' routines associated with darkness and light, morning and evening, weekends, weekdays, workweeks, holidays, and vacations.

Only when caregivers interact with outsiders—beyond the confines of their immediate caregiving situations—do they begin to realize that other people's patience is a threat to the urgency of their day-to-day lives. *"I'll just wait until tomorrow."* Nothing important can be delayed until tomorrow. *"I am so bored with my life."* Bored—what does that even mean? You don't see what I see—the urgency of now when I have no faith in tomorrow. *"Let's talk about it later—there is no rush."* We will never be ready. Later is now, and now needs to be addressed. The luxury of delaying and waiting until another time makes no sense. *"Sleep? I'll sleep later. Live it up."* Sleep, what I would give for an hour of uninterrupted rest. But even when I try to sleep, I can't let go of what I'm thinking about because I know someone is always depending on me—whether I'm sleeping or awake, their needs know no rest. When caregivers' beliefs that every moment needs to matter—must matter—are met by others' indecisions, delays, and unending comfort with inaction, understanding the world beyond can begin to fracture. When caregivers feel as though everything is "on" them and them alone, other people's lack of urgency can become suffocating as it only reminds caregivers of their growing differences with others.

Caregivers experience such intense, life-altering experiences with their loved ones that to not cry or become emotional seems like a reminder of other people's inauthenticity. Other people's perceived detachment from approaching their everyday moments with abandon is difficult to endure when so much of a caregiver's experience is deeply felt. Surrounded by people who live in categories defined by either "good" or "bad" days or "happy" or "sad" experiences, vulnerable *and* strong caregivers traverse these traditional boundaries, living in an "all of the above" category of emotions and feelings that can't easily translate when they respond to the simple question, *"How are you?"*

(Un)Certainty and (Hyper)Vigilance

Experiencing uncertainty about what will or won't happen is an inescapable part of the human experience.[2] However, the manner in which caregivers manage ambiguity contributes to an ever-increasing sense of isolation. Based on daily, care-based experiences, caregivers can begin to expect the worst—not because they are more negative than others, but as a by-product of their care experiences. When in the presence of uncertainty—What will tomorrow bring?—the inevitable tendency is to begin crafting a response.[3] Caregivers, like non-caregivers, wonder what will happen next. Unlike others, however, not preparing for what might go awry might lead to peril when the stakes of the caregiver role are so high. "What might go wrong today?" isn't a sign of negativity; rather, it is a context-based orientation informed by an acute awareness of the ongoing fragility of their situations. Caregivers' proximity to illness provides a deep appreciation of what could go wrong and what might not be right and of the underlying seriousness of health situation(s) that most other people do not see, hear, or witness on a daily basis. Cumulatively, these care-based experiences shape what caregivers expect—or what they can expect—to happen.

An always-on mentality means caregivers attempt to predict and anticipate all that could go wrong as a way of protecting themselves and their loved ones. Caregivers' experiences of uncertainty more intense than those of others who believe in the uninterrupted flow of experience from one moment to the next. Caregivers' hyperawareness regarding the differences between today and tomorrow and this hour and the next, means their care situations ask them to recognize that the possibilities of what could happen are always greater than what others might anticipate. When caregivers daily care experiences expose them to what can happen, it is impossible to unlearn what one knows, creating a constant alertness that denies the luxury of believing that everything will work out.

The habit of interpreting uncertainty as a threat, rather than a possibility, creates a hypervigilant awareness since caregivers know care responsibilities may fall onto them—alone. Whereas hope is a valid and celebrated response to uncertainty, it also presumes a willing rejection of preparing for all that could happen that doesn't bend to one's desires, a luxury that can have serious consequences for caregivers and their loved ones. Preparing for the "worst" means constantly being primed to respond to events that can unfold in unexpected ways.

When those around you ignore the parts of reality that you see and live, connection is jeopardized. What others don't mention or acknowledge is *your* reality, and it's hard not to notice how frequently your orientation is different from others'. When others get up in the morning, they think about possibility. When caregivers get up in the morning, they think through all of the possible ways in which things might go wrong. When the phone rings, others view possibility, while caregivers anticipate bad news. Other people talk about wants and desires. Caregivers stay close to what needs to be done. Others may view an incoming email as just another message, where caregivers may see this as a sign of the overwhelming and unrelenting tasks associated with their role. For most, a text message might be viewed as an opportunity to connect with a friend or family member, but for a caregiver, a text may represent the emotional challenges of having to maintain existing relationships in addition to the innumerable tasks of caregiving. As a response to uncertainty, hypervigilance isn't about being "negative" as much as it is a reflection of ongoing attempts to maintain a semblance of control at the very moment when responsibility means accounting for the endless possibilities of what could and might happen.

(Inter)dependence

Total care isn't simply a matter of tasks; it's an orientation changer because it makes explicit the interconnectedness between a caregiver and another person. Caregiving means acknowledging that the person you care for is as much a part of you as you are a part of them. This relationship of interdependence is often denied or overlooked because it is contrary to the ideal of the free, autonomous individual.

When other people talk of themselves, it is often done in a language free of challenges, limitations, or boundaries. Disconnected from relationships and relational commitments, dreams of accomplishment and adventure are articulated as ideals of freedom as the "I" becomes a complete and pure expression of desire detached from others' influences. Listen to anyone long enough, and it's easy to recognize that very few dreams are relationship grounded; rather, they are about something far off and distant, away from where one currently is, and almost always about an individual *choosing* to become something other than what they currently are. When other people talk about choice—and choosing—it is based almost exclusively on desire and opportunity.

Choice, when talked about in individualistic and non-relational terms, can't help but appear senseless to caregivers, whose notion of choice and interdependence is so much more nuanced. Caregiving is both a choice and non-choice. Few people proactively seek out the informal caregiver role. At the same time, it doesn't mean that the role can be accurately and fully defined by obligation alone, as that would deny the component of relationship loyalty that had once characterized your pre-caregiver relationship. Caregiving entails a relationship that people don't necessarily want and also a role they feel they can't say no to because it needs to be done, and without you, it wouldn't be done.[4] Thus, the motive for caregiving is a cloudy combination of simultaneous reluctance, care, acute awareness of need, and competence mixed together, defying most other relationship types where motives are clear, mutually beneficial, and well understood. Caregivers are keenly aware that they are tethered to their loved ones. An "it's me or no one" awareness permeates how caregivers think of themselves, even when not physically present with a loved one.[5] Whereas other people talk of vacating, physically and mentally, their everyday work and family responsibilities, caregivers know their deep connectedness stays with them wherever they are. Not being physically present with a loved one does not free them from responsibility—rather, it only exacerbates it in ways few others can understand.

"At home, I am this type of person so I can focus on what I need to do. At work, I need to be this type of person so I can accomplish what I need to." Caregivers may have little tolerance for this kind of compartmentalization talk that denies the realities of their experiences. This compartmentalized construction of the self builds barriers between home and work and personal life in ways that are not possible when caregiving is context transcendent rather than context specific (e.g., work, home, personal). Caregivers know that their responsibilities do not respect boundaries between personal, work, social, and family lives.[6] Instead, responsibilities are omnipresent and ongoing factors that shape what can (and can't) be envisioned in all domains—work, personal, home, and so on.

Caregiving isn't simply confined to changing, feeding, bathing, and making doctor's appointments. Rather, it rearranges existing relationship connections—complicating what it means to be a spouse, son, daughter, mother, father, sibling, parent, employee, and so on. Care, or the deep awareness that care responsibilities defy other people's boundaries, can make it difficult to tolerate others' representations of "life." The constant, hypervigilant attention the care role requires can become all consuming, upending any distinctions that once guided actions and expectations, making it difficult to be in the company of those who speak of home, work, personal, and family life as if they never intersected.

"Downtime" is usually understood as a temporary capacity to escape the obligations associated with a particular role. Away from responsibility, one can decompress and liberate oneself by thinking about other facets of life. Relaxation and downtime, however, become meaningless when responsibility is ever present. Getting away and going on vacation makes no sense to caregivers, simply because it may seem impossible to find time and opportunity (even temporarily) to remove oneself from one's daily responsibilities.

Complete interdependence, not independence, means caregivers may feel it is impossible to be "away," even when they are not physically present with a loved one. Caregivers' simultaneous desire to be with their loved one and away from their loved one—a constant kind of unsettledness—is amplified. Whether one is at the grocery store or sitting next to their loved one, complete and utter responsibility can become claustrophobic as moments of panic descend without warning, rendering it nearly impossible to feel settled. Like a magnet, caregivers are drawn to their loved one, unwilling to endure the anxiety that exhausts them even when away. As the possibility of "getting away" from the caregiving role diminishes, listening to others talk about getting away—in mind and spirit—may be admirable, but increasingly foreign and beyond comprehension.

Interdependence doesn't just characterize the nature of the caregiver relationship, it also becomes imprinted into a person's identity, shaping what they are willing to do and whom they are willing and able to be around—even when they think they want to get away and be free. The identity of a caregiver can't be easily picked up and put down when it's convenient because a loved one's needs know no boundaries.

Power(less)

Most people believe they can change almost any situation. As a result of diligence and hard work, a taken-for-granted belief is that all things can be made better. This belief, however noble, can make caregivers feel excluded from participating, in the presumption that change is possible as caregivers lived experiences may constantly remind them that they, and their care situations, are excluded from most people's beliefs.

No one would deny the hope and possibility associated with cures and the advancements of science and technology. Yet believing in hope is different when you are near someone with a name, face, and body and a situation that may not be privileged to be part of medical, scientific, and/or cure-based hopes. Most people have a remarkably low tolerance for being with and near loved ones whose situations may evoke the limitations of change. Care, however, exists in these very spaces where the language of doing and action is confronted with the realities of care. Others talk in the language of doing—*"Something needs to be done. There has to be a cure—an experimental trial or some miracle of miracles?"* Doing receives standing ovations. Caregivers may realize that helping a loved one manage pain and enhancing comfort is often greeted with silence because what they do—caring, not curing—is too easily dismissed since it doesn't conform to what others want to believe about the heroism and valor of "winning battles."[7] Consequently, most people have a low tolerance for remaining close to another when they aren't able to "change" or "fix" the situation because staying, or caring in light of constraints, seemingly defies understanding. From afar, this kind of care is often labeled as "settling" or "giving up" or a "lack of will." Without malice, caregiving becomes politicized and threatening, a reminder that the fragility of life is not simply reserved for the unlucky few, but an inevitable reality that eventually finds everyone.

Throughout adulthood, culture celebrates an ongoing intolerance for acceptance. Never settle. Never accept. Never stop. Never stop wanting. Never stop trying. Never stop desiring. Never stop persuading. Never stop wanting something more than what is before us. Caring for people who may not fit under the label of "improving" requires a tolerance for acceptance that others find unacceptable. You aren't just caring—you are caring for someone who may not be on the road to recovery. Someone who can't be cured. In the process, you are tainted because your care may be viewed as an accomplice to "failure."[8] Others may marvel at a caregiver's willingness and capacity to care, but being labeled a "saint" is also a reminder of how differently you are viewed. Exceptional, beyond comprehension, otherworldly, the "saint" moniker is also a sign that caregivers need not be understood or listened to because they—and their role—are essentially different from what most people are willing to tolerate. Thus, they and what they do behind closed doors should remain sequestered and left alone, cheered on from afar, but left mysterious, for fear that who they are and what they do may somehow be contagious, injecting their lives with unnecessary doubt and uncertainty.[9]

Caregivers' thoughts and beliefs become chastened by a loved one's changing physical circumstances and the keen awareness that, at times, the world pushes them forward and around like a raft in whitewater. Alone, the river quickly teaches them that efforts to protest are sometimes futile when there are forces greater than our desires and efforts. Life is fragile. Bodies are fragile. Outsiders' beliefs are fragile, too. Suddenly, caring for another becomes threatening, a reason to remain silent, to remain away, for fear of what this realization might mean to them and their beliefs about their own lives.

UNANTICIPATED DIFFERENCE

Caregivers may begin to view family and friends around them through an ever-widening lens of difference, transforming familiar people and situations into examples of distance and disconnect. Not wanting to burden those closest to them, caregivers become increasingly aware of their responsibilities. More specifically, the response to the challenges of care is not a collective response, but an individual one—a deepening awareness that you are in this all alone, that there are limits to what family and friends can provide. Or limits to what you believe they can provide because they have their own challenges, families, worries, and constraints. A growing discomfort, when in the company of others who are believed incapable or unwilling to understand the caregiving experience, inevitably leads to a type of preoccupation with the emerging differences between you and everyone beyond your immediate circumstances of care.

Since loneliness is a perception,[10] it defies rationality and often feeds on itself in ways that exaggerate perceived differences over time. Left to your thoughts, watching others from the inside out, you can convince yourself that people must not care since they don't notice you. Over time, and without interruption from others, the desire to explain why people are acting and responding in the way they are becomes more compelling than any standards of accuracy or logic. Over time, and without interruption from others, you can convince yourself that people are avoiding you in your time of need. Over time, and without interruption from others, you can convince yourself that people simply don't care about your situation.

You may want someone to notice you. You may even have thought about screaming through the bedroom window to those you watch pass by on foot and in their cars. Most likely, though, you never yelled out— and people never looked in. They had lives to live. Places to go. Calories to burn. Mail to get. Leisure to enjoy. Lunches to make. Errands to run. Appointments to make. Meetings to attend. As a caregiver, the view flips. You no longer look at the world the same way because you begin seeing the world from the inside out, whereas most people see the world from the outside in. This inside-out view of the world can make you feel invisible, alone, isolated, and yes, like outsiders living in a world of insiders.

Feeling invisible to the rest of the world isn't simply about being noticed; it's also about how you orient yourself to those around you.

This cycle of vulnerability and perceived difference continues, unabated. The more you feel separated from others, the more reasons you may find not to connect with others. The more removed you feel from others, the stranger it feels to be in the company of others. Everything and everyone seems to move so fast, whereas you feel as if you are moving in slow motion, awkwardly a beat off from others' rhythms. Surrounded by people who suddenly look different and act differently, differences between you and others become the only thing you can see. They don't have your concerns. They have no idea of the life you are living. They have no idea what you are facing. They have no idea what you are experiencing, no conception of the stressors you are experiencing, no possible way of understanding what you worry about at night and what haunts you during the day. Their lives go forward, onward, and uninterrupted as the schism between you and them widens so that it seems impossible to overcome.

This transformation is disorienting because somewhere in the midst of a conversation with a friend or family member, you may realize something is strange. They are familiar, but the way you are interpreting what is being said (or not said) no longer makes sense. You clearly hear what is being said (and not said) by well-intentioned friends, family, and colleagues, but you also begin to doubt yourself with a simultaneous inner voice. *"Why do I suddenly feel so isolated even when surrounded by people who care for me?" "When did this shift happen?" "Don't they notice it, too?"* When difference is featured, uncertainty increases as the people you once thought you could rely on are injected with newfound apprehension, making those most familiar to us stranger than strangers.

A NEW WAY OF SEEING AND BEING

Although a hypersensitive awareness of how you have become different from others permeates your consciousness, this same shift in perspective can also help clarify and prioritize what and who matter most. In this way, care is the great editor of life—it helps shut out the world and its noise and focus your attention on who and what matter most.

What you once thought to be important and valuable may fall away when compared to the life-wrenching responsibilities and decisions that mark your newfound everyday reality. You know what is important—you don't need to look elsewhere. You don't need to go on a journey to find it. It's not somewhere far away—in a distant land. It's not about celebrities you've never met and sports figures whose fortunes turn without any impact on your life. What is important and valuable and vital is where your attention is focused. There is nothing abstract about a caregiver's purpose when care makes an immediate impact on someone you love. Your compass for action and inaction is growing clear—clearer and more pronounced than it could have ever been before, when boredom and procrastination and a false sense of certainty may have diluted the way you embraced the day.

Something else may happen as well. As your tolerance for others' beliefs and expectations diminishes, everything and everyone who enters your loved one's world is vetted through this very tangible and specific lens of a fledgling caregiver's orientation. Prior to taking on your caregiver role, you may never have thought much about who and what was around you, or what you allowed into your consciousness. Mere accident, proximity, and shared history were the only criteria. Now, a newfound set of criteria is possible as the stakes of access to your loved one have never been more paramount.

Making It Personal

A LETTER TO FRIENDS AND FAMILY
FROM A CAREGIVER

Dear Friends and Family,

This is a letter you'll never receive, but it's something that those closest to you may be thinking and feeling and experiencing—even though they may never tell you. Not because they don't want to. It's just that they—we—can't. Or maybe it's we don't know how to. This isn't a letter to make you feel bad. Rather, it's a letter to explain the inexplicable, or what sometimes happens to us when we care for someone who isn't getting better . . .

I've told you what is happening, but what you don't know is what is happening to me. I'm not even sure what is happening to me. I'm trying to make sense of it all—taking it in and trying to find the words that will be understandable. Coherence takes time—it's not something I can do myself—so I will need you. Right now, I'm thinking through how what I'm experiencing might sound like to you if I tried to explain it. I desperately want you to understand, but I also don't want to scare you. Please don't interpret my silence as a lack of care. I care about you, and that's why I'm trying so hard. Even though the harder I try to put my experiences into words, the more jumbled it all seems. What I'm seeing and experiencing and feeling—it's so raw and all over the place that it will take me time to translate it in a way that I can share. Please be patient with me. Please.

I'm sorry we're drifting apart. I really am. I'm not picking up my phone or answering my messages these days. Half the time, I feel like I'm too busy. The other half of the time, I see when you've called, but I don't have the energy to even listen to a voicemail message. It's not that I don't want to. It's just that I feel like I can't right now. I'm here, but I may not even answer the door if you come by. It's not that I don't want to. You want to help and for that, I am deeply grateful, but being near illness is changing me. I want to be called. I want you to text. I want you to want to come by—even though when you do—I may not answer.

I'm avoiding not just you right now—it's everyone. Please don't take it personally. I get anxious these days. Not about the big stuff—I see that up close and personal all the time. It's the little stuff that's tripping me up. I'm embarrassed to admit it, but I get nervous when someone asks me something as simple as, "How are you doing?" Yesterday, a stranger asked me that question as I was waiting in line at the pharmacy. It was as if I couldn't speak. I don't know how to answer that question without tearing up and feeling like I'm tearing apart. I wish I could give you a clean and neat response when you ask me how I'm doing, but nothing right now is clean and neat. Because I care about you, I can't simply allow myself to say, "I'm okay" or "I'm doing fine." I'm not there yet, and right now, it feels like I'll never be there, so I'm sparing you and me the pain of lying.

I don't worry about what others seem to care about. The nightly news. Or the election. Or the Kardashians. I want to care about what everyone else cares about, but I don't. Is it because I'm all cared out at the end of each day? I used to look forward to so much. But now, I've completely lost perspective. Not in the way most people lose perspective. I used to get nervous about the silliest of things. Talking to new people. Meeting new people. Getting up in front of people to talk about something. Now, I don't know what I get nervous about. Everything is blurring together, and I am looking at a horizon I can't explain to you yet. I wish I could, but I have a filter that doesn't allow me to see what you see anymore. I wish I could forget for one moment. Fun. Get-togethers. A dinner out. A movie. Thank you for the invitations, but I can't forget right now. It's not that I don't want to—it's just that I'm focused on that horizon, beyond the everyday. You see the grandeur of everyday life and get consumed in it. I look at everyday life and see something beyond it. I know I'm missing more than I see—and you're a part of what I'm missing.

I want you to be near me. I want to hear your voice. Please don't misunderstand me. I'm here, but I'm gone. I may be near you, but I can't listen to you the way I once did. You may hear me and think I sound the same, but I don't. I didn't choose this way of looking at things; it feels like it chose me. I just wanted you to know what's going through my mind. I just wanted to explain myself without making everything so awkward. I wish I could have told you this in person—not an apology—just a way to explain. Soon enough, I hope to reach out and smile and give you a hug. Right now, so much is working its way through me. But thank you for being near me so that when I'm ready, you'll be there, knowing I will need you to help me begin making sense of myself again.

Love,
Me

4

AUDIENCE BETRAYAL

When life as you once knew it becomes interrupted,[1] the first instinct is to try to remind yourself that you are not alone. Someone must be told. Someone must know. The search for a supportive audience begins as the situation you find yourself in envelops you in ways that could never have been anticipated.

There's nothing more painful and bewildering than being misunderstood by people you care about and who you believe care about you. When the people you most want to understand don't (or can't), there is fallout, not only to your relationships but also to your ability to navigate your care situation. Families are essential in helping caregivers make sense of what is happening and in providing a deep and abiding reassurance that their understandings of the world are validated.[2] However, when there is audience misalignment—a perceived disconnect between what you want and what others around you (can) provide—caregivers may feel deeply alone, even when in the company of family and friends who once provided comfort and strength.

Family and friends are the people we most expect to be there for us and with us. At the same time, family and friends—the people you think you know best—are often the most likely to let you down, as their inability to provide comfort and support in ways you most want transforms you in ways never expected. Surrounded by people you once believed would provide so much support, this caregiver transformation can make caregivers feel like strangers to themselves, trapped by a desire to share, but painfully reminded that what they are going through feels impossible to explain when those closest to you disappear or aren't there for you in the ways you expected. When the people you know best disappoint, whom can you trust? How is it that family and friends seem distant and aloof when you need them most? Why is it that the people closest to you can hurt you so much with what is said or not said? How is it that you can feel utterly alone even when surrounded by people you know so well?

WHAT MASK ARE YOU ASKED TO WEAR?

The people around us have expectations of *us* just as we have expectations of *them*. We are aware of other people's expectations most intensely when we perceive a disconnect between how we feel and what we believe others need from us. In the midst of struggle, we all wear a variety of masks that present the parts of ourselves we believe others want to see and hear.[3] For caregivers, putting on a mask isn't something that just happens on Halloween. Caregivers don't go to a costume shop to buy masks; rather, they are ingenious in disguising their authentic feelings, worries, fears, and uncertainties because of a widening gulf between how they feel and what they are thinking, and what they believe others will allow them to be, given their circumstances.[4]

If caregivers believe they can only reveal parts of themselves while hiding essential truths about their feelings and care experiences, exhaustion and frustration are likely by-products. There is an endless variety of masks caregivers "put on" (or are pressured into wearing) in the company of others; however, there are certain masks that are repeatedly "worn" that not only shape what caregivers believe can be shared and explained, but also impact the quality of support they can receive when interacting with family and friends.

The "Saint" Mask

Saints walk into difficult situations when most others walk away and serenely endure when most others shudder. Saints seemingly embrace struggle with such elegance that their compassion and endurance are proof that they are otherworldly when coping with suffering. This mask is so admired because it is greeted with awe. Saints are revered, but reverence doesn't necessarily equal understanding.

Appreciation happens from afar, but it doesn't require others to step toward caregivers. Instead, others are encouraged to remain comfortably distant, placing those wearing the saint mask on a pedestal, rationalizing their distance with an awareness that caregivers are so different because of their unyielding willingness and compassion. *"I can't believe you are doing so much." "I couldn't endure what you experience every day." "I don't know how you do it. I'm too emotional."* This praise, though appreciated, also situates caregivers as different, distinct, and even aberrant because they are engaged in something that is believed to be extraordinary. But someone who is worthy of acclaim doesn't need to be understood or listened to, only admired at arm's length because the nomination of sainthood disallows connections that only come with a voicing of everyday struggles and difficulties.[5] Because the saint label doesn't allow for moments of self-doubt or lapses of faith, wearers are required to remain silent so that they can live up to what others need them to be—admirable but remarkably unusual. In the process, this mask traps its wearers into adhering to what others want to believe about them, implying that saints don't need to be listened to or learned about because, after all, they're saints—not people.

The "Everything Is Okay" Mask

This disguise is shaped in the image of people's expectations because it allows others' beliefs to remain unchanged. This mask allows others to feel comfortable knowing that life, however challenging, is still within control. Despite what is happening, everything is presented as okay so that the people around you will not have to contemplate what might happen if life doesn't return to normal or if parts of life don't always fit within the category of "okayness."

This mask is appreciated by family and friends because it doesn't ask anyone to recognize how the care situation is changing everyone involved. If this mask is worn long enough, it may prevent wearers from allowing themselves to be changed by the experiences they are enduring. This mask highlights, in every conceivable way, the compulsion to return to life as it was once lived and to return to one's job as it once was, and to reclaim relationships exactly as they were before the caregiver experience. This mask can feel uncomfortable, and even smothering at times, because authenticity is sacrificed at the expense of others' needs. *"Your positive attitude is so inspiring." "Once everything gets back to normal, we can get together again." "I am so impressed that you are managing everything so well."* Since the wearers of this mask devote unending attention and effort to maintaining the appearance of normality, other people are not invited to appreciate how a caregiver can be positive *and still* devastated, coping *and still* overwhelmed, a totally different person *and still* the same person. This mask asks wearers to deny vital parts of their experiences by immediately cleaning up any doubts or contradictions so as to be able to give others what they want to hear, which oftentimes conflicts with what the wearers of this mask are experiencing.[6]

The "Fighter" Mask

The fighter mask conforms to the belief that all challenges can be overcome if the wearer has an absolute and unwavering desire to fight at all costs. Fighters fight. They are expected to be relentless and single-minded in their focus on beating back whatever threatens them and their loved one. This mask is welcomed by family and friends because it allows people to connect to caregivers using almost exclusively the language of cure and the ongoing search for solutions. *"Okay, here's what you need to do." "Have you checked out this treatment; it's worked for so many people I know." "What's your plan? Everyone has to have a battle plan." "If you want this enough, you can make it happen." "You've got this!"* Solution-chasing audiences believe the world is filled with problems requiring solutions. Because these audiences care, their willingness to provide solutions is seemingly a sign of sincerity and good intentions. Solutions are wonderful except when they are treated as the beginning and ending of engagement with the wearers of this caregiver mask. Audiences that approach only with solutions act as if they know you, or know enough about you and your loved one, that they no longer need to listen to what is being said and not being said.

Those who live with this mask can feel particularly anxious and on edge when the only form of connection others seek involves "warlike" solutions to defeat the enemy. When every conversation is about a cure, or a possible cure, this mask denies wearers the possibility of exploring life between "battles"—if only for a moment—because there is always something that needs to be done and some war that needs to be initiated. In the process, caregivers are resigned to "soldiering on" and "waging another battle." The fighter mask makes it difficult for caregivers to acknowledge anything but pure victory consistent with a "never settle" mentality so acclaimed by others.[7] When caring for someone with a chronic illness, however, ongoing care experiences simply don't fit within "winning" or "losing" mentalities, rendering wearers silent because so many of their experiences seem beyond translation.

Since other people demand hope at all times, the fighter mask excludes possibilities for sharing about nonfighting care experiences like intimacy, fragility, and moments of peace. Deviations from the rigid adherence to the never-settle, always-fighting mentality are often greeted with bewilderment and disbelief. *"What do you mean there is no cure?" "She's going to live with this for the rest of her life?" "There's got to be something you can do, right?"* Reflection and attempts to make sense of what is happening in the moment aren't allowed to be a part of these discussions when others expect the "fight" to be the subject of all conversations.

When interacting with others, caregivers who wear these masks may feel compelled to minimize or distort their stigmatized care experiences for concern that their care role will make them feel different and even more socially isolated.[8] They exert incredible emotional energy in attempting to maintain the appearance of regularity in hopes of protecting themselves and their loved one from unwanted and harmful attention while also wanting to authentically communicate what they are experiencing. To minimize awkwardness for themselves and their loved ones, they quickly become masters of euphemisms— *"We're both making it through"* and quick redirects— *"But how are things with you?"*—to avoid talking about their situation in ways that may be met with disbelief and discomfort. Instead of allowing vulnerability to bring them closer, others' expectations can prevent caregivers from fully benefiting from support, understanding, and connection.

FIRST AUDIENCES

All of these masks highlight that caregivers aren't simply shaped by their care experiences. Rather, the people around them—family, friends, and colleagues—also determine what is (in)appropriate to think, perform, and share about the care experience.[9] In the process of interacting with others, caregivers, like other stigmatized identities,[10] may feel compelled to perform, act, and respond in ways that interrupt possibilities for authentic and satisfying social support as some masks are viewed as less "appropriate" than others.

Feeling supported can protect caregivers. Support from others can reduce stress, boost resilience, and improve caregivers' beliefs about their ability to positively impact their experiences.[11] Yet how caregivers think, feel, and respond to their care situations is evaluated, in part, by perceptions of support from the very people they care about. Giving and receiving support comes in many forms that blend into one another. Practical support might mean providing a meal or transportation. Emotional support involves providing connection by listening to understand those in need. Informational support can be provided through accessing and sharing information, while companionship entails a willingness to be with someone throughout life's challenges.[12] These varying types of support, among others, can be sought from and provided by a variety of audiences.

Family, in all of its various manifestations, is most people's first audience because we are born into a family (functional or dysfunctional) that creates shared history and experiences. You believe your family knows you like no one else. Family members know who you are and what you are like in a multitude of situations and in response to a variety of stresses. Your family has likely seen you at your "worst" and "finest," when you are "off" and "on," in public and in the intimacy of the home setting where you are most likely to feel that you can be raw and unedited—seemingly free of masks. Family members also have multiple points of reference to inform who they think you are and how you have evolved because they have witnessed you develop over time.

Family members are not only witnesses but also coauthors who have shaped who you are and who you are becoming. Family relationships are often thought of as different from other relationships because they are expected to be present throughout one's life, transcending circumstances and context. Family ties don't simply bind us to one another; they provide constancy among the choice-based relationships we become a part of (e.g., friendships, marriage, work-based relationships) and fall away from (e.g., breakups, changing friendships, divorces) throughout life. Family members are the people we believe we can count on because they know us longer than most others, and we believe we know them, too. As a result, we find comfort in knowing that, even if everything else around us changes, there is one constant in our lives.[13]

Not only are we relationally tied to and mutually influenced by family members as sisters, brothers, mothers, fathers, sons, daughters, spouses, and so on,[14] but we are also shaped by a common family system that remains influential long after we move away. These family templates for making sense are rarely written down but are reinforced through countless conversations and experiences throughout the formative family years, shaping perceptions about what is (in)significant, what should be (not) talked about, how we should (not) handle stress, what we believe is (not) expected of family members, and a myriad of expectations for how we should respond to the world beyond.[15]

WAVES OF AUDIENCE DISAPPOINTMENT AND DESPAIR

Despite the best intentions of the audiences we go to first—family and friends—there are limitations to what they can do for us when it may be impossible to fulfill our needs and expectations for support.[16] When the people you most think should be there, the people that you most want to understand—aren't—you can't help but feel betrayed. What are you to feel when family members simply assume *you* will be the care-giver—believing somehow you are the most equipped because *their* life situations immediately disqualify them from the role? What are you to feel when certain family members initially ask you how you are doing, but then are unwilling to continue inquiring about the depth of your unfolding care situation? What are you to feel when family members openly talk about vacations and family get-togethers and everyone as-sumes your choices and freedoms are the same as theirs? What are you to feel when your care is questioned, doubted, or contradicted by those far away—those who've never once asked you for details of the care situation you know more intimately than anyone else? These unfulfilled expectations can't help but make you rethink everything you once believed about the people you thought would always be there for you when you needed them most.[17]

What happens when the phone stops ringing? What are you to believe when texts from friends that were fast and furious in the beginning of your care role are now only an occasional trickle? What are you to feel when promises of coming over to your house to spend time together over coffee begin and end in disappointment—leaving you thinking that each ring of the phone is someone reaching out to you? And what are you left wondering when friends ask you to go out to dinner or see a movie and you have to constantly say no or gently remind them that you can't, only then to be questioned as to why you can't find someone to take care of your loved one?

Caregivers don't think about their care situations in isolation. Rather, they evaluate care situations along with how supported they feel.[18] When the people you believed would be present and supportive disappoint, your closest relationships are injected with unexpected uncertainty, lessening the likelihood that the people already in your social networks will be able to fulfill your social support needs in ways that are satisfying and meaningful.

WHAT ISN'T SHARED

Disappointment and feelings of betrayal from audiences closest to you affect what you are willing to communicate with friends and family. In most relationships, the more you share with someone, the more you are likely to feel close. For example, romantic partners mutually disclose their interests, passions, fears, and dreams in hopes of enhancing intimacy. We open ourselves up to be known by another by sharing a variety of topics and revealing information about ourselves that might not be shared with anyone else.[19] Although most other relationships are characterized by a willingness to share, from the obvious to the most intimate, private, and exclusive information,[20] the caregiver relationship is distinctive because of what *isn't* or *can't* be shared with others. The nature of the caregiving relationship affects what can (and should) be disclosed, complicating caregivers' ability to seek and receive satisfying support from friends and family already in their social networks.

Saying No to Support

Family and friends can provide deeply rich and satisfying support.[21] However, receiving support from these audiences also means having to negotiate support in a relational context. Even the most well-intentioned comments cannot be received apart from unavoidable judgment, expectation, and emotion that burrow into every conversation, visit, phone call, action, and text message. The relational meanings associated with social support from friends and family are why the simplest acts of attempted comfort—such as a hug—can also be sources of emotional exhaustion that represent so much more than the hug itself.

Caregivers might find themselves retreating from family and friends, even though doing so seemingly defies the benefits of feeling supported by those they care most about.[22] They may reject invitations to temporarily take a break and get out of the house, receive a visitor, or talk on the phone. Caregivers reject offers of support, not because they don't want to feel connected, but because of what they believe accepting support requires from them. Not feeling as though you have the stamina to endure all that is associated with merely drinking coffee with a particular family member highlights how difficult it can be to untangle support from how you think and feel about your relationships with the people making the offer. Support from people you know comes with conditions, even though the conditions may never be explicit. All social support from family and friends is interpreted through the lens of the past—a long-standing but never talked-about grievance, a belief that a family member isn't helping you as much as you think they should, or hurt feelings because another family member has a habit of arriving in town unannounced with "answers," only to quickly leave with chaos in their wake. A caregiver's calculus for the costs and benefits of social support is deceptively difficult to determine. Already feeling vulnerable and at the edge of exhaustion, the anticipated social stamina needed to manage frustrations, needs, expectations, guilt, and relational histories may be reason enough to be less open with family and friends.[23]

Seeking to meet the anticipated needs of family and friends requires focus and stamina when caregivers believe they have little, if any, to spare. The energy associated with not saying or doing something that will upset someone you care about must be carefully and cautiously budgeted. The need to "put on a happy face" or to "not show how upset I am that you haven't called me for the last two months" might make the difference between letting a phone call go to voicemail or answering it just to hear another's voice. Caregivers' desire not to upset those closest to them (and the people they need to maintain an ongoing relationship with) can become a reason to avoid family's or friends' invitations. Over time, saying no to companionship may be filtered through the lens of emotional conservation, as the mere thought of getting together with friends, or participating in family activities, or answering emails, may be too much to endure. Everyday offers of support may be experienced as not just exhausting but also overwhelming. When communicating with people you know well, everything that is (not) said and (not) done is instantaneously charged with meaning that matters, justifying a retreat farther and farther away from others. Trying to reduce the possibility of making a "mistake" or overreacting in a way that might have long-lasting relational consequences that cannot be undone makes support sometimes feel as if it doesn't hold you up as much as it pushes you down.

A paradox of receiving support from family and friends is that they know you so well that they may understand you better than anyone in the world. At the same time, they may know you so well that their words (or lack of) can wound you in ways that can both surprise and devastate. *"It must be nice to be home all day. I wish I could do that."* *"Why are you so tired? All you do is watch your loved one sleep."* *"You're not acting like your normal self. Come on, you used to laugh a lot more."* *"Why aren't you returning my phone calls and emails? It's not like you don't have the time."* Being hurt—by words—is an occupational hazard of caregiving that can strain relationships and can contribute to caregiver isolation. Words hurt people all the time, but why is it that caregivers are so prone to getting wounded by people they know the best?

When deprived of sleep, anxious, overwhelmed, and vulnerable, what people (don't) say matters to us more than it might under so-called normal circumstances (caregivers never care in "normal" circumstances). We pay such close attention to what others say or don't say because we are looking for solace. We want others to make us feel better. We are looking for reassurance. We are looking for understanding. We are looking for our burdens to be temporarily lifted. Simply put, we are a perfectly exposed audience for others' words because we are *deeply* listening to what others are saying or not saying.

Unfortunately, caregivers can listen too well because we can't let go of what has been said to us. Under different circumstances, words may be forgotten almost as quickly as they are uttered. Under the influence of caregiving, however, families' and friends' comments are more likely to stay with us throughout the day and into the night. They are played over and over in our minds, and with each passing moment, they become louder and louder until their words are the *only* words we hear. It's not their fault, but they don't see what you see. They don't hear what you hear. They may not even allow themselves to hear because you are close to someone in ways that might make them uncomfortable. If they knew, they might look at you differently, not out of disrespect, but because they are afraid of what and whom you are around, what you see, and what you experience that they won't allow themselves to even contemplate.[24] They don't know what your moment-to-moment existence is like. They have no idea that their words will stay with you longer than they can imagine.

The people we know also know us. And this can be remarkably comforting when so much else is in flux. Yet others' deep knowledge of your past can also discourage you from seeking support from family because they can't separate their reactions to your particular situation and challenges from their perceptions of you. You, the person they have known so long and (seemingly) so well, is, ironically, what may keep them from fully being able to understand and appreciate what is being said and what you may need or want. People in your close-knit network of family and friends may not be able to understand what you are going through because they haven't experienced it. Family and friends may be too similar to who you once were and unable to help you with what you are feeling, thinking, or doing because your changing experiences defy what they know, or even what they believe you should be doing.[25]

When What Is(n't) Said Hurts

The physical and emotional exhaustion associated with the care role intensifies caregiver vulnerability and dramatically escalates the stakes of every encounter. Sincere messages and well wishes can still hurt. *"Oh, is your wife better now?" "Is he still sick?" "You knew what you were getting into." "When will you be able to get your life back?" "Well, everything happens for a reason."* These messages can be so painful to endure and difficult to dismiss because vulnerability means caregivers are both remarkably open—needing others' support—and defenseless against the shards of well-intentioned comments that make it nearly impossible to distinguish good intentions from the harmful effects of relational judgments. *"Come on, you've always exaggerated—is it really that bad? Don't you think you are being a bit too dramatic?" "Why not just think about a facility?" "You always have been a negative person."* Unfortunately, the people who know you best are more likely to minimize your concerns and challenges than those who don't know you at all because familiarity not only breeds judgment—or anxieties about judgment—but also an inability to untangle words from the person speaking.[26]

Caregiver vulnerability associated with emotional exhaustion isn't limited to what is said; rather, it encompasses a deeper awareness of what isn't said or noticed that you believe should be. Only when communicating with family and friends, the people we know best, can *not* saying something wound. Questions that aren't asked, or questions you believe should be asked, sting. Assumptions that remind you that your situation is profoundly misunderstood can hurt even when they are unintentional. And topics that aren't addressed, when you believe they should be, can offend when they remind you that those closest to you may not desire understanding. When caregivers are emotionally exhausted, it is difficult not to respond in the way you feel at that exact moment—*"I can't believe you never ask me a question about what's really going on!"* If you respond in this way (how you feel at the moment), you also risk negatively impacting not only this particular conversation but future conversations and the ongoing relationships with people you care about. When everything that is (not) communicated has relational consequences, support isn't just something that you receive and give, it's also something that can vandalize relationships. Caregivers know better than most that the benefits of support can never be separated from the overwhelming awareness of the possible costs of engaging family and friends when you are exhausted and emotionally susceptible.

THE CHALLENGES OF SHARING

Even when given the opportunity to share and benefit from social support, caregivers face communication challenges that are believed to be difficult to overcome. Caregiving often defies assumptions associated with other medical crises. There may be no well-recognized markers that let others know when the caregiver role started, how long it will continue, and when, if at all, it might end. The fact that there is so much ambiguity about the processes and trajectory of caregiving means caregivers themselves must create, from scratch, their own beginnings, middles, and ends for others to recognize.[27]

As a result, friends and family are likely to wait for caregivers to initiate discussions, creating an ongoing communication burden. If someone was caring for a loved one going to a hospital for acute-care surgery, reaching out to family and friends would have clear(er) benchmarks for communication. Knowing what and when to communicate is clarified by the date of your loved one's surgery, and the nature of the surgery has meaning within the context of recovery. This communicative clarity associated with acute-care situations isn't just helpful for caregivers. It also allows others to more fully participate. Other people's offers of help and support have bookmarked moments—leading up to the surgery, the surgery itself, and the transition home—reducing uncertainty about when their help and support might be most needed.

Without such clarity, caregivers in chronic situations are less likely to reach out to family and friends because of ongoing uncertainty. In chronic-care situations, when should you ask for help? How often should you update others, especially if there are no "significant" changes that may be recognized as worthy of sharing? Help and support is so often thought of as having clear beginning and ending points. When the need for support is ongoing, caregivers are left without the words to express the notion that help knows no holidays and defies predictable ending points. In this void, in a world between help and helplessness, the lack of distinct opportunities for others' involvement encourages a kind of "wait-and-see" attitude, creating an ever-widening gulf between caregivers' concerns that others just "won't get it" and outsiders' assumptions that "they will tell me when they need help."

What Can Be Done?

Trained in responding to acute-care needs, well-intentioned friends and family often lead with questions focusing on what can be *done* to help. This sincere and apparently simple request—*"What can I do?"*—may be difficult for caregivers to authentically respond to because the question itself reminds them they can feel helpless even when attempting to respond to such a simple inquiry. Caregivers often believe that if they accurately and fully respond, friends and family would be repelled because what they most need is not what people feel comfortable providing (e.g., feeding a loved one to provide an hour of respite, bathing a loved one, driving a loved one to and from appointments). To avoid awkwardness and reduce the likelihood that others would think they are asking for the impossible or something inappropriate, caregivers must try to figure out how to articulate their needs and desires for help without overwhelming others' good intentions.

Not wanting to insult others' questions about what can be *done*, the depth, breadth, complexity, and contradictions of caregiving are more likely to be distorted into clichéd responses—*"Thank you but I think we're fine right now"*—because we believe that sharing anything approximating the complicated realities of care situations is more than others want to know. Each time a caregiver replies with a *"good"* or *"okay,"* the gulf between what they believe they can share and what they wish they could share widens. In this ever-widening chasm, each conversation becomes a disorienting reminder of the divide between what they are experiencing and what they are able to explain. Eventually, not knowing *how* to share is substituted, without warning, for something else—a lack of desire to want to share.

Superimposed Realities

For caregivers, the challenges of communicating experiences do not just apply to family and friends. To remain close to the person receiving their care, they believe that concealing, rather than sharing, is essential. The caregiver relationship is complicated because it involves previous, but still ongoing, types of relationships (e.g., spousal, parental, child) that once depended on mutual sharing as a way of enhancing and maintaining connection. This existing relationship template never disappears but must be layered within an existing caregiver role. This layering increases complexity because it requires simultaneous negotiation of at least two relationship models with accompanying sets of expectations that don't disappear as much as they compete with one another. Negotiating the desire to meaningfully disclose to a loved one must constantly be balanced in light of the possible harms of disclosure.

Most relationship partners value openness and authenticity to create shared realities, common goals, and understandings of where they are and where they hope to be in their relationship. Closeness is achieved through sharing.[28] Yet the caregiver relationship is different. Connection becomes radically altered and may not be possible or even desirable with the person you once bonded with through the sharing of concerns, hopes, worries, fears, and joys. To prevent a loved one from feeling guilt about how your care relationship may be impacting other parts of your life, you may value omission more than honest and open sharing.[29] For example, you might have previously shared a problem at work, when you were interacting within only one relationship type. Now, when assessing what to share, everything becomes more complicated because the caregiver relationship is superimposed over your original relationship. It's not because you don't want a loved one to know but because you feel as though you can't, even though you know that the absence of sharing is irrevocably changing your relationship.

Independently, each type of relationship has its distinct rules and ways of working, but when they must exist simultaneously, they are often experienced as contradictory and tension filled, each demanding its own prominence without any guidance on how they might mesh with one another in any meaningful way. Superimposing two relationship types means everything changes. Relationship rules are upended. Presumptions are erased. Routine and proficiency are replaced by doubt as you must try to reconcile how these two relationships can exist together, inevitably making you question not simply what can be communicated but how you should communicate. *"I want to tell you and I don't want to hurt you." "We used to be so honest with one another and I know we can't now. It's not right for you or me." "I so want to ask you what your silence means but I don't know how to because part of me is afraid of what you might say."*

What was once a clear way to achieve connection—sharing with your loved one about a work problem—now becomes complicated with contradictory meanings. A problem at work, stemming from lack of sleep and exhaustion, may now be concealed rather than shared because it might initiate guilt in your loved one. Suddenly, disclosure is not a means of achieving closeness; it's a source of unending stress for a loved one who has no capacity to change their condition. And it's a source of stress for you because you know you are being deprived of sharing possibilities that were once so important to your pre-caregiver relationship.

The expected reciprocity of give-and-take that once defined your relationship needs to be reimagined when the caregiver role is added to your already existing relational bonds. Protection,[30] rather than enhancing closeness, becomes a new reality that explains why the very person you are caring for may also contribute to an increased sense of loneliness. When disclosure is no longer a choice, but a threat and ongoing relationship tension,[31] caregivers feel compelled to edit the very realities of their caregiver situations and difficulties for fear that their raw and unedited disclosures would be interpreted as attacks or indictments beyond their loved one's capacity to change.

Though caregivers may not be able to freely share with their loved one, the desire to connect via disclosure never disappears as the caregiver role does not change your awareness of what was once possible. Though the same person may be before you, the relationship is altered because there is so much you might want to say, but can't. So many difficulties or frustrations about the disease or condition that you'd like to share, but know you cannot. There may be so much you are thinking about and want to share, but can no longer say out loud because you wouldn't want your loved one to hear for fear that simple descriptions of care challenges might devastate them in ways you would never intend nor want.[32] No greeting cards are written for the people we love who are physically present but not whom we remember them to be.

Suddenly, or over time, this transformation can make you feel alone, even when surrounded by people you love and care about. Loneliness does not simply happen because there are no audiences around you; rather, it emerges in ways you cannot ignore because you feel distant from the very people who are around you. Family, friends, and loved ones can still be enduring sources of social support because of a shared relational past,[33] but the people closest to you and the ones most likely to be with you throughout your experiences may still not be the right audiences to understand and appreciate your care experiences.

A NEW WAY OF SEEING AND BEING

Disappointment in family and friends is an emotional reaction. It can also be informative—helping you better understand one paradoxical truth of caregiving. Your existing, pre-caregiver networks of family and friends are vital parts of your life. Family, and some friends, will likely be in your life throughout your care experiences.[34] Yet, perhaps for the first time, you are coming to the uncomfortable conclusion that family and friends, alone, cannot suffice. It's scary knowing that there are limits to what your friends and family members can do to support you. It's disorienting to be faced with the reality that there are parts of your experiences, and you, that are beyond the understanding of those closest to you.

The mere thought of reaching out to others who are not family and friends might feel like an act of betrayal because it might look like you are rejecting the very people you know best. Yet, if no one in your existing network is or has been a caregiver, or if no one in your family or friend network is experiencing the type of care experiences you are in the midst of, expecting deep understanding may be unfair to them and you, even though you most want family and friends to be your first (and only) audiences.

Making It Personal

It shouldn't have happened. Not from her. A friend. More than a friend—someone who had been one of my wife's best friends for the last ten years. She had been through a similar situation. Her husband had been diagnosed with cancer, too. I thought she, of all people, would understand what we were going through. We had just received the news that we never expected. It was cancer. And it was aggressive. We were going to begin radiation treatment the following week. I greeted my wife's friend at the door. I was comforted by her presence as we were walking into uncharted territory. Our grown kids were home, too. They had all come home for the weekend. My wife was in her wheelchair in the back room of the house when I walked her friend in. They hugged and cried and then began talking. I left because I felt it was best if they had some time alone.

Only minutes later, I heard what I thought was a different type of crying. I walked back into the room, and I'll never forget the look on my wife's face. Her swollen face looked childlike, scared in a way I had never seen before. My wife's friend told me that they had been discussing what would happen. What radiation would be like. What the cancer might do. What the cancer had done to her own husband. The pain that it had caused him. The suffering that it brought to their family.

I didn't know what to do. I didn't know what to say. This wasn't a stranger I had let in. This was our friend. My wife's friend. I kind of went blank after that, but I remember telling her it was time to leave because we were exhausted. Once she left, the crying began again—uncontrollable and inconsolable. My entire family was now gathered together in one room, but all I could think about was that I had let this happen from the one person I would never have expected. I was expecting comfort, and I don't know what happened. I was responsible. I had let her in; I never thought this would happen. But from that point on, not everyone was welcome in our home, even people with good intentions.

5

WHO AM I BECOMING AND WHY AM I SO HARD ON MYSELF?

Inevitably, you've been asked the question *"What do you do?"* Not long ago, perhaps, this seemed like an easy question to answer. You went somewhere every day to work or engaged in some kind of activity every day, and then each evening, you came home to something and someone awaiting your return. What you once *did* seemingly fit nicely into a very clear and simple sentence: *"I am a . . . ."*

Now, this question is much more complicated. Your working days aren't only spent somewhere else, away from the home. And you don't come home from work to relax or recharge. No, now your home life is as challenging and exhausting as anything you've ever experienced. Work is now inside your home.[1] People who care aren't supposed to place "care" and "work" next to one another in a sentence. But caregiving is a preoccupation that totally disrespects sane working hours, union rules, salary increases, benefits, vacation time, or any other perk you can think of in which others acknowledge the value of your efforts and attention.

The question *"What do you do?"* is totally deceptive. Saying *"I am a caregiver"* isn't the whole truth. It just isn't. No one specializes in caregiving. Yes, you are a caregiver *and* you are also something else. No one has the luxury of solely being a caregiver. Roles help us know what we are expected to say, how we are supposed to act, and how we should relate to others.[2] From work roles to family roles to relationships, we want to know how we are doing and whether we are living up to the expectations for how we think a particular role *should* be fulfilled. Roles are not simply given to us. They are learned and negotiated in everyday conversations and responses.[3] Roles are helpful because they allow us to know what should be included or excluded from our attention.[4] At work or at home, roles tell us when we *should* pick up that phone, open an email, or look at the most recent text, or when it is okay to ignore them. The multiple roles we inhabit shape not only how we think about our experiences, but also what we think is possible and desirable.

Caregiving isn't a role you step into as much as a role that steps into you. The caregiver role is relentless. It is with you at night, long into the darkness, arises with you early in the morning, and stays with you throughout the day. It respects no boundaries. It doesn't account for schedules, nor does it have any concern for sleep or holidays. It does not respect aspirations and couldn't care less about timing. It doesn't care who you were before the role and doesn't acknowledge that you have other relationships. It can't be contained as it trespasses all boundaries.[5] This transformational moment isn't simply about what caregivers *do*. It's about what happens to you when you feel as if you are losing parts of yourself in the process of caring for someone you love.

THE CARE ROLE ALWAYS TRESPASSES

Most people believe in a world of carefully crafted boundaries in which different parts of life can be separated and balanced. They believe that work life can be partitioned from home life. And home life from personal life. And personal life from family life. And family life from romantic life. And romantic life from public life. And public life from online life. And online life from spiritual life, and so on.

Usually, we seek to maintain boundaries between different life roles through a variety of subtle, but influential, cues.[6] Location is used to help compartmentalize and solidify "appropriate" identity responses.[7] We *go* to work. We *drop* our kids off. We *head* home. We *get away* on vacation. These scene shifts, along with accompanying wardrobe changes, clarify the roles we are occupying at any given time, including what we are expected to do and what we (should) pay attention to. Think of the opening scene in *Mister Rogers' Neighborhood*.[8] From his public life, Mister Rogers walks through the front door and into his house, dressed in a suit. Then, he prepares himself for a different role by donning a cardigan, exchanging his dress shoes for house shoes. This location and wardrobe change provides clarity for Mr. Rogers as he is letting go—temporarily—of his public role, and assuming his informal, relational self. These minor but important location and wardrobe changes also signal to us, the viewer, that our relationships with Mr. Rogers will be defined by informality and friendliness, setting the stage for authenticity and connection.

Caregiving renders the compartmentalization of these so-called different aspects of life meaningless because the different roles we inhabit can no longer be kept from influencing one another. For the first time, you may feel that the care role is creating work-life distortions that require you to think about work, not as something that occurs at a particular place or during a specific time, but simply as an additional complication in which your care role demands ongoing attention without any relief. *"How flexible is my supervisor?" "Do I need to change jobs?" "Can I even keep my job?" "Can I get home on lunch break to make sure everything is okay?" "Will anyone notice if I'm checking my phone during meetings and subtly sending texts?"* The care role complicates clean role distinctions, blurring boundaries and removing the possibility of neatly distinguishing one aspect of life from another. Unlike most roles, the care role is always flexible because it can, and must, be enacted across multiple settings (home, doctor's offices, work) with an always-on time expectation (late into the night and throughout the day). Creating strict boundaries—"care begins here and ends there"—is beyond comprehension because the needs of the person you care for and the needs of managing your care role with other simultaneous obligations mean that physical location tells you very little about how to manage your care role. Care is a more about a set of expectations and needs that must be fulfilled despite whatever other roles you may also be inhabiting (spouse, parent, child, employee, student) or wherever you may be (at work, across the country, in different time zones, on the telephone, texting). This kind of always-on access constantly reminds you that wherever you are and whatever you are doing, the care role will create ongoing confusions because there aren't—and can't be—any parts of life and living that are off limits to care.[9]

The care role knows no boundaries as it rearranges the ways in which space can be used to achieve both connection and independence. What happens behind closed doors is considered private and no one else's business but ours and those we willingly allow in. Though the home space has historically been the site of activities believed to be beyond the categorization of work,[10] the caregiver role rearranges relationships inside the home just as it rearranges what is deemed possible outside the home. The home environment can also become imbalanced by the caregiver role. Stairs may become impediments, reminding inhabitants that even at home, some spaces are inaccessible. Bedrooms on the second floor become unused, museums to memories of what used to be possible. Wheelchairs may remind loved ones that hallways are too narrow, and carpets can become a kind of quicksand. No spaces, public or private, are unaffected by the care role.

Sharing a bedroom is one way a spouse or partner can demonstrate relationship commitment. A bedroom creates expectations of particular types of exclusive sharing and intimacy that call for the occasional separation of you, as a couple, from others in the family. Through the closing of bedroom doors, partners expect to be able to share space as a way of encouraging closeness and intensifying their relationship. Spouses that might normally want to be in the same room and in the same bed may find themselves needing to relocate to separate rooms in the house because of changing physical conditions and difficulties sleeping. Relocating rooms, not by choice but by necessity, reinforces a perceived disconnect initiated by the care role that begins to affect what is believed to be possible in the relationship as you once knew it. Loving someone in a romantic relationship used to mean sleeping in the same room and in the same bed. Now, loving someone as a caregiver and partner may mean sleeping in a separate bed or changing rooms completely. Such "small" changes don't simply indicate changes in location. Rather, they also reveal that the relationship that once defined you and your partner's connection can no longer be what it once was as new routines usher in not only new behaviors, but also new ways of interacting.[11]

Loving someone as a parent may have previously meant respecting a child's privacy. Now, loving someone as a caregiver and parent means there can be no privacy because you have to think of your child's safety. For a child, privatizing space within a home (e.g, "that's my room" or having a space in the home where they can "be alone") may be used to designate a growing expectation and need for independence. Growing into adulthood is often associated with the shutting of doors and the claiming of privacy as a means of differentiating one's self from others, even in the space of the home. Yet caring for a child with disabilities may mean that the prospect of using space as a way of communicating independence must be reimagined as the machines, devices, and cords, often accompanying the care role, do not respect architectural layouts.[12]

Inside the home, the care role alters what constitutes private and public acts. Going to the bathroom, for example, is believed to be a private act that requires shutting the door so dignity can be protected from the shame of bodily functions. The very access to your loved one's physical needs that the care role requires feels wrong because it creates access to a loved one's body in ways that infringe on what you once believed should be seen or not seen, given your preexisting relationship. Beyond the caregiver role, shutting people out from such bodily necessities is a way of creating boundaries and maintaining role clarity. But care does not respect the closing of doors, nor does it account for the initial shame that you and your loved one might experience when the boundaries that were once adhered to so meticulously to protect the sanctity of your relationship can no longer exist. Loving a parent may have once meant respecting their authority as a sign of respect. Now, loving someone as a caregiver *and* son or daughter means making decisions for them and violating previous notions of dignity.

Wiping. Relieving. Expunging. Digesting. Sores. Smells. Groans. Labored breathing. Cries. Whereas other roles and relationships ask people to avoid being witness to the body as it is, the care role requires up-close and personal attention, asking you to witness what others want to avoid. The care role does not allow for the respect of boundaries crafted by what is purposefully hidden. *"I don't want you to see me when I'm not at my best." "I want you to be attracted to me, not see me like this."* Instead, the care role requires transgressing the categories of respect, decency, and humility that (mis)guide so many others. Close and ongoing physical proximity to the body changes not only what caregivers witness, but also how they conceive of their relationships.

RELATIONSHIP CONFUSION

Caregiving never occurs in a vacuum. It always takes place in a relational context informed by an existing relationship. If love is a motive for entering the informal caregiving relationship, the superimposition of the

care role onto an already existing relationship ruptures the clear guidelines and expectations that were previously assumed and relied upon.

Physical acts of care necessitated by your care role are now charged
with meaning in ways not previously thought possible. The care role
requires a type of multitasking that defies expectations of "appropriateness." It may necessitate the feeding of loved ones. The bathing of loved
ones. The dressing of loved ones. The care role doesn't simply require
multitasking, it necessitates transgressive tasking, or doing something
you believe goes beyond the boundaries of relational expectations.[13]
The care role doesn't conform to what was once considered appropriate,
given your previous and ongoing relationship, it simply demands action
even though violating decorum may leave you feeling confused, uneasy,
and unsure of how such simple acts might change how you can relate
to your loved one.

Relationship confusion is what can happen when the care role
asks caregivers to act in ways they feel are inconsistent with preexisting
relationship guidelines. For example, the care role of bathing a spouse
can change how you think about your relationship. This one act can become charged with meaning that threatens relational identity. No longer
is physical intimacy and touch designed to enhance your relationship.
Rather, the caregiver role changes the meaning of physical intimacy,
from enhancing closeness to fulfilling a need. Over time, this one act
can create relational confusion and resistance because it deeply unsettles
the way you once viewed your relationship as a spouse or partner. The
reorientation to your loved one's body required by the caregiver role,
from intimacy to tasks, can threaten your own sense of identity because
it suggests a zero-sum dilemma: *"If I bathe my spouse, then I feel more like
a nurse. Even though I know my spouse needs to be bathed, caring for my spouse
in this way may make me feel like something other than a spouse."*

The care role does not acknowledge, nor does it respect, previous
relational boundaries. This incongruity can become a threat to a preexisting relational identity, fracturing who you can be with the person
you love. The more you engage in care tasks, the more you may feel
as though you are betraying your capacity to act and respond consistent
with your original and preferred, non-caregiver-relationship identity.
In the midst of such confusion, questions inevitably emerge that present themselves as either-or threats: *"Am I still a daughter? Or am I only a*

caregiver? Am I really a spouse? Or am I more like a nurse? Am I a parent, or am I more of a doctor/insurance specialist/advocate?" Yes, you may still be a spouse, daughter, or parent. But you are also a caregiver. And because of this reality, it feels as if you are violating the very relationship rules once believed to be sacred in the midst of the increasingly large shadow of the ever-expanding, boundary-breaking caregiver role.

Relationship Recalibration

Role expectations are never fully erased, even though the capacity to fulfill them may no longer be possible. You may feel as though you are no longer a son in the same way you once were since you began caregiving for a parent, but expectations of what a son-parent relationship *should* be don't disappear as much as they exist in an ongoing competition with the care role requirements. While caring for a loved one, you are also involved in something no one can know—a struggle of relationship expectations. This competition is disorienting because it changes how you think about your relationship and yourself. First, it occurs while you are still in a relationship with your loved one, initiating a different and unanticipated confusion. *"How can I be lost when I am in a relationship with the same person?"* Caregivers not only provide acts of care, but they also must wade through the paradox of knowing that the care they are providing is necessary, but also menacing, to the relationship they once experienced.

This kind of relationship recalibration would make more sense if caregivers were able to reintroduce themselves to their loved one because this emergent relationship defies categorization. It exists not as any one particular type of relationship, but as a hybrid that is a strange concoction of the familiar and unfamiliar, the known and the unknown. In some ways, the relationship is similar. In some ways, the relationship is different. In some ways, your loved one is different. In some ways, your loved one may be the same. In some ways, you are different. In some ways, you are the same. You and the person you care for—together—are the same and different but never the same as you used to be or so completely different that you might walk into the relationship without preconceptions of who the other person is and who they should be. But you can't reintroduce yourself. You are expected to act as if this relationship continues, unchanged, with the addition of your care role. But it isn't. You know this in ways others can't or don't.

This unwanted relationship recalibration occurs at the very time when communication and sharing between you and your loved one may be dwindling because of cognitive or physical incapacity, or because you feel that you can't share what you are seeing or experiencing out of concern or fear for how it will be received by your loved one.[14] Disintegrating relationship expectations won't—or can't—be talked about, even though it feels as if everyone will notice how awkward and strange it feels for you. For the first time, you may realize that it's impossible to try to live up to the expectations of your competing relationships because you are responding to desires and assumptions and habits operating in multiple dimensions, beyond others' capacity to notice.

When caregivers live within the confines of one relationship type—parent, child, friend, spouse—there is a set of relatively clear instructions guiding what merits attention and what doesn't. When engaged in both relationships, however, neither relationship feels right. They don't work in harmony, but as silent adversaries that only you notice but could never explain to others. It's like seeing images on Facebook of someone you know so well but also recognizing that the pictures they are posting aren't them. They're real, but not authentic. People who don't know your friend like you do—off stage,[15] between their posts—might think everything is fine because of the smiles and the extravagant locations of their posts. You know something other people don't because you don't simply see the pictures themselves, without context. You also know of the experiences and challenges they *aren't* posting.

As a caregiver, you are living in multiple realities that can't be forgotten because you feel them when the blurring lines of expectations bump into you. The realities of the care role that you weren't prepared for are now rearranging everything you once held sacred and true about your preexisting relationship. But, to the outside world, your relationship is the same. Or not changed enough to think that anything is really that different between your pre- and post-caregiver relationship. Here, in this moment, lostness is knowing that though you are in the same relationship and family system, everything is different. Here, in this moment, you know you can feel desperately lost in a relationship you've been in for years.

The rules of the relationship that once told you what to do and how to act to remain loyal, faithful, loving, and fulfilled now no longer make any sense. The rules are still there, present and never going away, but every time you "violate" the rules that once seemed so sacred to your relationship, you can't keep yourself from questioning what is happening to you and what you are becoming in the process. Self-doubt becomes magnified as competing role expectations inspire questions about you and your relationship that may no longer be able to be shared. *"My loved one needs this to be done, but I don't want to do it, not because I don't want it to happen, but because it has consequences for how I see myself with this person."*

Caregivers face ongoing role dilemmas few others can notice or appreciate. The care role isn't simply about tasks. It also involves a type of divorce from other relationship expectations that can be rejected, but never forgotten. This ongoing tension involves trying to negotiate what you know was once possible in your relationship with your loved one but may no longer be able to be realized in the caregiver role. The multiple roles we inhabit shape not only how we think about our experiences, but also what we think is possible and desirable.[16] This overlaying of contrary relationship expectations—what you wish would happen contrasted with what is needed and what you remember contrasted with what is before you—can't help but influence how you think about and experience the caregiver role.

ROLE EXHAUSTION

In relationships, when someone *needs* you, what *you* want takes a backseat. When you are in a relationship characterized by need, rather than preference and choice, everything one does or does not do is clarified by a standard of necessity that makes most everything else—especially your own wants and desires—pale in comparison. Constant attention to a loved one's needs can create guilt the moment you even begin thinking about yourself apart from the caregiver role.

Caregivers can feel as if they are disappearing into the care role because when choice is upended by need, how you view yourself changes. There is no rebuttal to need when you, as a caregiver, are close enough to appreciate a loved one's needs in ways that others don't or can't. Constantly responding to a loved one leaves little motivation to see beyond immediate circumstances. Nothing else matters, as almost everything else exists beyond your peripheral vision, allowing you to see only what is immediately before you—the needs of the minute, the needs of the hour, and the needs of the day. Seized by this absolute focus, everything else, including you—is in danger of being excluded. Somewhere in this process, the care role doesn't just change what you do, it changes how you *think* about what you do.

Never Enough

Caregivers are likely to feel that whatever they do in the face of unending need isn't enough. Whatever their efforts, however much they sacrifice, however long they go without sleep, or whatever extent they go to in an attempt to forgo other aspects of their lives and relationships, it never seems enough. The needs of the care role seem unquenchable, especially when caring won't necessarily change the outcome or even reduce the challenges or suffering your loved one may be experiencing in the moment. Over time, caregivers can feel "used up"[17] as beliefs about what one is doing or is capable of doing become distorted by feelings of inadequacy.[18]

For most other roles, there are measurable goals of accomplishment. Creating goals and metrics of accomplishment allow people to make sense of their day as it focuses attention on what is deemed worthy of remembering and highlighting. *"I did great today. I crossed everything off my list." "All of the work I've been doing finally paid off. Today, we made the deal." "This is our 25th wedding anniversary. A day truly worth celebrating."* Definable and achievable targets push us to get up early or stay later at work, and they provide incentive to make it through the more challenging aspects of our roles. *"If I can only get through this day and fulfill today's objectives, then I can take a deep breath and pat myself on the back for a job well done."* When caregivers feel as if their efforts are unworthy of assessment, acknowledgment, and feedback, they are like runners who are asked to run endlessly, without mile markers, with no watch to pace their efforts, and no destination to propel their bodies forward even when they feel like stopping. Without guides to make sense of their ongoing experiences, caring without benchmarks of meaning and renewal can quickly become exhausting and overwhelming.

Caregiving defies traditional standards of measurement. *"How can you talk about accomplishments when your loved one is still ill?" "Care shouldn't be measured—it's just something you do." "How can I reward myself when there's always something more to do?"* Goals and criteria for accomplishment make sense for public roles. In the private, home-based world of relationships, however, the care role exists without discernible ways for caregivers to find traction in role-based accomplishments. Since caring for a loved one often means a willingness to be present with another, even when a cure may not be possible or a change of outcome is not viable, caregiver "accomplishments" seem implausible and inappropriate. And so, caregivers care without such markers of accomplishment.

The role also seems immune from assessments of quality. Since caregiving is believed to be something one engages in because of a prior relationship connection, even contemplating what it might mean to be a "good" caregiver is disallowed. *"Talking about being good at being a caregiver—that's strange." "What is there to feel good about when what you're doing doesn't change your situation?"* Any discussion of performance is believed to be exclusively associated with desirable roles (e.g., nurse, doctor) that lead to positive outcomes. The possibility of trying to understand how someone can be a "good" caregiver in challenging situations asks people to accept the incongruous reality that assessments of quality can coexist alongside suffering. And so, caregivers care without guidance or role direction, preventing them from finding refuge in knowing that their daily efforts might be met with acknowledgment and appreciation, if only for a moment.

Role performance is often informed by feedback from others. In work roles, feedback is provided by supervisors, managers, and peers. Feedback for the care role, however, is not encouraged when the role is over-personalized and often labeled a *calling*, not a role. If care is only considered a calling,[19] reserved for special people,[20] rather than a role anyone can inhabit, it denies the possibility of talking about the challenges of caregiving because the focus is only on the incredible and extraordinary abilities of the person in the role. People who respond to callings aren't supposed to complain. Conceiving of caregiving as a calling excuses the possibility of even having to consider caregiving apart from the person who occupies the role. Consequently, feedback from others is discouraged. No one will tell you that you are doing a "good" job. And no one will ask if you are doing a "good" job. Though they may be individually celebrated, caregivers care without benchmarks, leaving them unprotected from being overwhelmed by an inability to mark their everyday experiences as meaningful.

Feedback from the very person you are caring for may also be limited and incomplete because they may not be capable of distinguishing what you are doing from what they need. Even if cognitively and physically capable of providing feedback, loved ones receiving care are remarkably vulnerable. They may recognize your ongoing care efforts and appreciate that their lives and comfort are (completely) in your hands. Yet they may also be aware that they can't change the situation they are in, nor can they lighten your load or reciprocate in any comparable way to what you are doing for them as a caregiver. As a result, seeking role feedback from your loved one is unfair because it asks them to risk jeopardizing the overwhelmingly uneven, one-sided dynamic of the care relationship. Yes, they want you taking care of them, but they also need you in ways that constantly remind them of the power you have over every aspect of their lives.[21] And so caregivers care in silence.

Under the Influence of Emotional Exhaustion

You have been *on* all day—attending to your loved one's physical and emotional needs. You've returned several calls and texts to family and friends who had left messages days earlier, hoping to get the latest update on your loved one's condition. You've made three meals, cleaned the house, and spent almost an hour trying to get in contact with the doctor about changing pain medications in hopes of helping your loved one sleep through the night. Finally, it's 9 p.m., and for the first time all day, silence. It's dark outside, and you hardly noticed what the weather was like all day. In fact, you're not even sure of the day of the week. Your weary body finds the pillow and then your eyes close. Darkness and exhaustion are the perfect breeding grounds for toxic and inaccurate generalizations that mysteriously distort the most innocent of thoughts into permanent and devastating so-called truths.

"*Today* was so difficult" becomes "*Every passing day* will get more and more difficult." "I am exhausted *right now*" becomes "I don't have the energy to do this *anymore*." "I feel so alone *right now*" becomes "No one can *ever* truly understand what I am going through." "I forgot to go to the bank *today*" becomes "I can't remember anything *anymore*." "I was expecting a phone call of support from *my good friend* this morning" becomes "*All of my friends* have moved on with their lives." Toxic generalizations about you and your care situation are most likely to occur when you are exhausted because, when under the influence of exhaustion, you are more likely to transform a momentary feeling or experience into permanence.[22] The more you think about your experiences at night, alone and exhausted, the more likely you are to believe in the permanence of your thoughts, even though these so-called truths may be completely inaccurate and unhealthy.

Under the influence of exhaustion, caregivers are prone to feel as if their unending, daily efforts are meaningless because there is no way for them to feel good about what they are doing or accomplishing. Not being appreciated for one's work, especially when someone is wholly devoted to a loved one, can create unyielding stress. Feeling inadequate in the role that you are in, whether physically present with your loved one or not, inhibits caregivers from the privilege of closing their eyes at night knowing with complete confidence that they, in fact, are not only doing a good job, but also from even knowing what doing a good job might mean.

The voice caregivers use to talk to themselves when exhausted and alone isn't supportive and encouraging. It's nasty and unrelenting. It's usually full of contempt and almost never self-forgiving. In the silence of their own thoughts, caregivers are vulnerable to treating themselves in ways they would never treat others. Distorted by exhaustion and isolation, the self-voice—the one no one else hears—never, ever apologizes. Apologies are born out of an expected response to others, not to ourselves. When one's voice emerges and is left unchecked, it isn't forgiving. It is free to fling generalizations and absolutes without regret, transforming whatever challenge is being experienced into an immutable truth that leaves no room for mistakes or self-understanding. If and when you are the only audience to yourself, the voice you hear can become distortive and repetitive, completely misreading and overplaying what you believe you can't do, or what you feel you aren't living up to, a constant reminder of individual inadequacies and failures. Even though the more you hear your inner voice, the more persuasive it sounds, what you hear is incomplete as your voice leaves no room for correction, adaptation, and perspective.

When the care role and the person in the care role are indistinguishable, caregivers can feel overwhelmed and consumed in their situations, making it more difficult to differentiate how they feel about themselves from their ability to adjust, respond, and cope with the situation at hand. In the midst of silence, role exhaustion can begin to distort how caregivers think about their experiences and the conclusions they reach about themselves when they don't know how to—and don't believe they deserve to—find self-compassion.

FINDING YOURSELF THROUGH SELF-COMPASSION

Many people in your existing networks may talk about the importance of self-care— *"You must take care of yourself." "If you don't take care of yourself, you won't be able to take care of your loved one."* This is all true. But you also are more likely to dismiss their advice because you interpret their statements as evidence of misunderstanding, given everything you have to do and all the responsibilities that cannot be postponed. However, this very same advice from those who are also caregivers will be listened to differently because someone isn't simply telling you something, they are living it. And you may listen anew, too, knowing that advice, information, and insights from people who have shared experiences, not a shared family history, can't simply be ignored or rejected. Their words are grounded in shared experiences, not simply advice from afar.

Most people recognize the importance of having compassion for others and approaching them and their situations with kindness and understanding.[23] It is much more difficult, however, to grant compassion to yourself, especially when who you are and what you are doing in the care role are indeterminately mixed together. The recipe for such a mixture often provides little, if any, protection from a kind of unrelenting self-criticism that reveals more about one's tolerance for self-compassion than an accurate, objective analysis of how someone is managing the care role. Just because you become accustomed to what you tell yourself about how you are doing in your care role, self-compassion means risking hearing and learning something that may change what you thought about yourself. Contrary to what most people think, self-compassion isn't a selfish act, but a necessary buffer to protect oneself from the occupational hazards of the care role: defensive and emotional thinking that negatively impacts one's ability to provide quality, ongoing care to themselves and their loved one.[24]

Making room for self-compassion also means making it possible to better understand how your role is shaping you in ways that are more accurate and objective than could ever be rendered when you are mired in the cycle of inadequacy and unfair self-criticism. Self-compassion does not mean freeing yourself of responsibilities. Instead, it allows you to open yourself up to others, making it possible for you to communicate with people who have a clearer perception of your situation than you might ever be able to have because you are in it, exhausted, criticizing yourself, over and over, until it becomes a reality you accede to, not because it helps you or because it's accurate, but because its unending repetition simply becomes familiar.

Self-compassion is an invitation to allow yourself to connect with others by finding the "we" and "us" in a role that can often make you feel alone and disconnected. Finding yourself within your role means risking thinking about yourself differently by being able to share with other caregivers who will allow you to find perspective through commonality of role challenges and joys. Self-compassion isn't about feeling sorry for yourself. It's about finding yourself in others, with others[25] and allowing yourself to give voice to what can't be stated to friends and family: the profane and the joyous aspects of the care experience that need to be voiced. Perhaps most importantly, self-compassion may permit you to begin creating enough distance between you and your role so you can begin to see the parts of yourself that you haven't allowed yourself to fully appreciate.[26]

A NEW WAY OF SEEING AND BEING

The care role that you find yourself in requires a reclaiming of metrics that will allow you to think about yourself, and your role experiences, in sustainable and authentic ways. Though others may use values of "perfection" and "outcomes" to guide them, these same metrics make no sense to the care role. Instead, caregivers must lean on values consistent with their role. Connection and mindfulness, not perfection and outcomes, are more appropriate markers and guides for your role because they emphasize the need and importance of the care role and how the role changes how you think about yourself.

Mindfulness encourages ongoing, non-labeling awareness of experiences, thoughts, and feelings as they occur throughout the care role. Instead of using outcomes as a metric of analysis, mindfulness requires a willingness to nonjudgmentally reflect on how you believe you are responding to unfolding situations and yourself.[27] Mindfulness is a value consistent with the care role because it is not dependent on outcome, results, tests, or end goals. Mindfulness refocuses attention by asking you to reflect on what is—rather than what isn't, what could be, and what should be. Below are some reflection questions that will help you get started thinking and writing about your experiences in ways that remind you of your role value in mindful, self-compassionate ways.

Today, what experience or moment did I appreciate that was enough on its own terms (without concern for what will come tomorrow)? What was it specifically about this experience that was so meaningful?[28]

I got really upset today. Now, in trying to better understand why I responded the way I did, I was really curious that my response was probably influenced by . . . .[29]

How was I kind to myself today? I was kind to myself today when dealing with . . . . I gave myself the care I needed today when I . . . .[30]

Making It Personal

I know why sleep deprivation is used as a form of torture. Our son is nearly thirty now, and he has never slept through a night in his life. A brain injury causes him to have seizures or cry out in pain or stop breathing until someone rubs his cheek. Seven years ago, our young man moved into a nearby care home where a nurse remains awake at his bedside, attending to all his nocturnal needs. But for many years, our family had no such support—my husband and I simply stayed awake in shifts.

In 2004, my husband was traveling often on business. I was attempting the impossible: staying awake to care for my children both day and night. One chilly, dark November morning, our part-time personal aide rang the doorbell to get our boy dressed and ready for school. It had been a particularly hard night, and I'd only slept for perhaps an hour. I heard my daughter answer the door and call after the dog who escaped through her legs, running across the street to the high school sports field. "Mom, Goldie escaped! What should I do?" "Get ready for school and I'll be down in a minute," I slurred. "Ask the helper to go get the dog and bring her back." I stumbled to the stairs, pulling my dressing gown around me and called down, "Is Goldie back now?" "No, Mum, the helper left. She told me to go get Goldie myself," said my daughter quietly. "She left? Why?" I began to cry. I threw my winter coat on over my pajamas and ran to the park, leash in hand. I cajoled the dog home, then proceeded to dress our son for school, prepare his medications and tube feeding supplies for the day and fill schoolbags with homework and snacks.

I was shaking when, after the children were safely at school, I telephoned the morning aide. "Why did you leave?" I was sobbing now. "What? Pardon? I . . . I'm not . . . supposed to look after pets," she stammered. I hung up, choking back my tears.

Later, I remembered an article I'd read about a palliative cancer patient who was also a mother of young children. She described her racking guilt to a friend, "I'm dying and I feel like I am abandoning my children," she cried. "Why is this happening? Did I eat too much sugar? Did my hair color cause my cancer? What did I do wrong?" Her friend answered, "Don't kick the baby. The baby is you. You are so fragile now. So don't kick the baby." I thought about myself, my body that felt like an aching shell. "Don't kick the baby. *Cradle* the baby."

The next day after school, my children asked to play in the park. "OK," I said, pushing our son's wheelchair out the front door with his sister perched on his lap. I held Goldie's leash around my left wrist and she pranced beside us. At the end of the driveway, I paused to look both ways before crossing, then pushed ahead. "I am so strong," I told myself, "and smart." I smiled and shivered as the chill began to penetrate my rain shell. "Cradle the baby," I thought.

6

WHEN "GETTING THROUGH" ISN'T GOOD ENOUGH

"**K**eep *your head down." "Keep going." "Grind." "Just get through it."* This is what we usually tell ourselves when life becomes difficult. This is how we seek to remain motivated when what we are facing is so frustrating and challenging that we must remind ourselves that something better is waiting on the other side. This is how we keep ourselves going when our bodies and minds tell us otherwise. *"When it's over." "When life gets better." "When things can return to normal." "When my relationship returns to what it once was." "When I get my life back."*

Survival mode has its benefits. It summons a type of complete focus and determination in an attempt to match the situation at hand. But exclusively relying on the *just get through it* mentality has consequences for caregivers because, as the hours and days pass, as one month blurs into months and seasons change, the *when it's over* mentality inevitably crashes into the realization that caregiving has become part of your life and part of who you are.

This urgency to make sense of your experiences seemingly comes out of nowhere, bumping into you without notice. *"Not now." "Tomorrow." "Soon." "When I'm ready." "Things are changing so rapidly. It's too early." "I will later."* These refrains, which may have guided you for so long, suddenly feel as if they are asking you to be indifferent to life—your life—that is passing you by because you've kept your head down, day after day. No one will give you permission to begin making sense of your experiences. After doctors, nurses, pharmacists, physical therapists, family, and loved ones walk and drive away from your situation or hang up the phone, or after they send an email or text, you are still in it. Other people will not find value in your experiences in ways that make sense to you. They don't have to—yet. They don't need to—yet. You have to—now. You must—now.[1]

This care transformation isn't noticeable. It isn't like a before-and-after reality television show where you can easily see the change by comparing what you look like now to what you used to look like. There are no big reveal moments when it comes to displaying how caregiving has shaped you and your beliefs. Internal makeovers are searing and silent. They reveal themselves slowly, and tentatively, not in bold declarations but in everyday conversations and interactions that are often met with disbelief rather than adoration. Care has been working its way *through* you, transforming how you think about what is possible and desirable. Care, deep care for another, can't help but transform. Care inevitably infiltrates every part of caregivers from their eyesight to their mind-set. It sets itself upon you in ways that begin to remake what you once took for granted. Your beliefs didn't come to you by accident. They were earned. They bear the signature of your care experiences.

ACCEPTANCE WITHOUT CONDITIONS

In adulthood, acceptance becomes a kind of dirty word. Never settle. Never stop trying. Never stop desiring. Never stop persuading. Never stop wanting something more than what is before us. This preoccupation with change inevitably finds its way into relationships. *"If you would only stop talking about . . . ." "If this is going to work, you need to do less of this." "If this is going to work, you need to do more of this."* This kind of conditional engagement with another is what is referred to as "care" and "love." Yet, relating to another in this way is built on the unstated belief that the people we care about are always incomplete.

Acceptance, as a relationship orientation, is so rare because it asks people to risk engaging with the person who is in front of them rather than who they want a loved one to be. Not where they need him to be. Not where they are asking her to be, but where she is now. Caregivers' desire for someone they love to improve and get better is always present, but caregiving relationships cannot be enacted with a strict change orientation because there may be certain realities that will not bend to any desire for change.

The "what *isn't* and *could be*" filter is intoxicating because it allows for connection based on the prospect of change or so-called improvement. An exclusive focus on this change orientation, however, means that so much is missed. This relational orientation does not allow partners to give their full attention to the person with them. The person before them, the unfiltered person and their story, is left overlooked, underappreciated, and inevitably undervalued when compared to what *could be* and what *might* happen. Though caregivers may initially have no option other than leading with a filter of acceptance, this relational orientation, or way of being with another, opens up a different way of seeing and connecting. Caregivers do not have the luxury of neglecting who is before them because care requires acceptance as a type of focused response to a loved one's ongoing needs.

A relational orientation featuring change creates unnecessary distance between people, perpetually plotting satisfaction and connection just out into the future, one step removed from where you are and whom you are with. The capacity to enter into a care-based relationship, then, is an act of disruption to the change model that most others can't even contemplate. *"How do you do it, really?" "I couldn't do it, I care too much." "I would start crying every time I enter the room."* Perhaps these well-intentioned comments from others hint at how caregiving experiences shape you differently from others. Through an orientation of acceptance, caregivers are more prepared to direct their attention to the realities before them than to the endless possibilities of what might be, what could be, what should be, and what may never be. Caregivers' openness to acceptance can be unsettling to others because it also means rejecting the idea that what is happening now is less important than what we wish would happen. Genuinely engaging another is intimidating because it means rejecting strategies of distraction that blind us to the needs of the person before us. It also means acknowledging that the person near us is worthy of being themselves in ways that may contradict who we thought they were and who we want them to be.

Acceptance is a radically disruptive orientation to most people because it asks us to risk engaging with another on *their* terms, not where we want them to be. Not where we need them to be. Not where we are asking them to be—but where they are now. Caregiving is a response to a call to accept loved ones as they are: cognitively, physiologically, and relationally. Rather than ignoring these realities, caregivers must develop the capacity to simultaneously mourn what can't be changed, recognize what can be changed, *and* accept their situation so that care and comfort can be provided.

A filter of change doesn't permit an investment in any given moment wholly and completely because a preoccupation with change serves as a type of insurance between now and later. The change orientation protects relational participants from fully attending to the present in hopes that an elusive possibility will allow them to hedge bets and only partially commit to the person and challenges staring at them. Expecting and demanding change—constantly—from another is a recipe for indifference. It is a reluctance to commit entirely to this one person at this particular time in the hope that tomorrow will come to the rescue and mitigate the need to adjust to who your loved one is now.

Caregivers' unparalleled proximity to loved ones in the midst of suffering and need encourages an unlearning of what most others ignore. When the filter change is temporarily removed, caregivers more fully allow themselves to experience the intensity of the present. The filter of acceptance that caregivers must embrace to enact their caregiving duties, however, means that there is no protection from the challenges of the moment. Yet this commitment to the situation at hand and person before them also means that their experiences may be more intense when compared to those equally invested in the present and the future, the person before them and the person they want them to become.

BEYOND COSTS AND BENEFITS

Throughout life, many relationships are based on an unstated arrangement: we engage (and remain) in relationships with others when we believe there is more to be gained from being with someone than not being with them.[2] This type of reciprocal exchange makes so much sense when relationships are perceived as equal— *"I'm giving as much as I'm getting and I'm getting as much as I'm giving."*

When it comes to caregiver relationships, however, everything is turned upside down. The unquestioned assumption that we should only engage in relationships in which we believe we gain as much as we give does not fit within the caregiver model and can quickly become difficult for others to understand. *"Let me get this straight—you care, day after day, and you get what in return?" "What are you getting out of this?"* Your care and willingness to be with another without assurances that you will gain advancement, fame, money, solace, comfort, fulfillment, or even reciprocity can't help but make others uncomfortable because it ruptures the unstated expectations imported into almost every other type of relationship.

The caregiver relationship defies a rational, cost-benefit analysis— *"I should engage in this activity because the rewards will outweigh the costs."* And yet, caregivers care hour after hour and day after day. The caregiver relationship, therefore, says something about an emerging value system that perhaps you have not yet allowed yourself to notice or fully appreciate. Your care means you are willing to be involved in a relationship that does not lead to more comfort, rest, assuredness of appreciation, deep understanding, peace of mind, or reciprocity. Your ongoing willingness to care, despite the fact that caregiving contradicts relational cost-benefit models that guide so many, means that something else must be involved.

Self-interest alone cannot be sufficient to understand the reason(s) why someone remains in a caregiver relationship despite the lopsided cost-benefit equation. Shared history and love for another cannot be compelled into *a* benefit because care is a transcendent relationship value that includes, but is not limited to, the caregiver relationship. It is also an extension of a previously existing relationship (spouse, child, parent). Costs *or* benefits, therefore, aren't easily labeled when the person being cared for has a name, a face, and a shared history. Caregivers realize that costs *or* benefits are always tainted by an inability to untangle one from the other because neither can be quarantined from a larger context of care that is informed and complicated by an evolving relationship.

The caregiver relationship calculus complicates this formula when framed in a more comprehensive and holistic context of value. When other people dream of making a difference in the world beyond—work, politics, art, or entertainment—impact is so often viewed as happening away from where you are and what you are currently doing. Instead of looking exclusively to the public space for purpose, value, and meaning, caregiving cannot be fully appreciated as only a relationship. It is most definitely a relationship and yet it is also something more. It's also a value statement that transcends any assessment of cost and benefit apart from an emerging system of meaning.

As another person's lifeline, caregiver responsibilities are immense and, at times, overwhelming. But the gravity of this felt responsibility is also a sign of role importance and value that is rarely, if ever, experienced by people seeking a reminder of why they do what they do on a daily basis. The courage to care for the most vulnerable—especially when it doesn't conform to measures of self-interest—doesn't make most people's bucket lists. Bucket lists are usually about individual goals and experiences only dreamed about—travels to faraway places and incredible adventures. Caregiving isn't likely on anyone's bucket list. Few people ever dream of caring for someone who is ill or disabled. Caregiving is about what currently exists—not what's out there in the abyss of possibility. Caregiving is grounded in the everyday, not in the imagination of vacated realities. It's situated in the real, not the ideal. It takes place within your home, not on a grand stage in a destination city. It takes place with someone you know, not someone you hope to meet.

In the act of caring for someone, values are being created that are shaping not simply how you care in your role and relationship, but also what you expect in the roles and relationships beyond caregiving. Overhearing others talk about what they are going to do and who they are going to become is alluring, but it also excludes the possibility that value can emerge from something other than the exotic and distant. It can also arise within already existing relationships, from the routine and the local. That person nearest to you, not people in general, but this person, now, today, may not be on most people's bucket list, but your care for another may be remaking what you believe should (not) be on your bucket list. For caregivers, making a difference isn't about what happens tomorrow. Or when you are ready. Or when you are done with your education and your finances are in order. Or when you feel fully prepared for what is to come. Making a difference is all about what you are doing and who you are becoming when no one else is watching.

BEFORE AND AFTER WORDS

Listening is one of the most potent forms of communication because it allows people to become closer and develop a deeper connection.[3] Even though most people put "listening" at the top of their résumés,[4] those of us who are in caregiver relationships know that listening isn't just about remembering something, and it surely can't be reducible to a "skill." For caregivers, it's so much more.

Caregivers' experiences highlight the limitations of words as a way of knowing and understanding. In general, the moment we open our mouths to speak, we limit our ability to fully observe and appreciate our surroundings and the people in them. Situational awareness disappears into the background as arguments and abstract thought take center stage. Speaking seeks to change perceptions of situations. It isn't necessarily designed to understand people and create connections. Speaking can divide people from one another because we only open our mouths to say something when we want to correct or alter the world and the people around us. When done "right" or "persuasively," speaking silences the other. *"I win, you lose." "My argument is better than yours." "I totally shut him up with my thesis."* Statements and propositions attack and can poke others into antagonistic relationships that position people in static and deceptive categories of creator and listener, I versus you, offensive and defensive postures, winner and loser, and them versus us.[5]

Too often, people rely on words to make them feel less alone by filling the silence. Caregivers understand listening in much more nuanced and dynamic ways. Listening is the anti-abstraction. Listening has no past and no future. It can't be used as a weapon to unload on another. It doesn't allow for the purging of frustrations and angst that someone has been holding onto. Listening always takes place in the company of others (or their messages). It is the ultimate human act of *now* because it fastens you to the moment and opens you up to understand all that is before you. Even thousands of miles away, on a phone call, listening can make you feel as if as if you were next to one another. Understanding is a natural off-spring of listening because it is a constant reminder that we are not alone. Unlike most others, caregivers in close physical proximity to a loved one appreciate nonverbal communication as the language of communion.

Words, not touch, are the language of the spectator. Communicating with one another at a distance (4 to 12 feet) has become the new normal. Our intimate space (within 18 inches around us) and personal space (1.5 to 4 feet)[6] are so often left empty in everyday, relational life that people too easily forget how to "be" when someone is close enough to us that we can touch them and they can touch us. And when intimate space is breached, it's usually in the form of an inconvenience as we're passing by others in crowded spaces to get to where we really want to be. Since caregivers regularly interact in a space of intimacy with their loved one defined by close proximity and intimacy, words can seem more harsh and oftentimes defy the appropriateness of the moment that calls for closeness, not persuasion.

Words are given so much attention because they are proof of an interaction and can be summarized, explained, and shared with those not present. Comprehension is valued because facts and information can be recorded and transcribed, memorized and regurgitated. Speakers prepare for what they are going to say because the spotlight will be on them. They prepare, in advance, the right words and the right arguments because speaking is a public spectacle to be seen and heard as far as a voice will project. And it isn't just what is said that matters. Speaking is also a referendum on the speaker. *"How did I do?" "What do people think of me?"* Listeners don't prepare for listening. It isn't showy, even though listening never stops as it is always unfolding. It's subtle. It doesn't draw an audience as speaking does. No one will gather to watch someone listen. There is nothing to be seen. No standing ovations. No curtain calls. Listening, in relationships, requires no amplification because it draws people nearer without conditions in the way speaking does. And listening isn't a referendum on the self as much as it is an invitation to create something together.

Listening isn't about a perfectly eloquent sentence. It isn't something that can be recorded for posterity and shared with others. When listening, we can't help but find ourselves turning our attention and presence toward another, where the *I* and *you* mysteriously transform into a *we* that is often impossible when one person is speaking *at* another. Caregivers, as invitational listeners, create conditions for sharing and understanding because they open themselves to what exists before them. This involves a willingness to be close enough to another person to invite the possibility for genuine and authentic sharing. And sharing isn't only about words—it's about an awareness of another that allows for understanding to occur beyond the exchange of information. The kind of listening that caregivers engage in is distinct because it isn't only about what is said, but also about what is made possible.

SILENCE AS AN INVITATION

Just the two of you, but nothing is said. There should be so much to talk about. So much you want to say. So much you thought about saying on the drive over to visit. But here you are, sitting only feet from your loved one, and there is nothing but silence. A caregiver may interpret this situation very differently from someone for whom silence is viewed as a threat to connection. Within a silence-as-threat interpretation, panic ensues during prolonged interpersonal silence. Muscles become tense as silence becomes a breeding ground for disconnecting attributions. *"Is everything okay?" "Is she mad at me?" "Did I do something wrong?" "It was a mistake to visit." "I'm never doing this again."*

For those not informed by caregiving relationships, silence is one of the great social fears when in the company of someone we care for. Most people are taught that silence is a sign of something gone wrong. So, it's no surprise that interpersonal silence is believed to be an inevitable sign of something that must be terribly wrong because if there isn't talking, relating cannot be possible. If there is an absence of talking, someone must be upset. If the person you are with doesn't have anything to say, the visit is worthless. If you don't have anything to say, the interaction must be a waste of time. Most people are highly educated when it comes to knowing how to make sense of others' words—but too often, they are unprepared to make sense of the meanings of silence between words. Words are believed to equal reassurance. From this mind-set, silence introduces the cascading of doubt about yourself, the other, and what is happening between you and another. When this is the default way to interpret silence, is it any surprise most people allow themselves to endure this surge of awkwardness for only a matter of mere seconds?

Silence, however, is a language caregivers understand because it is an essential part of their relationship with those who are tired, ill, or unable to speak. Silence can bring people closer together only when silence is viewed as a means of knowing rather than a sign of awkwardness. Caregivers know that awkwardness quickly flows into appreciation when they trust in the knowledge that what is being shared together may be more important than anything that could be put into words. Caregivers know what most others don't—talk is just as effective at keeping people "distant" as it is in drawing people near. If others were able to witness how you, as a caregiver, create and maintain closeness with your loved one, they would likely question the value of the interaction. *"I don't get it, nothing happened? Nothing was said."* What outsiders might dismiss as awkward—*"I don't get how you can spend time with someone who can't talk or express themselves?"*—your experiences lead you to a different conclusion.

Silence, in the company of someone you already know, can be sacred. Connection can happen without sharing a single word. Silence is a social act of sharing that reorients you to openness without holding you or the other person hostage to a detailed examination of someone's history, background, or résumé. Silence, with an accompanying willingness and desire to be present, can sometimes communicate all that needs to be said. Presence, without words, can focus attention in ways that no words could ever inspire because it reveals a truth that caregivers learn from their experiences. It is talking, not silence, that camouflages what we already have in common with one another. It is talking, not silence, that dupes us into believing that words are necessary to find commonality when common humanity already exists.

From this orientation, silence isn't a description of what *isn't* happening between two people as much as it is an invitation to appreciate what *is* being created between two people. Openness to what is possible is scary to most people because it means not being able to predict or control what will happen in an interaction. This is one reason why invitational listening is rare. Invitational listeners learn how to temporarily reject the world beyond by completely and wholly embracing the person they are with. By temporarily rejecting others not present, caregivers allow themselves to more fully embrace *this* moment, *this* person, and *this* possibility for connection—*now*. This willingness to risk *being* where others are unable or unwilling to venture makes you a pioneer of the spaces between people that, when encouraged through silence, allow the revelation of new possibilities.

Caregivers' enhanced level of comfort with silence can give a loved one the greatest gift of all—permission to be themselves. They don't have to put on a show. They don't have to "get up" for meeting you. They can be authentically themselves. Knowing that they can sleep peacefully in your company or listen to you without having to give you verbal feedback means you are different from most others, whose presence requires them to be something other than they are feeling or experiencing.[7] Your comfort with silence is an incredible gift of peace, an invitation to grow into a moment that isn't for anyone else but you and the person you are with.

The willingness to listen through silence is a radical act because it often occurs when the world beyond no longer believes your loved one needs to be listened to. You—and your presence and attention—disagree. You know something others don't—listening is transformative for both you and your loved one. Transformation through listening isn't a public act to be seen and liked by others. Transformation unfolds when you open yourself to being near another while temporarily rejecting the temptation to be accessible to others not present with you in that moment.

Silence is always lost in this translation. The interaction exists for itself because it was valuable on its own merits, not because it would necessarily be meaningful to others. No one can have access to that particular moment as it was experienced. No picture can capture what was seen and felt. But then again, the fact that what was shared can't be replicated is what makes invitational listening through silence so compelling. Certain shared moments created between you and your loved one are exclusive to you both in that particular moment. Yes, it's vital to be able to explain the value of your interactions to others. But it's equally important to know that those moments between you and your loved one are meaningful precisely because they can never be fully translated.

Integration, Not Competition

The values of competition so revered in public life don't translate to caregiving because competition's focus on difference inhibits the maintenance of curiosity, interest, and collaboration. Competitive accomplishments look and sound impressive. But these same accomplishments also give the impression that accomplishments are the only aspects of a person that matter. The language of competition fits nicely within a cure-based care model because it marshals energy, strength, resources, and attention toward a future that offers something that the present does not. *"When I get to where I really want to be, then . . . ." "When I get the respect I think I deserve, then . . . ." "When others finally appreciate me for what I've been doing, then . . . ." "When there is a cure, then . . . ."*

A cycle of competition is incompatible with caregiving because it asks people to stand apart from the world, even though the person you love might be right next to you. They may be next to you, but you are not, as your mind is scanning the horizon for respect and acclaim and appreciation miles away from the voices, needs, laughter, and concerns of those you hear and touch. *"Am I doing better than others? Worse?" "I'm not where I thought I would be."* Competition distorts the world around you when dealing with others, reducing people and experiences to perceived threats and opportunities. When viewed through the lens of competition, others are either with you or against you, transforming the people in your life into objects worthy of retreating from rather than walking toward.

Caregiving makes it possible to see others, not as threats but as allies. Caregiving invites viewing others as whole people with a multitude of life experiences and perspectives that don't ask to be changed or converted—just appreciated. A framework of collaboration, rather than competition, opens caregivers up to finding comfort in a shared humanity. Rejecting a competitive mind-set means focusing, not on how you may be different from others, but how you are alike. The collaborative orientation necessary to caregiving recognizes the importance of integration, not distinction, as it values a willingness to become a part of people's experiences, not to become the center of attention. Competition is showy. *"Look what I did." "See how I'm better than the rest."* Standing above others, the competitor thrives in the glory of the limelight, eventually allowing value to be reduced to others' adoration.

Competition seemingly creates the need for confidence, or the perceived ability to walk into any scenario armed with an unwavering belief in an ability to influence people and solve problems. Confidence becomes an important way in which people are assessed. Yet confidence, conceived in this way, is incompatible with caregiving because it requires the belief that confident people are better, smarter, more knowledgeable, and more competent than everyone else. It presumes that the confident person already has the answers and always knows what's going on—as if confidence was something possessed for all times and all situations. Confidence, then, must be constantly "proven," and this is almost always assessed by how someone looks, sounds, and performs *in front of others*.

Caregiving is anonymous. It thrives in the middle of the night when no on notices. It continues on without being heralded. Much of what is accomplished in this role is achieved by adjusting to situations, people, and expectations in which accommodation is required in an attempt to maintain the appearance of coherence and continuity.[8] Caregiver confidence isn't about what happens in front of a general audience. It's about what happens when you are with and near those you love, beyond the scope of others' awareness. Caregivers don't "build" their confidence because it isn't something one person can possess or own. Rather, confidence is created *with* others in response to social situations—not the situation anybody necessarily wants. Not the situation they believe should happen. Or the situation they wish would happen.

This type of confidence doesn't allow for the luxury of making grand proclamations promising to solve a loved one's problems and frustrations and suffering. Instead, it is grounded in a radical humility earned from a willingness to adjust and integrate into complex situations that transcend any one context (i.e., doctor's offices, rehabilitation centers, hospitals, treatment centers, hospices, homes) or any one relationship category (i.e., spouse, parent, child, caregiving). Confidence isn't about what is said or done as much as it is a willingness to be present throughout evolving situations. Comfort, not confidence, endures more powerfully than any standing ovation could ever last.

AUTHENTICITY—NOW

Telling people what you think they want to hear *now* makes you shudder every time you hear yourself out loud because it is too far from the truth of your everyday experiences. Camouflaging how you feel about your experiences no longer seems sustainable.[9] Nodding along with clichés no longer seems palatable. While others may see the value of leaning toward others with only their strengths, accomplishments, and apparent invulnerabilities, caregivers' desire for authentic connection means finding audiences capable of appreciating the full scope of your emerging values and experiences, including weaknesses, joys, vulnerabilities, and fears.

There are risks in being vulnerable when sharing with others—especially with family and friends.[10] But now, the risks of *not* revealing your full, unmasked, caregiver experiences feels more compelling than they once did. At this point, sharing can no longer be filtered by what you believe others need to hear, but by what you need to hear yourself communicate to others. "*I need someone to know I'm worried about what is happening at work.*" "*I no longer want to hide that I'm still grieving over the death of a loved one.*" "*If someone can't know me—the whole me—not just the partial me I've hidden from others, then I don't want to waste my time with that person.*" Without warning, what it means to connect has shifted. Waiting can no longer be respected. The *something better* that you once wished or hoped for is replaced by an obligation to make valuable what your care experiences have taught you. Without notice or appreciation, *later* has become *now*, and *now* can no longer wait.

This yearning to connect isn't simply about sharing challenges. Vulnerability also means wanting to find audiences who will allow you to communicate those experiences that go beyond clichés to include so much more than what others think is happening. Beyond sadness and struggle. Beyond progress and recovery. Thoughts that can't simply be shared in a Facebook post. The desire to explain the joys you are experiencing. The newfound sense of value to your life. The laughter and deep connection you feel that can't be translated or captured in a photo on Instagram.

This transformation marks the time when you begin actively looking for people who are willing to laugh with you about the profane, trivial, and profound parts of your experiences that you've had to edit far too long. No longer do you feel as if you are different from other caregivers—too old, too young, too well off, too distressed, too overwhelmed, too capable, too supported, too occupied with other obligations, too busy, too. . . . The people you had once dismissed, and the *caregiver* title (and all its manifestations) that you so rejected, may now look and sound different. Suddenly, it feels as if the only people you want to connect with are the people you didn't initially want to identify with. Now, you need to voice the parts of your experiences that are seemingly beyond translation to someone who isn't also in a caregiving situation. It is time to find those who, for the first time, are like you in ways you may have never considered.

A NEW WAY OF SEEING AND BEING

Beliefs aren't produced in a factory. Values don't emerge when thoughts are detached from lived realities. Beliefs and values are reflections of experiences that are shaped by responses to recurring experiences. Eventually, beliefs are mistaken for reality, as it appears as if they were born with us even though they weren't. They were earned. These taken-for-granted beliefs can't help but become mistaken for enduring truths that are used to guide priorities, relationships, and choices. Caring for someone changes caregivers.

Along the journey, caregivers can't help but become disoriented as the beliefs and values that had once guided them now appear jagged and dangerous, requiring constant questioning. But these beliefs and values have been reshaped by your care experiences just as a moving river reshapes the sharpest of edges into looking and feeling as if they were always that way. Care changes. Care changes you. Care changes your loved one. Care changes your beliefs and values. And care changes what you see when you look in the mirror.

Most people believe looking in a mirror allows them to see themselves. And it does. But only partially. Looking in a mirror to note the physical contours of your face is incomplete. What you see is true *and* deceptive. Real *and* incomplete. When caregivers look into a mirror, they aren't alone. They see themselves, but they also see their loved ones. They also see the care experiences that have shaped them in the darkness of night and in the private spaces of challenge and joy. What stares back at them in the mirror aren't those experiences alone, but an emergent set of beliefs and values that can't be readily recognized by others as much they are felt by you, every day. The people others see is not the person you are or have become. Creatively reclaiming the value of your role means recognizing the values of caregiving that will help you recognize your new self in the mirror—surrounded by others.

Among the few respected public rituals remaining in contemporary life are college graduations. It's beyond unfortunate, however, that we don't ritualize life's other markers beyond graduation. In honor of life's often overlooked but life-altering transitions, here's what a ceremony for caregivers might look like.

What Are We Honoring?

Our ceremony will honor our willingness to respond to life roles that we were drafted into—unexpectedly. That's right, the roles that called us to care that didn't occur within our expected time frames and didn't conform to our plans. These care roles weren't the roles that we spent our lives sculpting our résumés to attain. Explaining care doesn't go over well at parties—trust us, we've tried—because people don't know how to respond. Care isn't a position. It's not a company. There are no promotions. It's not a bucket list item. These life roles came at us, whether we were ready or not.

Honoring care authentically doesn't mean we would individually walk across a stage for a handshake and picture. For our "graduation" ceremony, that would be deceptive and impossible—we'd never fit everyone in the camera frame. Invisible life transitions like caregiving are always social—our responsibilities and connections highlight how we are rooted in and grounded with others. Instead, our ceremony will call attention to the fact that our lives aren't defined by other people's beliefs about ambition. No, our ambition isn't neatly packaged. It's private and public, familial and stigmatizing, life altering and life affirming. This ceremony will honor our willingness to walk not simply toward our goals, but also to open doors into people's lives when few others would.

Who Would Speak?

Commencement speakers are the celebrities of college graduations. Carefully chosen and vetted, a person speaks for the graduating class. An inspiring figure. A celebrity we've seen on television. A politician or sports figure who comes from afar to tell us about the art of living, armed with sweeping answers and clichés to rid of us of our uncertainty and tell us there is nothing really to fear because the world beyond is for the taking.

For our ceremony, we'd do things much differently. Importing a national figure to talk about our everyday, lived experiences wouldn't make sense to us. When someone tells us they have the "answers," we tune out. We don't have the energy or patience for such speeches.

We're not even looking for answers, and we're not keen on listening to others who charismatically clean up and organize our lives in fifteen minutes or less before heading out of town. We're used to messy—clean clichés wouldn't work.

Instead, perhaps all of us in attendance would write out a line or two about our experiences and challenges, or draw a picture or create a tune, integrating our creations into a babble of voices and representations. It would be noisy, no doubt, but whatever is created would be connected to others' creations. We would be both creators and audience—our words and creations and images and sounds and presence would be our rousing anthem. Not a Katy Perry kind of anthem, though. Unlike college graduates, we're not waiting to be inspired. We know too well the expiration date of inspiration. Our experiences tell us that inspiration without love and care and a commitment to others rings hollow. I'm talking about an anthem of our own making that allows us to pause time long enough to mark our care transitions—however confusing—while surrounded by others.

What Would Be Said?

This is so very complicated because we know graduation speeches always include a brief shout-out to the past and an unending preoccupation with what is coming, where people are going, and who they hope to become.

Our ceremony couldn't help but be drastically different. We don't think like most college graduates—we don't see ourselves as unbounded, floating in the wind of mere possibility. Our roles connect us to those we love and care for. Sometimes we feel our connections constrain us, but we also know they are the life-fulfilling necessities we wouldn't want to live without. We aren't free agents. We are social agents. That's what will be said. And shared. And felt. And celebrated.

Most people dream of where they will visit and what sights they might see and experience after graduation. Grief. Loss. Anger. Loneliness. Silence. These experiences are typically not invited to graduation speeches. But these are the places we have visited, and these are the places that have visited us. They have compelled us to expose parts of ourselves we didn't want others to notice. They've made us vulnerable, inspiring us to endless self-questioning and doubt. They aren't glamorous destinations but they are necessary parts of our journey that shouldn't be omitted because leaving them out would mean erasing vital parts of our experiences. Let others edit their words of wisdom to only include inauthentic half-truths. Not for our ceremony though.

What About Moving Your Tassel?

Today, during our celebration, we don't need to mark our care transition with the ritual placement of our tassels because we are already marked. We don't have to tell people we are important by reminding them of the awesomeness of our yet-to-be-lived future. We don't have to strategically self-present like college graduates and tell the world what we think they want to hear. Today, we are as we are. We are what it looks like in the midst of disorientation and resilience. We are college students' future selves. The only difference is that for the first time, we can see and appreciate who is around us. We are no longer consumed with looking through people to find a glimpse of the future. We can appreciate those around us—that's right, you—for who we are now. Yes, this is where we need to be, here—complicated. Tangled. Connected. Grounded. Not out there beyond—but right here. Yes, right here. Not valuable for who we are going to be. Valuable for who we are and what we are doing now.

Excuse us, but we're going to stay here a bit longer. Unlike a college graduation, we don't have a party to attend. Nothing to run to. Not anymore. Do you notice what's going on? People are still arriving at our ceremony. The seats around us are constantly being filled because there are no onlookers—no spectators or visitors—just participants engaged in this thing called living. Stay with us here a bit longer, would you? We want to close our eyes and feel the presence of acknowledgment and shared struggle. Grab a seat, there's one right next to us.

Making It Personal

Sometimes the people we love talk to us in silent ways if we are lucky and if we are closely attuned. My son Nicholas has severe cerebral palsy and chronic pain. He has always been a poor sleeper and, frequently, he would awaken screaming and crying. He would need me to reposition his body or rearrange the covers, some nights as often as every twenty minutes. I remember that, sometimes, I would wake on my own, in a quiet house. I would tense because I knew that somehow Nick would be alert to my wakefulness and call out to me. How I longed to be left alone in the quiet to go back to sleep! But I felt that some enchanted string for listening connected our rooms and he would *know* that I was awake. He always knew. And I could anticipate his needs, sense his discomfort, and discern his boredom or frustration. I mastered this knowledge without conversation. I simply "knew."

The state of acute listening that caregivers employ can be called "telepathy." It can be called "listening with the total self" or "seeking deep connectedness" to another. Whatever you name it, that cord of unspoken communication is the very essence of intimacy. Not many people ever experience it—but caregivers often do.

Pay attention to the way a caregiver speaks. At the beginning of a care experience, she is likely to use the third person to describe a loved one's symptoms or actions. "He has pain when he climbs the stairs." Over time, that "he" becomes "we." "We" were in the hospital for surgery. It went pretty well for "us."

Nurses trained in the "old days" use this turn of phrase with their patients: "And how are we today, Mr. Smith?" they might inquire. That use of the third person may sound quaint and even ridiculous today, but I bet it came from the ingrained idea that in caring, we are in this together. The "I" is always "we" because we are bound by a promise to abide with another and listen carefully as they confide to us their suffering.

PREFACE TO CHAPTERS 7–14

Reorientation and Advocacy

M*erriam-Webster's Dictionary* defines wisdom as the ability to "discern inner qualities and relationships," or demonstrate sensible action or judgment.[1] Understanding the complex web of relationships in caring for those we love forms the springboard for sensible action. What kinds of acts can caregivers perform that will result in an easing of heavy burdens? What does advocacy in caring look like, and how can anyone in the midst of chaos at home identify achievable goals that will result in stress relief and enhanced well-being?

Making meaning of the care experience is a giant step forward in the process of becoming a wise caregiver. But alone, it is not enough. Sensible actions must be identified and tried out—an exercise that is impossible without first discerning the inner qualities and relationships that are central to creating a personal care narrative.

The course of a disease or the aging process may be uncontrollable, but we can exert influence over how we manage our emotions and the activities of daily life in caring. We can systematically mine the community for resources. We can map our care relationships in order to reveal potential partners and allies. We can leverage familial and social ties to create a circle of personal support. And we can coordinate those efforts so that help is helpful. Wisdom in caregiving is achievable when insight is coupled with judgment.

7

MAKING MEANING THAT
MATTERS NOW

When the stories you have become accustomed to telling about your caregiver experiences make you feel like a stranger to the life you are living,[1] it's time to take notice and do something. When the stories you (over)hear—the ones your friends and work colleagues tell when speaking about your experiences—no longer make sense because you can't find yourself in what they are saying, it's time to take notice and do something.

The stories you tell others and the stories you tell yourself are vital because they will allow you to make sense of your experiences in ways that keep you going and remind you—and others—why you are doing what you are doing. Cultivating a coherent, authentic voice is a social act. Authenticity doesn't find you, it's always the by-product of interpretations you try on, practice, revise, and continue modifying as your experiences evolve. Translating your experiences into an evolving caregiver narrative means that the way you think and talk about your experiences must be believable (truthful and reliable) and cohere (fit together) with your day-to-day care experiences.[2]

Clichés are often interpreted as offensive because they highlight what happens when other people's values and experiences—the values and experiences of non-caregivers—are assumed to be universal when, in fact, they are context, role, and relationship specific. Take any un-welcomed cliché you've ever heard or been handed when someone tries to reduce your experiences to one sentence. *"You are a better person than me." "But look how much you have grown." "It's divine will that it's turned out this way." "You are so special." "We call you superwoman!"* Sincere clichés are interpreted as meaningless (and even cruel) because they are incoherent and divorced from your experiences. Even though they are directed at you and seemingly for you, they also exclude you—or the parts of your experiences that can no longer be separated from who you are. They are imposed on you, not created with you.[3]

Unlike clichés, posttraumatic growth demonstrates a "wisdom about life" born from meanings gleaned from experiences that make possible a renewed narrative, or script, for rethinking life.[4] Posttraumatic growth is a type of transformation because it means that "development, at least in some areas, has surpassed what was present before the struggle with crises occurred."[5] People are transformed—not by experiences alone as much as by what they learned and discovered in an authentic remaking of meaning grounded in vulnerability and distress. These areas of growth, such as a deeper awareness and appreciation for life and priorities, enhanced relationships, an improved appreciation of strength and endurance, a heightened sense of possibilities and growth, and reinvigoration of belief,[6] cannot be handed to someone in a neatly wrapped cliché.

There is no doubt you have grown throughout the care journey. Some areas of growth are easier to notice than others. Some areas of growth are difficult to see. And other areas of growth are deeply felt, but so very difficult to know how to share. Yet, *post*traumatic growth may not accurately characterize your experiences. Chronic caregiving is defined by an ongoing, indeterminate notion of time that has no clearly defined beginning and ending points.[7] Unlike other kinds of growth derived in the aftermath of trauma, caregivers must make meaning in the midst of unfolding challenge and stressors. Rather than posttraumatic growth, perhaps a more appropriate characterization for what you are tasked with doing is posttraumatic *growing* because caregiving requires ongoing sense making as your experiences unfold. Though others may have the benefits of time and distance when seeking to make sense of their experiences,[8] caregivers often do not.

Learning how to notice, understand, and communicate experiences may be hampered because caregiving typically occurs in the privacy of the home apart from other caregivers.[9] Though caregivers may regularly communicate with a variety of people—a loved one they are caring for, medical providers, and family and friends—isolation from others in similar circumstances can limit the development of a preferred and distinct identity.[10] Since caregivers don't have the opportunity to engage with similar others in their immediate, physical environment, it's more difficult to recognize individual experiences as part of a role characterized by a common, caregiver perspective that transcends any one particular situation.

There isn't one magical approach to making authentic meaning from your experiences. Authenticity is what happens when you believe the stories you tell yourself, and the stories you tell others are the stories you want others to hear. Authenticity, however, doesn't guarantee that family and friends will understand you. It doesn't even mean you will be appreciated. There are specific factors, however, that may foster the capacity for you to begin creating coherence that does not deny the messiness of your experiences as much as it uses the messiness, ambiguity, and uncertainty to identify, interpret, and communicate growth meanings. These ongoing processes of creation, coordination with others, and revision don't necessarily mean communicating only with audiences you already know. Growth from your caregiving experiences, or the ability to rely on meanings that work *with* you, must be cultivated collectively within a community of caregivers because storytelling is a social creation, not an individual accomplishment.[11] Whereas clichés dismiss the particular circumstances and constraints of your lived experiences, finding people facing similar challenges is necessary to creating authentic value that resonates with you and others like you, before you can begin effectively translating your experiences to outsiders.[12]

Communicating a deep appreciation of meaning from your experiences in ways that move you on and forward, throughout your journey, rather than attempting to take you out of your experiences, is possible when you begin cultivating audiences that may not be in your already existing social network. This ongoing coordination depends on sharing, exchanging, comparing, and collaborating with others whose lives are inextricably connected to shared needs and disruptions.

CULTIVATING THE RIGHT AUDIENCES

Sincerity alone doesn't help caregivers make meaning from their experiences. This is a tough truth to acknowledge because it highlights what your family and friends can't do when it comes to helping you create coherent stories about your caregiver experiences. Consider a simple question such as *"What's wrong?"* Beyond the information contained in any possible response, something more is being communicated when family and friends ask *"What's wrong?"* The subtext to the asking of this well-intentioned question might go something like this: *"You are defying my expectations and making me uneasy because if there is anything I can count on in this world—it's you being the 'you' I already know." "If you are changing—then that means my whole world is changing. That means I'm going to have to change, and that's scary." "I'm worried that you're experiencing something that I feel powerless to help you with."* You may be asked endless variations of the *what's wrong* question by people you already care about or feel close enough for them to ask. Herein lies the paradox of this question.

The *what's wrong* question is only asked by people you know well and yet, this very question changes what can be created and shared because it demands loyalty to the past. Though asked out of concern, the question asks you to remain loyal to the person whom family and friends remember and seemingly already know. Judgment, then, cannot be separated from understanding, limiting what can be said, heard, and voiced. What others remember you to be (your reputation, past mistakes, previous relationship disagreements, and conflicts) and what others want you to be (how you are supposed to act, what is [in]appropriate to talk about) influences how family and friends receive what you are going through and how they are able to respond. Because they know you and can't let go of a shared history and an expected future, they are more likely to minimize your concerns than others who don't know you. Minimizing your experiences and your responses to your caregiving challenges isn't done out of malice but because they can't help but interpret you and your situation in a context of previous memories and ongoing expectations.[13]

When asking *"What's wrong?"* family and friends may be preoccupied with their needs, not yours. This question puts too much emphasis on the parts of you that are already known—not on the ingenious combination of how you are seeking to respond to the challenges affecting you now. Being asked *"What's wrong?"* overplays constancy because it falsely assumes that consistency is more important than who you are becoming. The people you already know may be valuable forms of support, but they may also be limited in their ability to help you communicate ongoing value from your distinct experiences because they can't separate you from your situation. Asking them to approach you and your situation without a shared history and projected future would ask them to do the impossible—to completely detach what you are saying from who you are.

When you and your situation meet family's and friends' traditions, values, or tolerances for different ways of thinking and acting, understanding can be an unintentional casualty. Unknowingly, audiences that approach you through a default lens of "what's wrong" may make it more difficult for you to find value and growth in your care experiences because existing relationship(s) may silence the necessary exploration of possible meanings and understandings facilitated by open, honest, and raw expression.[14]

In times of crisis and stress, we all need something from others even if we don't know how to communicate that need. We need people around us who will help us reorient ourselves to our experiences. When someone asks *what is happening*—not what's wrong—the question becomes an invitation to dive deeper, explore changes, and allow you to share how unfolding experiences are remaking you, even when that means talking about taboo subjects and emotional responses, and venting about frustrations that don't necessarily call out for a solution.[15] A shared history can be overwhelmingly reassuring because it allows caregivers to understand another person without having to say a word. At the same time, a shared history can be overwhelmingly alienating when it is used to expect loyalty and adherence to maintaining the appearance of understanding.[16] Sometimes, the people you know best can't help but ask, *"What's wrong?* instead of being open to understanding *what is happening.*

In these circumstances, finding audiences who share a common stressor, not a common past, may make possible the development of growth and understanding in response to recurring stressors. These types of relationships take place among individuals whom you interact with but who aren't in your already existing networks of family and close friends.[17] These audiences may be more open to you and your situation because they too must respond to the challenge of caregiving and because they are different from you in so many ways, except for common caregiver challenges. Consequently, engaging with others who don't know you but do know the challenges of your situation and role is more likely to open you to expansive and diverse ways of responding to common realities that can bring you closer to others and provide new and creative ways of responding.

To this point, you may have believed transformation was something that has been happening to you, but transformation is also a way to create meaning out of your experiences in ways that guide you. Transformation isn't only an individual experience that happens apart from others. Transformation is a social accomplishment created in response to and with others. Alone, we tend to overestimate what we can—or should—do in our role. Being with others, in this way, can allow you to more fully appreciate that constraints don't show what you can't do as much as they may help you realize how to creatively respond and accommodate to the boundaries of your roles and relationships.[18] Communicating with such audiences will allow access to a greater diversity of knowledge, insights, experiences, and responses not available in your already existing network of friends and family.[19]

Reaching beyond your existing networks may be the ultimate act of self-care because it allows you to find parts of yourself in others who have walked similar paths. Sometimes, sharing with someone you don't know frees you from the relationship complications associated with confiding in family and friends. Without having to worry about how everything you say or don't say might jeopardize existing relationships, you may be empowered to talk in detail, focusing on those very aspects of your experiences that are most difficult to talk about with family and friends.[20] New and expanded ways of responding can only be fully explored when constraints are not camouflaged but openly responded to with audiences who are different, but purposefully similar.

CREATING COHERENCE

One way to improve caregiver empowerment involves creating opportunities, in the face of restrictions, for understanding choices and then competently advocating to address you and (and your loved one's) interests.[21] Though caregivers may not be able to change their situation, translating "distress" into meaningful language can help caregivers better understand their experiences and themselves.[22] To maximize the ability to foster growth-based meanings,[23] caregivers must collectively create opportunities to connect, learn from, and try on strategies that help them adjust, endure, and find sustenance, even in the midst of the most challenging of situations.

Reclaiming Meaning

Beginnings can be difficult to draw energy from because caring for another is so inextricably associated with waiting. Special rooms are named in your honor: waiting rooms. You wait for a visit. Wait for clarity. Wait for hope. Wait for information. Wait for tests and more tests. Wait for results and for the interpretation of those results. Wait for the person you love to return to who they once were. Caregiving seemingly exists without clear beginnings or endings, trapping caregivers in a state of perpetual postponement. Against this backdrop of deference, reclaiming the energy of creating beginnings can positively contribute to perceptions of control.

Events can't be depended on to define beginnings; caregivers must. A quick look at a calendar of caregiver responsibilities might remind you that there is nothing so dramatic or noteworthy that seemingly necessitates a beginning. But beginnings must be marked, as almost all beginnings are manufactured. Waiting for a calendar to tell you what is important or worthy of others' appreciation hampers renewal. Although Mondays might signal the beginning of a new workweek for some, for caregivers, it might be Saturday morning or Friday night. Reclaiming beginnings means a willingness to rewrite calendars as an essential step in fostering renewal benchmarks throughout the care journey.

Beginnings are also typically marked by rituals. The first pitch of the new baseball season. The introduction of names on the first day of class. Shopping for clothes in advance of the first day on the job. Ritualizing beginnings allows participants to inject a particular moment as distinct from the countless other moments that will seek to crowd it out into just another moment. How will you ritualize your beginnings? Will the first hour of your mornings be an opportunity for a new beginning—a time for reflection and awareness and appreciation? Will you dress differently? Will you sit somewhere special? Will you sip your morning coffee differently than you do the remainder of the day? Marking difference out of the continuity of the everyday means regaining some control in determining how you will experience life rather than habitually deferring to what others tell you should be noticed or appreciated.

Celebrating is another marker of meaning that must be reclaimed. The looming anticipation of a beginning can be as intoxicating as the event or experience itself. Marking an event or experience sometime in the future reinforces value, as doing so creates anticipation. Marking an event too far into the future, however, may mean that its eventual reality is doubtful. Each week, schedule something to look forward to that doesn't depend on waiting on others. Scheduling a visit to a park? Planning on visiting with old friends? A bike ride on a nearby trail? Writing reflections in a journal? Marking beginnings means reworking your schedule so that the hours and days leading to newness allow you to prepare yourself and your senses for the experience itself.

Newness amid routine habits can become charged with meaning when it is socialized. Ask fellow caregivers how they create moments of significance. Tell others how you are preparing for an event or experience that you are injecting with the significance of something different from the everyday. It need not be grandiose—just properly marked and named as distinct. Put it in your planner and phone. Invite others. The more you talk about it, the more real it becomes. The more real a beginning is treated, the more likely you are to create a reality that both you and others respect as worthy of attention and presence.

The energy of embracing engineered beginnings will linger long after the experience itself. Don't inhibit this energy. You deserve this afterglow of lightness because it is a reminder that self-created moments of breathing space can be a moving response to life's limitations. Don't be rational about it. Don't squash excitement. Allowing created beginnings to energize and nourish you through challenges may momentarily free you to see yourself and your caregiving situation through different eyes. If caregivers only wait to be lifted up by others' beginnings, they risk feeling trapped in an endless series of waiting and deferring and obligation, only further reminding them they have no capacity to influence their everyday. Creating the possibility of newness even in the midst of life's most challenging moments is a reminder that though you must respond to life's events that may be beyond your control, you are also capable of imprinting your hours and days with distinct signatures of your own making. Reclaiming control about what your care experiences mean also requires communicating with audiences who allow you to freely voice the full breadth of your experiences.

Voicing the Full Range of Experiences

Seeking and finding audiences who share challenges will allow caregivers to more fully share, vent, explain, and voice the full scope of their experiences. Caregiving is full of challenges, but outsiders' inability or unwillingness to be receptive to the parts of your experiences that don't fit within stereotyped beliefs about what can happen during caregiving neglects vital opportunities to render value and purpose. When communicating with fellow caregivers facing common challenges and constraints, what can be thought and said, out loud and in writing, without judgment, opens up possibilities for illuminating aspects of your experiences that are too often camouflaged when you are interacting with family and friends. When unedited responses are shared with fellow caregivers, including the profane, funny, joyous, resented, sad, trivial, monumental, and grievous, you may find that what you believed only *you* felt and experienced really wasn't only about you. When shared with a community of caregivers, the profane may not really be so profane when shared with others under similar circumstances. A resentment, when voiced with similar others, may simply be revealed as a typical response. This type of connection, built on the possibility of sharing the full breadth of role experiences without concern for how it will affect your already existing relationships, can bring you closer together with a community of caregivers and foster renewed understandings of the stressors you are responding to.

At some point, it may be too much to seek to overcome outsiders' misconceptions of your role. Though outsiders may believe caregiving can *only* be sad, tragic, depressing, and unenviable, your realities tell you that it is much more dynamic and complex. Either-or conceptions—*either* caregiving is only noble, *or* caregiving is only sad—don't accurately characterize the full texture of your experiences. Communicating the full breadth of caregiving means making sense of all parts of your experiences, especially the parts others find difficult to acknowledge, but call out to be explored in ways not reducible to caricatures.[24]

It may be difficult for outsiders to understand that life is being lived and memories are being formed beyond their limited conceptions of caregiving. The "good" of your caregiver role and relationships, the very elements of your role that have changed how you think, must find a place to be shared, heard, and named, or these aspects of your role risk becoming lost among others' unknowing dismissal of lived experiences. If others believe that what you are doing is—and must be—depressing, so much is lost in translation because you know caregiving is complicated, as joy may exist alongside deep sadness in ways that defy outsiders' conceptions of a logic of consistency. Yet, authentically sharing the breadth of your experiences, including the redemptive aspects, may mean that others don't simply dismiss what you are saying but also negatively judge you.[25] Outsider perceptions may restrict you from highlighting the rewarding aspects of your role that may exist simultaneously with the most challenging aspects of caregiving. Too much camouflaging of these necessary, but apparently contradictory, features of your role can make you doubt the validity of your experiences when, in reality, it is others' expectations and beliefs that should be questioned.

Using euphemisms to describe your everyday can also have a dulling effect on your ability to render meaning from your experiences because, over time, there is a possibility that the perspective of the outsider becomes the only frame you use to reflect on your experiences. In the process, you may deprive yourself of necessary in-group, or caregiver-specific, meanings invisible to outsiders, but necessary to addressing the full breadth of experiences, including the role's joys and rewards. When in the company of those who are faced with common challenges, however, you can begin to create and experiment with insider frames of reality that allow you to articulate a much more nuanced rendering of your care role and relationship.

Caregivers may leverage metaphors to reflect on their evolving experiences by comparing their new situations to familiar experiences.[26] Metaphors are creative responses to novel situations that reflect an insider's perspective, especially when insider experiences may upend and expand traditional ways of thinking and acting.[27] Outsiders don't need to compare their new situations to familiar experiences when they are in sync. Yet, when caregiving experiences no longer can be reconciled within old frames of reference, new ways of understanding must be constructed, and metaphors provide not only a new way of seeing but also a corresponding language to describe multiple and overlapping realities. New audiences beyond friends and family provide an invitation to begin expressing and shaping how you want to articulate these emergent values. Yet articulating materializing values requires practice, the freedom to risk, and an audience who can provide impartial feedback and a common motive to make meaning from care situations because, like you, they need to.

Practicing Value Articulation

Caregivers may find it difficult to communicate the value of their presence against a cultural backdrop that associates time, attention, and effort with discernible outcomes. Since doing and curing receives attention and accolades, articulating the value of your role may be met with others' prejudices. As with other care roles,[28] shifting the focus away from what is *done* to what you are learning from being a caregiver not only may expand others' understandings of your role, but it may also highlight what you are gaining from your experiences. This shift in emphasis may allow you to more fully communicate your distinctive and innovative relational insights because they help tell a compelling story about what it means to connect with another human being.[29]

A willingness to venture forth *with another* without the comforting predictability of what will come next is a relational innovation that is becomingly increasingly scarce. This kind of innovation takes courage and risk, and caregivers are an embodiment of those willing to risk closeness without knowing what will happen tomorrow. While others fret over the possibility of losing control, care innovators like you continue caring even when controlling what will happen next is impossible. By featuring what can be understood only as a result of care interactions, caregivers can situate themselves as pioneers venturing into deeply authentic interactions at a time when most others are finding it increasingly difficult to know what it means to be with another. When thinking of your experiences as a type of invention, rather than simply a requirement or set of tasks, caregiving can be repositioned as a desirable source of insight. *What does it mean to be needed?* Doesn't your care relationship make you imminently qualified to be able to help others begin to understand what a relationship based on love, need, and care looks like and how it shapes a relationship? *What does it mean to live a life where procrastination is not possible?* Aren't you an expert here because what you experience with your loved one can't be delayed because care needs can't be put off? *What does it mean to make a difference in the world?* Don't you have so much to say here because you've been thinking and living and reflecting on this question so much more intensely than others who have to be asked this question? You are living it. Throughout, not only have your experiences been shaping you, they also became a means by which you can begin teaching others in ways that only you can teach—what it means to make a difference by being with another.[30]

Wanting to make a difference in the world is a near-universal refrain among young people yearning for an understanding of value. Making a difference is an incredibly admirable goal, but what if *being* rather than *doing* was conceived of as the ultimate way to make a difference in ways only caregivers can help others understand? Acknowledging the individuals who shape our everyday realities is often neglected because we're told, in a variety of ways, that people are irrelevant to goals and accomplishments: *"No one values my interactions with colleagues because they have nothing to do with my quarterly evaluation." "No one cares about whom I care for and about. They just want to know if I get my work done."* But caregivers know that the people we devote our physical presence, time, energy, and thoughts to also shape us. The contours of our lives are not reducible to abstract goals; they are determined by the relationships we make and sustain in our everyday lives. We emerge every day, not out of nothingness, but from the layers of care and attention of those that surround us.

Caregivers know that when we only talk about what we are doing to make a difference, we set ourselves up to be perpetually disappointed. *"Just wait, I'll be noticed once the project is done." "I know I'm nothing now until my work of creation is completed." "Once I finish my education, I'll be worthy of other people's respect."* If we truly valued presence as a type of accomplishment, would we delude ourselves into thinking that satisfaction will only come to us sometime in the future? Your presence with others is both process and product, complete unto itself and, at the same time, always shaping our futures. If presence was truly valued as sufficient and meaningful unto itself, then the kind of meaningful presence caregivers experience as a vital part of their role would drastically change the questions we ask one another at the end of a day. Instead of trying to assess the quality and value of our days by asking, *"What did you do today?,"* we should be asking a much more profound question: *"Whom did you devote your time and attention to today?"*

Fame is too often confused with importance, to the extent that *making a difference* is believed to happen in a community far away. Fame is the intoxication of making a difference in the lives of those who do not know you. In a world of numbers—likes, subscribers, followers—making a difference has become shorthand for how many people are impacted. Caregiving, however, shows a different way of assessing significance and cultural value. Caregivers model an alternative to the *making* a difference mentality. *Being* a difference means creating deep connections with people who know us best. *Being* a difference doesn't only mean changing people's lives, but it also means enhancing the quality of people's lives, including your own. From this perspective, life doesn't call for brilliance or engaging in incredible feats of heroism; rather, it invites us to be engaged and connected to people. Being connected to others doesn't require special qualifications. It doesn't mean waiting for approval. It doesn't mean having to qualify or apply. It isn't reserved for the special, the few, or the privileged. It's not a scarce resource that needs to be found; it's available and present in every neighborhood. In every stage of our lives. It's available when things are going well. And when things aren't going well. But it does require a willingness to walk into people's lives when they are vulnerable, and an openness to the value and importance of the people around you. Yes, that person. The value of one. The value of this day. That one person. This very day. Now.

A NEW WAY OF SEEING AND BEING

Making sense and creating value from your experiences in ways that work for you is not simply an opportunity to reclaim control, but also a way of keeping you going in ways that are consistent with who you have become. It reminds you that you are learning something others may not even know is possible. It reminds you that you are experiencing something others don't know how to appreciate. It reminds you that you are gaining something others may not be capable of because they have not lived, experienced, or shared what you have. And it invites you to begin thinking about what you have created with someone that others may also find meaningful and valuable.[31]

Telling coherent stories doesn't just happen; it is created and refined and revised. It is a collaborative act.[32] When we listen only to the voices in our head, we hear the same refrain over and over again. Hearing the same thing over and over again is deceptive because the more we hear it, the more we believe it must be reality because no other alternatives are provided in the unending loop of repetition. There are expiration dates to stories. Old ones may not necessarily make us sick, but they can make us uneasy, disoriented, and exhausted.

Reaching out and connecting with audiences who are purposefully different but share a common challenge and need—caregiving—is vital to encouraging growth meanings and to the voicing of the full range of your care experiences. Meaningful, aligned connection positions you to access more objective and accurate feedback so that you can better assess how you are responding to your care situation. With fellow caregivers, you will be able to try on new stories, as others make it possible for you to see your experiences from a different perspective, allowing you to begin giving yourself permission to be self-compassionate in ways that only others can encourage. For the first time, you might also realize that though you may feel as if you are totally alone in your responsibilities as a caregiver, you don't have to be alone in learning how to respond and take care of yourself so that you can continue caring for others.

REMAKING YOUR RÉSUMÉ

What's your title? Where did you go to school? Where did you get your training? Who are you connected to on LinkedIn? How many bullet points do you have on your résumé? Specialize? Focus? Become an expert at one something in particular? Résumés are the ways people relate, connect, and navigate the everyday of our occupational worlds. Titles and credentials help us know where we want to be and whom we want to meet. Most importantly, résumés are documents that mean something to others (and inevitably us) because they make real what and who we are in ways others understand.

Making It Personal

At some point in our lives, the standards and markers of other people's résumés can become meaningless and even counterproductive. Typical résumés don't work when we think about the skills, qualities, and characteristics that address the values and capacities of the care role. If we were to reconstruct a caregiver's résumé (and turn the traditional résumé upside down in the process), emphasizing values and skills more consistent with the caregiver role, here's what a caregiver's résumé might emphasize.

Values (Not Just Education)

Instead of concerning itself with where someone received an education (Harvard, Yale, Princeton, community college, state school) or how much education they completed (associate degree, bachelor degree, LPN, BSN, MSN, MD, PhD, MBA), a caregiver's résumé would be informative only if it conveyed a person's values:

- Who is important to them?
- Whom have they listened to without judgment?
- How much compassion do they have—for themselves?
- Could others count on this person in times of need?
- Whom do they laugh with?
- Whom have they cried with?
- Whom do they choose to be with, not because of advancement or prestige, but because of whom they value being in the company of?

Life (Not Just Work) Experience

This section on a traditional résumé seems to make so much sense. What relevant experience does a person have that will make him or her a good candidate for a specific job or industry? Where did she receive her training? Experience? Under whom? What did he do? What can she do?

Yet, for caregivers, traditional work experiences don't make a whole lot of sense. Experience for an informal caregiver? None needed. No special qualifications. No advanced training. A management-training program? Not necessary. But what is needed is probably more rare and growing even more scarce by the day—willingness.

To care for a loved one is an act of courage—by saying "yes" to a loved one, you are in turn saying "no" to other so-called opportunities that receive acclaim and attention. Opportunities for advancement. Opportunities to relax. Opportunities to stay in your routine. Opportunities to outsource your care. Opportunities to hide yourself from the reality that we have more to offer our loved ones than a job skill.

Interpersonal Openness (Not Just Skills)

On a traditional résumé, skills usually advertise to a prospective employer what makes you different from others. These items almost always focus on individual skills followed by powerful verbs. For a caregiver's résumé, skills are also vital. But the skills of difference that you highlight from your work life don't fit here. Informal caregiver capacities should almost always focus on relational skills that situate you with others, emphasizing what you have in common, rather than what separates you from them.

- Are you present when in the company of others? Do you always have to be the center of attention?
- Do you use "we" to describe your life, or are you stuck in "I"?
- Are you willing to be with and near another human being when association with that person won't necessarily provide any special attention or privileges?
- Do you have the capacity to walk into another's life when most others are walking away?
- Do you have the interpretive skills to find value and meaning in care-based relationships when most others dismiss these experiences as *only* depressing, sad, something to be celebrated, but from afar?

Availability: Always and Everywhere

For most résumés, this is the section where you indicate when you can start or when you will be done with your current job so that you can be ready for the next opportunity. Or when you are willing to work. Days? Nights? Weekends? Part- or full-time?

For a caregiver's résumé, availability is not something we come up with. Rather, the need for care compels us and is characterized by how we make sense of experiences when love meets need.

- For an informal caregiver, the question isn't about when we are available, it's about when another person needs us. And it's not something that we agree upon in advance. It will change depending on the type of needs (acute, chronic, terminal) of our loved one.
- Availability means the willingness to know that care can't be contained as something we do or give or think about in the morning or the evening. It infiltrates. It becomes a way of being at work, with others, when absent, when we're far away, or when we're up close.
- Part-time? Full-time? *Always*-time is more like it.

Endurance and Courage (Not Just Honors and Leadership)

Winning awards and being recognized is so important to a traditional résumé's value because it reminds others that you are doing something distinctive that others acknowledge. Being "better" than others is the stuff of medals and awards and claps and cheers.

As a caregiver, an honors or leadership category doesn't quite fit. Caring for someone you love means doing work that few people care about. There is no competition to care for a loved one. No way to distinguish yourself as special. No way to highlight how you are better than others. And gold medals? Awards? Close-ups? Slow-motion replays of your performance? No, not for caregiving. Not in this culture.

Caregivers, with courage, develop their own metrics of goodness apart from outcome and applause, in the company of those who understand common role experiences and challenges. They endure, and in the process, create community from shared challenges, not simply shared aspirations.

8

BEGIN WITH THE BASICS: WHAT IS MY ROLE AT HOME, WHAT DO I *WANT* IT TO BE?

Sometimes, it feels like we're in a less-than-seaworthy boat, but not too far from shore. The seas are calm, the weather warm and clear. The off-the-radar fragility is almost peaceful. Out of nowhere, I notice that we have drifted further out than I had planned. Even that does not matter so much—it is tranquil and the busyness of care keeps me focused. Then, as quickly as the winds shift, the seas begin to get rough. The skies darken, the wind picks up and the effort in the boat becomes enormous. I would like to head to shore, but I have to focus on what happens in the boat. It is harder now, with the unsteadiness and fear. I adjust to it enough to steady the course, all the while knowing the storm will not last forever. The worst happens instead—the boat springs a leak. For every pail of water I pitch out to sea, two more enter. The fatigue is beyond bearable, the constancy of effort, without any progress. Does anyone know we are here?—Diane S. (who cares for her twenty-six-year-old son, who has a traumatic brain injury).

It is clear that we are transformed by caring for someone we love, but what or whom have we changed *into?* Pre-caregiving interests and hobbies are frequently necessary sacrifices to a life that is tethered to home. And it is easy to lose sight of possibility and positivity in a life of intensive caring. It may be that we feel "too far from shore" to bother sending up a flare.

After understanding the transitions inherent in shifting from loved one to caregiver, it's natural to ask "Who am I now?" and "How can I craft a life that I value, given the givens?" Beginning to exercise control over a life that seems hopelessly adrift in a sea of unmet needs starts with an understanding of what lies beneath that sea and of the experience of floating in it. "What now?" or even "So what?" are the existential questions that flow from comprehending the caregiver experience. How can an individual whose role allows so little in the way of personal choice use self-knowledge to springboard into wisdom and advocacy? The answer may be in another set of questions.

There are certain questions that a caregiver has difficulty answering. The first is "What do you do all day?" Every caring day is so heavily weighted by tasks related to another's needs that there is little time to pause with satisfaction about what's been accomplished. So much is unplanned. The day unfolds as a series of responses to needs that arise like ducks in a shooting gallery. The caregiver's imagination and the ability to act on the basis of personal choice or preference are natural casualties of the caring role. The second question we have trouble answering is, "How do you know what your loved one needs?" We're likely to answer, "I don't know how I know. I just know." Our creative imagination might be on hold, but our intuition is in overdrive. The necessity to monitor a loved one's health contributes to the creation of a near-constant state of hypervigilance. With so little opportunity for reflection, daydreaming, or other forms of mental refreshment, it's no wonder that caregivers lose their capacity for self-awareness. It's no wonder that caregivers cannot answer the question, "What do you do all day?"

Awareness of what we do and how we do it gives us a road map for directing our life. Naming tasks and deciding how we feel about them is an important first step in understanding the caregiving life and learning how to control it (as opposed to it controlling us). Often, we don't give ourselves credit for all we do in a caring role. And certainly, health care professionals are frequently unaware of the range of tasks in the caregiver's day—their sole focus is usually on just the small part of family life that involves their interventions.

Consider the list of care tasks below. There may be tasks in the list that you enjoy and some you don't. Some of these may be necessary to undertake multiple times every day and others may be required occasionally.

PHYSICAL ASSISTANCE

Physical Assistance/Mobility (Indoor)—Providing an arm for balance in walking or a lift to aid in chair transfers may be a natural part of caring. Likewise, ensuring mobility aids are nearby or pushing a loved one's wheelchair may be necessary.

Physical Assistance/Toileting—Changing pads in the case of incontinence, helping on and off the toilet, and assisting with hand washing are duties that many caregivers carry out on a daily (and nightly) basis.

Physical Assistance/Bathing—Caregivers may need to help with showering or bathing, hair washing, shaving, and with dental hygiene.

Physical Assistance/Dressing—There may be aspects of dressing that a loved one cannot manage independently such as buttons, zippers, winter boots, and coats or jackets.

Physical Assistance/Eating—If a loved one has impaired hand function, cutting food as well as assistance with eating and drinking will be a caregiver responsibility.

Physical Assistance/Outings—Even if a loved one is ambulatory, he or she might require assistance with outings, including entering and exiting the vehicle and managing the seat belt. Wheelchair users will need tie-down restraints secured or the folded wheelchair lifted into the vehicle after the loved one has been assisted into the vehicle seat.

NON-PHYSICAL CARE

Behavior Support—In the case of a loved one's challenging behavior due to confusion or dementia, calming strategies might be required. Often, the caregiver brokers the relationship of a loved one to the rest of the world. A caring task will be to translate the world to a loved one and the loved one to the world.

Emotional Support/Stimulation—Chatting, playing games, and arranging and coordinating visits from family or friends all constitute emotional support to address social isolation. Diverting the attention of a loved one who is anxious, confused, or in pain is a particular talent that caregivers hone by practice.

Medication Management—Ordering medications, often from a variety of providers, and administering them is a key caregiver responsibility.

Caring for Other Family Members—Very often, caregivers are caring for other family members, apart from a dependent loved one. Nearly half of all Americans in their forties and fifties are caring for children as well as parents over the age of sixty-five.[1] "Sandwich caregiving" is becoming the norm in our society.

Enjoying Time Together with Your Loved One—Caring for a loved one sometimes means spending companionable time together, either by sharing an activity, reminiscing, or simply enjoying each other's company. Shared time, even in silence, is one way that caregivers combat the effects of isolation.

CASE-MANAGEMENT CHORES

Managing the Medical Diary—Making medical appointments and arranging for everything from transportation to filling post-clinic prescriptions is a key responsibility of all caregivers.

Medical-Record Keeping/Sharing—The caregiver is often the corporate memory for all the information relating to a loved one's encounters with health care systems. Case coordination and keeping track of multiple clinicians across disciplines nearly always falls to the patient or caregiver, who must master both digital and old-fashioned paper care-coordination tools.

Researching Medical Information—Caregivers are crack researchers by necessity. New symptoms, clinical changes, and disease progression are all factors that incite and require caregivers to gather information online. They conduct online research in an effort to avoid the emergency room, to seek a semblance of control and certainty, and to give the best care they can.

Paid Staff Procurement—Finding qualified home-care workers who are also a good match for the patient and family is challenging. Staff retention is notoriously difficult in the low-pay business of home health care, so caregivers are often in a continuous employee-search mode.

Staff Training—Home-care staff are trained in the "standard of care," as it applies to their professional qualification. But they won't know anything about the medical and personal particulars of the patient. Families and patients themselves (if they are able) provide those details. Caregivers deliver training, act as an ongoing resource, and provide the patient "corporate history."

Managing Staff Payroll—Paying home-care staff, managing shift schedules, and maintaining relationships with service-provider case coordinators are all typical caregiver duties.

The Role of the "Care Guarantor"—Ten thousand Americans turn sixty-five every day, and 70 percent of those will require long-term care for an average of three years. We know that families deliver 80 percent of care at home[2] to their loved ones with dependency needs, and we know there is a serious shortage of home-care workers.[3] Those demographics mean that, often, shifts cannot be filled because of staff shortages. When there's no one to help, families are forced to fill in as care guarantors or quickly find creative ways to fill necessary care gaps (e.g., when the caregiver needs to visit a doctor or is ill).

Managing Insurance and Other Funding Applications—Almost one quarter of all caregivers are caring for their loved ones more than forty-one hours per week, while 37 percent are caring for loved ones who have multiple health-care challenges.[4] It is this group of intensive caregivers who report experiencing high stress, at least some of which is due to their role as advocates with insurance providers and financial institutions.

Managing Communications in the Circle of Care—Communicating everything that everyone needs to know in a circle of care[5] is a fiendishly tricky but vital caregiver responsibility. Of all caregivers, 63 percent report their role as a circle-of-care communication facilitator as second only to their role in monitoring the health of their loved one.[6]

Specialized Supply/Equipment Ordering—In home care, a house can often look like a hospital. Supplies such as incontinence pads, catheters, dressings, monitors, and mobility aids must be ordered, maintained, counted, and ordered again by the caregiver. If supplies or equipment are eligible expenses under an insurance plan, the caregiver must complete the relevant paperwork to claim compensation (see "Managing Insurance and Other Funding Applications").

HOUSEHOLD CHORES

Food Shopping and Preparation—"Normal" family needs don't disappear when extraordinary needs emerge. Food shopping must be done as usual, but it will take longer if special diets are required for the patient. Alternative arrangements for food ordering and delivering must be explored if the caregiver isn't free to go out. Seventy-six percent of all caregivers report food shopping as a principal family responsibility, and 61 percent report the same for cooking.[7]

Managing Household Finances—Falling behind in bill payments and other duties of financial management can result in high levels of stress for the caregiver. Unpaid bills or taxes have a detrimental multiplying effect both financially and emotionally for the whole family.

Tidying/Light Cleaning—Caring for someone at home is a messy business. Days aren't spent at the office and meals aren't taken at restaurants. A patient with nursing needs lives at home, likely together with at least one family member. Being infirm and home all day means that dishes pile up in the sink, wastebaskets fill quickly, and spills are likely. Seventy-two percent of all caregivers report that they have sole responsibility for housework in the home of a loved one with care needs.[8]

Heavy Cleaning—The dependency needs of a loved one usually indicate an accompanying vulnerability to infection. The caregiver must ensure a very clean environment, which may require regularly sterilizing surfaces as well as cleaning more vigorously and frequently than usual.

Laundry—Loved ones with care needs generate a lot of laundry. Sheets, bibs, clothing, and cleaning cloths all require changing frequently. This is especially true when loved ones are users of incontinence products.

Driving/Errands—One of the principal tasks of a caregiver is to provide transportation to a loved one. Of all caregivers, 78 percent report providing this service as part of their role.[9] Often, frailty, mobility challenges, or cognitive impairment make it difficult for an older parent or ill spouse to travel alone or with an unfamiliar driver. When transport is required to medical appointments, caregivers take on emotional support and advocacy roles, so outsourcing the driving of a loved one is, for most families, not a viable option.

Yard Maintenance—Homeowners who are caregivers frequently find that yard maintenance is a major challenge. Keeping up with snow clearing, lawn mowing, and garden weeding may be important for personal pride as well as family safety. But when loved ones cannot be attended to outside, yard tasks may prove very difficult to achieve. Snow banks and overgrown yards contribute to social isolation and stress for the caregiver.

Banking—In the case of Alzheimer's and dementia, the caregiver often assumes power of attorney for the financial matters of a loved one. This means that caregivers are forced to assume responsibility for two sets of taxes as well as an increased workload in other areas of financial management.

Pet Care—When loved ones become ill or infirm, families do not give up their pets. A pet's need for nutrition, health, and fitness becomes part of the caregiver's daily responsibilities.

OTHER

Outside Employment—Six in ten caregivers are employed outside the home, and all of them report having to make a workplace accommodation as a result of their caring role.[10] Today many employers recognize the need to support their caregiver employees by offering flexible hours. Nevertheless, caregivers report high levels of stress when the need to be at home is in competition with the need to be at work.

Self-Care—Self-care is different for everyone. For some, respite might mean psychological counseling. For others, a break means working part-time or simply going for a walk. Caregivers are frequently told to look after themselves, but in light of other more urgent responsibilities, finding time and energy for self-care can be a challenge.

Peer Support (Online and Offline)—Caregiver peer groups can be a source of valuable crowd-sourced expertise as well as emotional support. For many caregivers, conversing with others who share an understanding of both the joy and the burden of caring for a loved one can provide a natural form of validation, friendship, and invaluable information sharing.

All of these tasks and duties can overwhelm because they become habitual. En masse, they crowd out the opportunity for mindfulness. In the absence of self-awareness, it is difficult to remember how a caring day unfolded, much less communicate how it did.

***What I do every day gives me clues about who I am at this stage in
my life.*** Mastery is an important concept in caregiving because being
very good at something can help us to like it and to sense control over
it. A caregiver daily-task diary can help reveal current realities as well as
possibilities for change. Use an hourly agenda, choose tasks from the lists
above, and fill it in. Examine your own caring workday. Which caring
tasks have you mastered? Which ones are completed by virtue of pure
luck and willpower? Next, consider more deeply which tasks you enjoy
and which you don't. Look at how your satisfaction is spread throughout
a twenty-four-hour period. If your afternoon is heavy with unpleasant
tasks, perhaps there's an opportunity to reorganize the day. There may
be no time for respite other than during sleeping hours. If this is the
case, look again at the tasks, and see whether any can be combined or
eliminated in order to create some breathing room.

Importantly, there may be tasks listed that could be off-loaded to
someone else: a paid supporter, a friend, or another member of the
family. It is not necessary at this stage to identify a person to take on
these tasks. This is an exercise in mining the daily diary for the potential of respite.

Quiet times in the day represent opportunities for self-care. "Me
time" looks different for everyone. For some, a "free" hour might be
the perfect time for a nap. For others, it's a chance to read a magazine or
knit a scarf. The key here is to seek opportunities in the day when you
can be intentional about doing something that feels relaxing and fulfilling, even if it's grocery shopping alone or calling an old friend for a chat.
The decision to insert yourself into your caregiving life by choosing how
to arrange your daily responsibilities does not mean choosing between
you and your loved one. Rather, it means considering your own needs
and those of your loved one. A critical look at a caregiver's day might
reveal that lunch is made, but only for a loved one. Caregivers often
develop a habit of thinking, "I'll grab a sandwich later—I can always eat
afterward when Mom is settled." Combining caregiver responsibilities
with one's own personal needs and preferences is possible. But shifting
priorities requires a set intention to be as kind to yourself as you are
to your loved one. And a deep understanding of what you do in a day
and how you feel about it makes it easier to choose tasks that could be
shared with others.

HOW TO KNOW WHAT YOU NEED AND GET
WHAT YOU WANT: LAYING THE GROUNDWORK

Every caregiver has a unique perspective on his or her role. An understanding of one's choice to give care in the context of personal and family history will determine how easy or difficult it will be to convert the facts of a caring life into an action plan—a plan to locate and secure help that is helpful. Below are a few trigger questions or statements that will help to form the beginning of creating that plan.

1. I am an expert in . . . .
2. I wish someone else would do the following tasks: . . . .
3. My favorite caregiving tasks are . . . .
4. My least favorite caregiving tasks are . . . .
5. Caregiving tasks that are too intimate or too risky for another person to carry out are . . . .
6. Caregiving tasks that another person could do with a little training and trust building are . . . .
7. I can enjoy a break indoors when I'm with my loved one. True or False?
8. I cannot enjoy a break outdoors if I'm with my loved one. True or False?
9. For me, a break at home would look like . . . .
10. For me, a break outside of home would look like . . . .

My Wish List

1. If I had someone who was unpaid to help me, I would ask him or her to . . . .
2. If I had someone who was paid to help me, I would ask him or her to . . . .

The answers to these questions will plant the seeds for a new way of seeing and being in the caring role. Awareness and understanding of possibility for a shift in thinking and doing is highly personal. Every caregiver is different, but the common certainty is that every one will feel better with the opportunity to exercise choice and access respite, especially when the caring role is intensive and performed over years.

A NEW WAY OF SEEING AND BEING

David Brooks, the *New York Times* essayist, describes suffering as a process of painful self-discovery.[11] He compares the experience of enduring traumatic life events to falling through the bottom floor of your personality, only to discover that there are more bottom floors below to penetrate. The strength to keep on living as we suffer teaches us that we cannot control our painful experiences, but we can respond to them. This discovery of strength in the face of great adversity is sometimes called "posttraumatic growth."[12]

For the caring community, posttraumatic growth illustrates the important paradox of caring for someone we love who is ill or infirm—it's the paradox that by suffering with our loved ones, we reveal our own hidden strengths and discover over time how to leverage them. Looking clear-eyed at all we do without judgment helps us achieve this objective of locating hope and possibility. Finding value in acts of caring calls on us to reflect on all the tasks we perform in a day. In this way, we can locate and reclaim our "lost identities" in our caring lives.

As we watch our loved ones struggle, we suffer in tandem. And as we suffer, the smashing through the bottom floor of our personality can transform us into advocates. Discovering who we are enables us to protect, cajole, nurture, and defend, and over time, we become able to introduce personal choice, however small, into everyday life. As we evolve into mindful caregivers, the determined purpose and meaning of our caring lives is revealed.

Making It Personal

In 2004, our family was in crisis. Our son Nicholas's care needs had increased exponentially after his severe cerebral palsy caused his right hip to dislocate painfully, even after multiple corrective surgeries. Nick's disabilities, in combination with his chronic pain and poor sleep, meant that my husband and I had become dangerously exhausted. We applied to a government-sponsored health and social services committee for nursing help at home—help we desperately needed. At the committee meeting, I read a list of Nicholas's daily care requirements to the assembled social workers and case managers. These are Nick's daily care tasks that I read that day:

- dispense nine medications via gastrostomy (stomach) tube 10 times per day, plus additional pain medications as needed;
- monitor and treat skin breakdown at feeding tube site in abdomen and at elbow and hip where pressure sores are common;
- reposition Nicholas in wheelchair every half hour for pain and discomfort (he is unable to reposition himself independently);
- lift Nicholas out of his chair into bed 6 times per day to alleviate pain from prolonged sitting;
- change briefs and clothing for incontinence 6 times per day;
- administer tube feeding 2 to 3 times per day given by pump over a three-hour period, plus dispense additional water given via syringe into the tube 10 times per day;
- reposition overnight for pain, seizures and/or sleep apnea, plus dispense pain medication on as-needed basis (at least hourly and often more frequently);
- record and report pain, seizure, and apnea symptoms for physician specialists;
- wash Nick's face and hands 4 times per day;
- brush Nick's teeth 3 times per day;
- shower Nick once per day;
- change Nick's clothing 3 times per day due to spills or incontinence;
- give total assistance for eating of oral snacks while monitoring for possible choking;
- perform frequent manicure/pedicure due to self-injury risk;
- perform massage and manual traction of limbs for pain relief as needed;
- offer communication assistance (Nick is non-speaking)—interpret each of Nick's efforts to communicate verbally and translate to others. Offer Nick oral presentation of all new information to compensate for his low vision, (e.g., read aloud newspaper, books, homework);
- offer social/emotional support: change television/radio stations, DVD, control computer and PlayStation (Nick has no hand function). Facilitate friendships and community interactions.

In preparing this list, I remember wondering, *"Do I do all this? Is this a picture of our family life and of my life?"* Naming all these tasks, including ones we felt might be unimportant to others—reminded me in a powerful way of our son's vulnerability and of the enormous weight on our shoulders to keep him alive, healthy, and pain free. I also made a second list of what would happen to Nick if each of these care tasks was ignored. The consequences were serious and in some cases, life threatening. Contemplating our family's vulnerability was humbling, and my fear of not accessing the help we needed grew. But with that fear came righteousness. My husband and I love our son, and when we looked at our duties of care, we knew we had the ammunition we needed to make an irrefutable case for help at home. In presenting our weaknesses, we felt strong. The list gave me a dispassionate way to see my life. "Please don't allow our family to fail before you help us to succeed," I said. "Help us now." And they did.

As I have advocated for those I love over the years, I've thought a lot about the lessons I learned that day. When I was faced with everyone saying "No," I asked myself, "What is my contribution to the solutions I want?" which made it more difficult for them to say "No" to supporting my family. My mindful reviewing of my caring duties proved to be an effective and empowering advocacy strategy throughout my life, time and time again.

9

IT TAKES A VILLAGE:
REVEALING HIDDEN ASSETS
IN THE NEIGHBORHOOD

People can't know what they need until they first know
what they have. —John McKnight

Isolation is a natural by-product of caregiving. Becoming vulnerable
often leads us to believe we represent the labels that are assigned to
us—labels such as "needy," "incapable," "dependent," and eventually,
"in crisis." We may believe that we have no capacities, gifts, or talents to
offer the world. We may even begin to believe that we are unlovable by
strangers or at least unlikable. Labels hurt. We may appear to ourselves
and to others as an empty glass. And that's because all of the labels assigned to us are based on how "badly" we're doing and what kind of
help we need. Of course caregiving families have needs, but we are not
the sum total of our needs. It's shameful that our overstretched social-
care benefits are based on a system in which we must demonstrate how
badly we've failed to care for our own before we are given the support
we need to succeed.

But this is not who we are, and these negative descriptors aren't
representative of our loved ones, either. Our loved ones have histories,
personalities, preferences, and talents—and so do we. Every living person has some gift or capacity to offer others. It is through recognizing
these capacities that we glimpse the possibility of community belonging
and living as well as possible, given health or aging challenges. Care is
reciprocal, so what are the gifts that caring families might offer others
in the community? Caregivers are expert purveyors of hospitality—we
know how to make people feel comfortable and welcome. Loved ones
who are nonspeaking have a special way of helping others slow down
by offering deep listening and nonjudgmental presence. Caring families

often contribute to the economy by paying the salaries of personal support workers. We model perseverance, ingenuity, patience and above all, kindness.

Knowing the value of what we have to give makes asking for help easier. Understanding personal assets gives us confidence to face the world and our neighbors. It also sparks ideas about what else we might have to offer in reciprocal relationships with friends and family.

LIVING WELL, GIVEN THE GIVENS

"It takes a village" is an adage that we usually apply to child rearing. But it's true of all family caregiving—caring is an activity that is best shared cooperatively among friends, family, and professionals (when their expertise is needed). But what kind of help is helpful, and how can community connections be forged to ease the burden of care and enable belonging? This question takes on urgency, especially in the early stages of caring, before exhaustion and desperation loom large.

The Asset Based Community Development Approach, or ABCD,[1] is a good place to begin thinking about the give-and-take of needs and assets in local neighborhoods. ABCD is about mobilizing the neighborhood so that people can find friendship and natural support locally. The approach builds on the assets that are already found in the community—it catalyzes individuals, associations, and institutions to come together to build on what they have, not concentrate on their needs. In the past when a person had a need, they went to their neighborhood for assistance. But today, the prevalent assumption is that a neighbor does not have the skills to help, therefore we must go to a professional. Of course, some families need professionals such as nurses or personal-support workers to help at home. But there are many aspects of helping us to live well that do not require a license or a university degree.

ABCD in Action

Richland County is in rural southern Wisconsin. When surveyed, older adults living there expressed the desire to live at home as long as possible, and they wanted to have a good life in the company of friends and family. So, in 2011, Richland Together Let's Connect[2] was born. Founding partners of the initiative were the Aging and Disability Resource Center of Southwest Wisconsin[3] and the Active Aging Research Center at the University of Wisconsin–Madison.[4] The project focused first on reducing loneliness. Using an ABCD approach to information gathering, the research team learned that older adults in Richland County liked to volunteer, spend time with family, and stay active by visiting friends, reading, and gardening. Most had some informal support of friends, neighbors, and family. They also reported having formal supports such as medical services and social supports such as Meals on Wheels. Challenges they identified were financial worries, driving (especially at night and in winter conditions), technology difficulties, and locating information regarding formal supports and social activities.

Richland Together Let's Connect took the assets and challenges of their older residents and decided how to innovate using community resources. They started a "little libraries" scheme of free book exchanges on street corners. To complement the little libraries, book clubs were formed. Technology was leveraged to organize friends, families, and neighbors who had something to offer one another. An online Neighborhood Time Bank[5] was created, where members could trade an hour of weeding for a knitting lesson or a toaster repair for snow shoveling. They also developed a regional website that included an easy-to-navigate calendar of local activities.

ABCD trains community organizers to be neighborhood sleuths. They gather information about residents' talents, interests, and skills. But they don't stop there—they ask which items on the list people are willing to share with others in the community. Then they organize ways for everyone to meet their daily needs through companionship and creative bartering systems. But what if an ABCD practitioner isn't available to help? Caregivers can take action themselves.

Be Your Own Community Connector

Here are some actions that caregivers can take on behalf of their own families. (A family member can be assigned some of these information-gathering tasks if the caregiver is too busy.)

1. Consider those who live in your city block or, if you live in a rural area, your close neighbors. Make a point of introducing yourself to three people who live nearby. If you know them already, make a point of getting in touch to say hello. Social connections turn into friendships. And friendships reduce social isolation. They also make people happier and safer. Our friends are our first and most valuable social safety net.

2. Contact your neighborhood association, community center, senior center and municipal government to see whether anyone is already working in your neighborhood using ABCD principles. If they are, ask how you and your caregiving family can participate in order to give and receive benefits from community sharing. If the community leaders you speak to are not aware of ABCD, use this as an opportunity to educate them about free resources on the relevant websites to help them learn to coordinate the assets of citizens where you live.

Sample call script:

> Hello, I'm calling to inquire whether anyone in your organization is aware of or is using The Asset Based Community Development Approach or ABCD. If you aren't sure, would you connect me with someone who is in charge of community development in my area?

Sample script to use if the government or association representative is not aware of ABCD:

> As a family caregiver, I know my family would benefit from a more connected community. Your organization is involved in community building, so perhaps you would like to know more about the Asset Based Community Development Institute. Their website has free resources and tools to help families like mine be less isolated and more involved locally. You can access those resources at www.abcdinstitute .org. Please let me know of any community building initiatives for family caregivers in my area.

3. Facebook often has group pages that are specific to communities. If there is a community page for your neighborhood, use it to trade services/ gifts. You might offer an hour of sewing in exchange for the same time of lawn cutting. Consider your skills and also the assets in your home. If

you have a garden plot or fruit trees, there might be apartment dwellers nearby who would like to plant, harvest, and share what they grow on your land. Most cities also have Meetup[6] groups based on interests and hobbies. There may be groups suitable for you and/or your loved one to share talents and make friends. In 2009, Dr. Kathy Marshak created a Meetup group called "Asperger Syndrome: Partners and Family of Adults with ASD" in her native city of Portland, Oregon.[7] On the website, she wrote: "I do hope you will join me and others to form a community for those of us who have this unique life of being in relationship with an adult on the Autism Spectrum."

Now, Dr. Kathy's Meetup has almost 2,500 members, but the feel is still intimate and personal. Today, Meetups are in almost every city. They exist to support most major disease or disability-family communities as well as to bring together any individuals who share interests or hobbies.

4. Consider all the institutions and associations in your neighborhood. Reflect on how you and your family might find friendship, belonging, respite, home help, and care within those entities.

Schools

Elementary schools may have a volunteer program for reading to children, or for children reading to an older adult. This might be a valuable opportunity for your elder loved one to add meaning and purpose to their week. Schools might have an initiative for intergenerational learning, empathy education, or a diversity program that could include individuals with disabilities or health challenges. Innovative teachers frequently use local seniors to enhance their history lessons. In Canada, the Memory Project[8] provides veterans of various conflicts the opportunity to share their personal experiences through oral interviews. These stories as well as artifacts are available for use by teachers, students, and the general public. Seniors are also called upon to share personal histories in person with students of all ages including on Remembrance or Memorial Days. It's worth calling the principal of local schools to inquire about opportunities to share knowledge, skills, and memories relevant to social and political history. Universities often have service clubs as well as disability-, disease-, or age-specific support groups that function locally.

Best Buddies[9] is an international nonprofit organization dedicated to establishing a global volunteer movement that creates opportunities for one-to-one friendships, integrated employment, and leadership development for people with intellectual and developmental disabilities (IDD). Best Buddies links university students (as well as other members of the community) with local people who have disabilities in order to achieve their goals of personal growth and inclusion. Community colleges or universities that offer health-care training, including personal support work and nursing, are potential sources of home help from students wishing to earn extra money as they bolster their CVs.

In 2014, a group of Chicago seniors began chatting online with students of English at a language school in Sao Paulo, Brazil. A video of members of the retirement community helping the students with their English skills through casual conversation went viral.[10] All universities and colleges have an office to support the needs of foreign students. It's worth calling that office to offer the services of an older adult or loved one with disabilities as a chat partner for students learning English.

Handy Tip: High schools frequently require their students to complete volunteer hours in order to graduate. Guidance counselors will have information on whether a student could assist with yard work, grass cutting, dog walking, or snow removal on a voluntary basis.

Community Centers and Senior Centers

Community and senior centers are the caregiver's best friend. Frequently, there are programs offered that range from post-stroke aquarehab to zumba with inclusive childcare. A creative community-center leader might have instigated an employment support and education program that trains (and pays) young adults with developmental disabilities to clear lunch tables, water plants, or greet members. For seniors, there are fitness opportunities for older adults and quiet swimming times designed for people with disabilities and their families. Some centers link swimmers with volunteers to help with changing and support in the pool. Senior centers offer a range of programming for all abilities, including activities in the domains of sports and fitness, hobbies and interests, travel, walking, and technology training, as well as daytime groups that offer respite to caregivers. Call your local center to see what's on offer for you and your loved one. If your personal financial resources are limited, ask whether they offer subsidies for membership (the YMCA offers this type of assistance). If you're not sure about the availability of financial assistance to join a center, ask for a fee schedule that includes information about subsidies.

Handy Tip: If your community or senior center does not offer the program you want, ask to meet with a manager to discuss including your preferred activity.

Faith Groups and Places of Worship

Churches, synagogues and temples are natural places of support and belonging. Ask your priest or rabbi whether there's an opportunity for you to worship while a volunteer cares for your loved one. Many places of worship have committees devoted to the needs of caregivers and the elderly or people with disabilities. Call and ask how the faith community might help your family and how you and your loved one can contribute to the faith community.

Handy Tip: Most faith communities offer home visits to individuals who request that service. They visit hospitals as well, and representatives from local churches or synagogues coordinate spiritual support with in-patient chaplains.

Municipal Services Including Parks and Public Spaces

People working in your local municipal government have a responsibility to know and support their most vulnerable constituents. Google your city government to see what public services are operated in your area—these could include local art galleries (often with specialized learning programs), outdoor swimming pools, parks, and even population-specific programs such as day activity groups for people with disabilities or dementia. All cities have municipal counselors or alderpersons who are responsible for governing the affairs of local neighborhoods. Alderpersons' contact information is listed on every city website—they are there to serve the needs of constituents.

Handy Tip: First responders can be helpful neighbors, too. Make an appointment to phone or visit your local fire station. If you support someone with mobility challenges, they will put you on an alert registry so that in case of fire, your home will be flagged as the residence of someone vulnerable who needs extra assistance in an emergency. Police departments often have registries for citizens with cognitive impairments who may be prone to wandering and getting lost.

Cultural Associations

Cultural associations are, by definition, dedicated to community building. As an example, the Federation of Italian-American Associations in Brooklyn, New York, offers the following services:[11]

> At F.I.A.O.'s main office our staff assists individuals and families with the preparation of applications, translation of documents, referral to agencies, visits to home bound people, and escorting non-English speaking clients to governmental agencies. We also assist those seeking Public Assistance (i.e. Food Stamps, Medicaid / Medicare), Housing (i.e. Section 8, IT 214 & Rent Increase exemption), Immigration (i.e. Citizenship Applications, Alien Card renewal), and HEAP (Application and Home Attendant referrals). In addition, representatives from the Social Security Administration and from the Italian "Patronato" are on site every first Thursday of the month.

Local cultural groups often have the kind of neighbor-to-neighbor support for all ages that is culture- and language-specific. Because cultural groups offer programs for children and teens, too, there may be opportunities for inter-age social inclusion and contribution.

Handy Tip: Cultural groups and associations rely on volunteers. Cultural-center hospitality, helping at events, and office work are just a few areas of community contribution that can give caregiving families a sense of purpose and belonging.

Museums and Other Arts Institutions

Most art galleries today host programs for vulnerable people and their caregivers. Frequently on offer are painting groups for dementia sufferers, sculpture classes for people with disabilities, and guided discussion tours tailored for audiences with communication challenges. Theaters and cinemas will often host special performances for unique audiences such as persons with autism and their families or mothers and babies. Local arts centers may sponsor choral singing opportunities for older adults and their caregivers, an activity shown to benefit the health and well-being of participants at any age.[12]

Handy Tip: Most municipalities in the United States and Canada host a 2-1-1 telephone service providing information about local programs including those that support the arts, seniors, caregivers, and youth. If the arts-inclusion program that you are looking for isn't offered in your area, seek out one that serves the general population and inquire with a manager about whether accommodations can be made to enable your loved one's participation.

Libraries

Libraries offer a range of activities that serve to connect local residents. Book clubs and writers groups (including memoir writing) are just two examples. Many offer film screenings, discussion groups, author talks, and newcomer support as well. If you or your loved one enjoys books, the library could be a place of community belonging and purpose.

Handy Tip: Google your library and click on "Events and Programs." If you or your loved one requires adaptations for accessibility, click on "Services."

Local Businesses

Sometimes a place of friendship is a local restaurant, coffee shop, barbershop, or pub. Regular customers get to know one another, and events like pub quiz nights can forge caring relationships that are enduring and meaningful.

Handy Tip: Pencil in regular visits to the same hair stylist or local café. Hair salons or spas are places of relaxation and intimacy. Relationships are built with frequent and regular visits to the same service providers. They may begin as professionals, but they often become friends.

Nonprofits and Social Enterprises

There's a new breed of nonprofit springing up in communities across the country. These are groups designed to battle the social isolation experienced by seniors, people with disabilities, and their families. *Men's shed*[13] is one of those initiatives. Men's sheds, or community sheds, are nonprofit organizations that originated in Australia to advise and improve the overall health of all men. The slogan for men's sheds is "Shoulder to Shoulder," shortened from "Men don't talk face to face, they talk shoulder to shoulder." In 2014, Professor Barry Golding coined the term "shedagogy" to describe "a distinctive, new way of acknowledging, describing and addressing the way some men prefer to learn informally in shed-like spaces mainly with other men."[14] Every men's shed will have its own unique aims and will focus on a certain subject. There are five different kinds of men's sheds: work, clinical, educational, recreational, and communal.

Work sheds are for those who want to remain active and have an overall goal. These sheds focus heavily on restoration and construction, while helping the local community. *Clinical* and *Communal sheds* have similar features, with the core of their aims focused on helping the local male community discuss their health and well-being. *Recreational* men's sheds are created to help local men be social. *Educational* sheds are aimed at improving skills and qualities. *Virtual* sheds provide an online capability where members from all men's sheds and other remote communities across the country or around world can actively communicate and be involved in numerous research, writing, and photographic activities. Men's sheds are also beginning initiatives to support men with dementia and Alzheimer's disease, especially in the early stages. Research supports the value of men's sheds to the "shedders" themselves. A 2007 research study[15] reported the following feedback from participants:

- 99.5 percent of men, "I feel better about myself."
- 97 percent, "I have a place where I belong."
- 97 percent, "I can give back to the community."

- 97 percent, "I am doing what I really enjoy."
- 90 percent, "I feel more accepted in the community."
- 79 percent, "I get access to men's health information."
- 77 percent, "I feel happier at home."

Approximately 30 percent of shedders are disabled.

Another trending neighborhood movement is Community Kitchens.[16] A community kitchen is a small group of people who get together to prepare meals for themselves or their families. The many benefits to joining a community kitchen include meeting new people and having fun, sharing ideas, taking home nutritious meals, learning new recipes, and saving time and money. Community kitchens are common today in most municipalities across North America.

Handy Tip: Google the name of your city followed by "innovation" and the name of your disease, disability, or aging challenge. You will be surprised by the hidden assets in your community.

Pets as Social Connectors

Dog lovers know that besides being "man's best friend," canines are terrific neighborhood relationship facilitators. Striking up a conversation with strangers is intimidating, but with a dog, it's easier. Gazes that might have landed on a mobility aid suddenly turn to a pooch. Conversation moves easily from praise for doggy cuteness to breed differences to best dog parks in the vicinity. Dog walkers in the same city block know one another and form friendships that often breach the limits of the dog walk. Associate Professor Lisa Wood of the University of Western Australia's School of Population Health has analyzed the results from telephone interviews with people living in Perth, as well as San Diego, Portland, and Nashville in the United States, which asked about pet ownership and social connections.

Dr. Wood observed, "One of our key findings was that if you owned pets you were more likely to meet people in your neighborhood." Respondents were then asked if they had met someone through their pet—someone from whom they went on to receive social support such as having regular conversations and receiving advice or information. "Across the study, 42 percent of people said that they had met someone through their pet that they could turn to," Dr. Wood said.[17]

If you don't have a pet and don't have access to pet therapy, offer to walk a neighbor's dog. They will appreciate the help, and you and your loved one (if they are able) will enjoy the opportunity for exercise and socializing without the commitment of pet ownership. If your loved one has mobility challenges that make walking impossible, consider the possibility of arranging home visits of neighbors' pets that are mature, friendly, and well behaved.

Handy Tip: Pet Partners[18] is a charity that places therapy animals in health care institutions and community-support agencies. Volunteers sometimes combine walking or reading with their traditional pet therapy activities to enhance the well-being of people of all ages with care needs.

How Can I Begin to Ask Friends and Family for Help?

Caregivers have a hard time making new friends (unless they are other caregivers). But most do have some relationships that are remnants of life before caregiving duties took center stage. What kind of help can members of our social circle offer? It's hard enough to ask for assistance at the best of times, but trying to match the needs of home and family with the skills and interests of friends and family is almost impossible in the fog of caregiving. Here are some skills, professions, and interests that could equate to help at home.

- An administrative assistant could help with managing bill payments, filing, medical records, and creating a shared agenda.
- A bookkeeper could help with the organization of payroll for home-care paid staff.
- A shop clerk could help with shopping for clothing with your loved one or ordering online.
- A homemaker could prepare and deliver one meal per week.
- An insurance salesman could help with navigating insurance coverage.

- A music lover could spend time creating a playlist for your loved one, and this "gift" could include a visit to enjoy the music together.
- A human resources professional could help with creating a hiring and training regime for paid home-care staff.
- A taxi or delivery driver could help with transportation to medical appointments.
- A pharmacist in the family could help to foster a connection with the community pharmacist and help to organize medications at home.
- A friend or family member who works in the construction industry might function as a handyman.
- Someone who works in the fitness industry could help with moving heavy objects at home, or they could create a light exercise regime for you and your loved one.
- Someone who sews could mend clothes or create adapted clothing features by, for example, replacing buttons and zippers with Velcro or snap closures.
- Anyone who works in government could help to locate services and patient/caregiver benefits offered by the city, state, or province and at the national or federal level.
- A friend or family member who is employed in food services of any kind could investigate grocery delivery and food preparation help in the community.
- Someone working in the area of information technology could set up apps or websites to facilitate friends and family in delivering food, visiting, accompanying a loved one on outings, coordinating medical information and care, and so on.

It might seem mercenary or cynical to mine the professions, talents, and interests of friends and family members in an effort to secure help for the family. But it's human nature that people will say "Yes" if they are asked to perform a limited role doing something they're good at or that they enjoy. And the fact is, people want to help. Often though, friends or family members are intimidated by the scale of need and by the specialized care that may be well outside of their comfort zone. Offering someone an invitation to share their gifts and talents is quite different from asking them to take on an open-ended job that they know nothing about and that could even go horribly wrong. The trick is to match time-limited tasks to the skills sets of friends, neighbors, and family who are already motivated to help but may be intimidated.

Handy Tip: Remember, the caregiving community has a vast amount of knowledge, wisdom, and experience. If you need help and aren't sure where to get it, ask another caregiver.

A NEW WAY OF SEEING AND BEING

If we are healthy, working, or busy raising children, we may not be aware of who and what is around us in the neighborhood. But caring for someone in the family may be an important reason to explore what and who is nearby. Beginning to think differently about gifts, assets, needs, and neighborhoods begins with a reckoning of what you would like your family to share with others. Putting that list together with needs is easier when answering the following three questions: 1) In my family, what are the things we can do by ourselves? 2) What are things we can do with a bit of help? 3) What are things that we cannot manage at all on our own? Answers to the first question about things you do well on your own will give clues about what you might consider sharing with others in order to foster friendship and belonging. Answers to questions two and three will guide your search for community members who would like to (or need to) offer help that also benefits your family. All cities and neighborhoods have institutions that offer assistance to those living with a particular disease or disability. But that assistance may or may not be what you need, or it may not be available when you need it. Arranging help that is useful is like putting together a puzzle—and in this case, the puzzle pieces are a mix of formal (institutional or medical) and informal (local community and often unpaid) resources.

Making It Personal

In 1998, much of eastern Canada and New England was declared to be in a state of emergency. Over the course of eleven days, almost forty millimeters of freezing rain fell, crushing power lines and toppling the entire power grid serving the northeast. As the temperature dropped and we huddled beside our fireplace, the realization dawned on me that without electricity, I could not feed Nicholas. Nick is tube fed, and his pump was electrically powered. His principal mode of communication at that time was a speaking computer, operated via head switches. Without power, Nicholas could not speak. Without heat in the house, he began to shiver. A natural disaster suddenly caused Nick to become much, much more disabled than I had ever known him to be. Suddenly, I began to fear that he couldn't manage another cold night. Then the phone rang (our land line). It was the City Public Health Department informing me that they were aware our son had severe disabilities and that it was unsafe for him to remain at home without heat. They suggested he be admitted to our Children's Hospital. Nicholas was so afraid of the hospital that he began to scream when we turned the corner into the parking lot. I said no. Then they proposed an "old age home"—again, I said no. I'd heard that some families I knew had already been offered hotel rooms, so I suggested that we be relocated to one of the few local hotels with electricity, along with our dog. They agreed, and we began our emergency evacuation, or as the children called it, the big adventure holiday.

Our local community center was a designated shelter, and that's where we went for kids' activities and socializing during the day. On normal days, the pool would be filled with the echo of children's gleeful shouts. The upstairs "living room" would be home to local mothers in yoga-wear chatting amiably with each other or with seniors who had perhaps just finished their "silver stars" exercise class.

But on the day we arrived at the center during the ice storm, the entire center was transformed into an overflowing, noisy, food-filled place of laughter, worry, and shock. It was as if our relatives (some of whom we had never met) had arrived from parts unknown to join us for some kind of bizarre reunion. These were our neighbors? A few of the families I knew had children in swimming lessons or were mothers who, like me, attended regular aerobics classes. But most of the people sitting on cots or chasing toddlers were strangers.

Yet it was an environment that invited chatting. "When did you lose your power? How long did you stay at home before you came here?

Is there anyone in your building who couldn't get out? You had to leave your cat at home? Oh dear, you must be so worried."

What struck me most about this forced gathering was the way that unlikely leaders emerged. One middle-aged woman looked worse for the wear—she had a smoker's voice and unkempt, gray hair. But her eyes were lively, and she was a natural caregiver We introduced ourselves and I learned that her name was Angela. "I'll take care of sweeping the floors," she said. "And when I'm done with that, I'll tidy the food tables. Do you see that lady over there? She has Alzheimer's and needs company. You go over and have a chat." This woman's talent for scanning the room and knowing who needed what was extraordinary. I learned that her residence was indeed nearby, but it was a world away from mine. Her building was a subsidized apartment building in the middle of our affluent neighborhood. She was the first person I had ever met from that building but she wouldn't be the last. Howard, a shy young man sporting a ball cap and baggy jeans asked if he could push Nick's chair in a game of ball hockey underway in the gym. Nick's eyes lit up. "Of course! Nick would love that, wouldn't you Nick!"

What I felt that day and in the days of the ice storm that followed was gratitude—gratitude for my neighbors, my new friends. I wanted to thank them for their teamwork, their generosity and their willingness to "step up" in the face of shared adversity. I hate to say it, but maybe we need more ice storms because what I saw in my neighborhood that January 1998 was the power of community.

ANOTHER STORY OF COMMUNITY

Four years ago, I was working as a community connector for a young family. My own family caregiving experience had given me the confidence and experience to mine communities for whatever they had to offer families like my own. "Brian," a widower, was struggling to care for his six-year-old son "Ian," who had severe disabilities and complex medical challenges. Because swallowing was difficult for Ian, experts recommended that all his food be chopped finely to minimize the chances of choking. Brian told me that caring for his son while working full-time at a demanding job as well as shopping and preparing a special diet was exhausting. He wanted help with food. I noticed a grocery store opposite the family home, so I decided to ask the manager if the store could offer services to help Brian and his son. They could. The manager told me he'd be happy to take Brian's weekly grocery order over the phone. Then he introduced me to "Helen" who worked at the salad bar. She could chop all the family groceries, and because the delivery address was close to the store, she would also deliver the order every week. Helen has become friends with Brian and Ian as well as with many of the home nurses who answer the door on grocery-delivery day. Ian always has a smile and a hug for his friend Helen.

But the story doesn't end there. Brian still needed help with cooking, so I decided to explore community kitchens in the area. "Betty" is a retired neighbor who partnered with "Liz" and "Susie" to organize a community kitchen. Members of their cooking group gather weekly in the local community center kitchen to prepare healthy meals for their families, and by sharing bulk ingredients, they save money. But they share more than just recipes—they exchange news about their children, favorite TV shows, and good books they've read. In short, the community kitchen is a friendship circle—one that decided to "adopt" Brian and Ian. Now, Betty, Liz, and Susie cook together for themselves and for Brian and Ian as well.

10

NAVIGATING THE ROUGH
WATERS OF TRANSITION

Our infant son's disabilities made swallowing difficult and even dangerous, so we opted for surgery to implant a feeding tube in his stomach. A few days after the operation, a specialist nurse took me aside. She showed me how to feed my baby boy using the tube together with plastic syringes, flexible bags to hold the formula and an electric pump. She showed me how to wash my hands before priming the length of tubing without flooding the tiny drip chamber in the pump. Next came the demonstration of how to program the pump with the desired drip speed, total dose and total volume. Nodding my head, I pretended to understand all the instructions. I wanted to be a competent, loving mother. But all I felt was a sick grief, gazing at the hole in my beautiful son's belly where now there was a flesh colored catheter, curling out of his diaper like a snake. When we got home from the hospital, I couldn't remember a single thing about how to use the equipment. I had no idea who to call—I'd never felt so alone. —Parent of a two-year-old child with a new feeding tube.

A journey of caring is never static. Small changes in a loved one's health occur every day. And over months or years, life-altering changes take place, too. A loved one comes home from the hospital after a stroke. A child with disabilities graduates from school, and suddenly a life with reassuring pediatric health-care supports morphs into the impoverished world of adult services. A parent moves from the family home into assisted living and a few years later is admitted to a long-term care institution. Perhaps the entire family has to relocate to another city for reasons that have nothing to do with illness, disability, or aging.

People are vulnerable when they move among the different parts of the health-care system.[1] Care transitions threaten patient and family well-being because they can increase the possibility of key providers losing critical background information. If new medical devices are introduced to the home, caregivers are frequently terrified that they lack the skills and training to operate them properly. But that is not all. Transitions require an increased degree of coordination, which may not be available, especially when the patient and family are in a new environment. Care coordination is suddenly the domain of the caregiver at a time when a loved one's needs have escalated and familiar supports have disappeared. At times of transition, patients and their families may "fall through the cracks." Accidents (and near accidents) may happen, sometimes leading to outright crises.

Caring, especially during patient transitions, is like putting together many pieces of a puzzle. The pieces might include learning new skills such as wound care, balancing employment, managing the family's needs at home, and liaising with health-care professionals. These puzzle pieces are hard to fit together—a situation that's made more challenging by the fact that others may be aware of only one or two of these pieces. The only person who is trying to create a whole picture with all the puzzle pieces is the caregiver. The caregiver is usually the only person who is invested in knowing about and influencing *all* aspects of the patient's life and illness experience, whether at home or in the hospital.

"Next Step in Care" is a United Hospital Fund online guide[2] designed to help caregivers and medical professionals work together to plan and implement safe and smooth patient transitions between care settings. It is one project that aims to fill the gap of training and support for families who may be using health technology devices at home for the first time, or who may need to know what to expect in a rehabilitation unit. The guide also seeks to help health care providers understand what kinds of support family caregivers need when their friend or relative transitions between care settings. And it's unique because it is written with a clear recognition that caregivers and families perform essential roles that systems cannot. There is no pretending that medical professionals or institutions can care for patients well without the contribution of family, especially during transitions.

The extra care that families provide during times of transition helps to ensure patient safety, but it also risks further isolating the caregiver and the family. Coordinated networks of support that existed before the transition may no longer be available. Friends and family members may not know how to help in new, more challenging circumstances. Transitions can be a very lonely time for caring families.

The most common experience of patients and caregivers moving through health settings is "going it alone." Hospital discharge arrangements are often completed in a hurry, at the last minute. The transfer of an elderly parent into a nursing home may be a very rushed affair because long waiting lists mean that patients must accept an opening immediately (that they didn't choose) or give up their place on the list. Even beginning a new day program can be a stressor for everyone in the family. Rarely in a caring life is everything smooth and predictable. It is no wonder that caregivers today report feeling that their lives are out of control.[3]

DRAW YOUR OWN ATLAS CAREMAP

One highly effective strategy for locating one's self and others who have a caring role inside and outside of the family is a process called "care mapping."[4] Atlas CareMaps reveal hidden truths about who is doing what in the circle of care, so they are enlightening at any point along the care journey. But at times of transition when relationships may be in flux, they are particularly helpful. And it's important to remember that becoming a caregiver is an important transition in itself.

Atlas CareMaps require no artistic talent. They consist of simple figures that represent a person's care "eco-system," showing who cares for whom and how. The process of drawing an Atlas CareMap and considering what it means helps people understand their existing care ecosystem and the multiple relationships within it (see, e.g., figure 10.1). For many, this leads to improved care, decreased anxiety, and more confidence in managing their care situations.

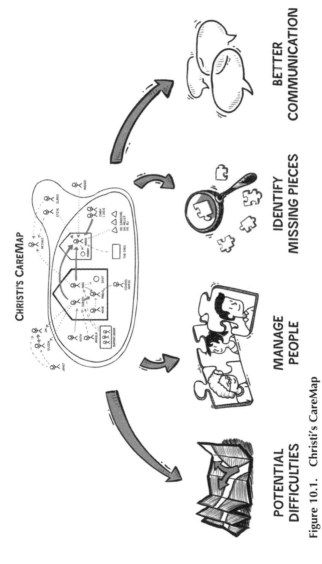

Figure 10.1. Christi's CareMap

Source: Atlas of Caregiving

Before drawing an online or paper-and-pencil CareMap,[5] consider the following questions and write down the names of individuals who play these supportive roles in your family. You may wish to write down your answers to the questions below in order to prepare for drawing your CareMap.

Who lives with you? Begin by listing everyone who lives in your household. Don't forget to list pets—they are members of the family, too!

Whom (all) do you care for? Most people care for more than one person, and in care mapping, it's important to think of everyone whose lives are enhanced by your active caring. Which of your activities are for the care of others (people or pets)? For example: Do you help anyone with medical activities? Do you provide social or emotional support to anyone? Do you help anyone with personal or household activities that they can't manage themselves? Do you help anyone cover some of the financial costs of health issues? Do you help anyone with advice on health conditions, treatments, and services?

Even if you are ill or frail, you might still be caring for children, spouses, parents, pets, neighbors, and friends. Sometimes there is no choice—you must help despite your own situation. Sometimes it is much more than that—caring for others can be a core part of our being. Some caregivers see their identity as being a caring member in a family and the community.

Who cares for or supports you? Who are the people whose presence in your life is important to your well-being? For example: Who provides important social and emotional support? Who provides medical support to you? Who helps with personal or household activities that you are unable to manage yourself? Who helps with the financial costs incurred because of health issues? Who helps you with ideas and decision making about well-being, health conditions, treatments, and services?

Who else cares for the people you care for? The questions you've asked yourself about who cares for you apply here as well. Consider everyone who also actively supports the people you care for. Your answers may include other family members, medical professionals (in home care and in clinical care settings), neighbors, friends, and community support workers such as staff at a day program.

Once you have a sense of your answers to these questions, you are ready to draw an Atlas CareMap. The Atlas of Caregiving website has easy-to-follow instructions on how to get started.[6] CareMaps are for anyone at any time because we all have caring relationships in our lives.

Maria's Atlas CareMap

When Maria and her husband, Angelo, are not working at their bakery, they are caring for their two grown daughters, Carla and Lori. Carla (26) has a mild cognitive impairment, but with Maria's support, helps out most days in the bakery. Lori is a single mother who lives nearby with her two young children. Maria cares for everyone in her family, but she gives extra support to Carla in the bakery, helping her to ice cakes and prepare orders for delivery. Maria also actively supports her father Frank (84) who has dementia and has recently moved into a memory care unit.

Frank is often anxious, tearful, and confused in his new surroundings, and Maria feels guilty and sad that her father is so distressed. Every weekend, Carla stays with her older sister Lori and her family. Lori's children, Luka and Sonya, love to play with their aunt Carla, and Lori always remembers to thank Carla for her help with the children.

Maria puts on a smile for her family and for her customers at the bakery, but privately, she admits to feeling exhausted and inadequate in meeting the needs of her husband and children (especially Carla), her father, and her business.

When Maria drew her Atlas CareMap (see figure 10.2), she was surprised by how much Carla contributed to both to the bakery business and to Lori's family. She also remembered to add the support of a regular customer at the bakery, Susan, who had recently begun to teach Carla how to use a sewing machine. Maria was reminded to include the community doctor who supported her emotional needs as well as the health of the whole family, including Frank's tumultuous move into the memory-care facility. Since Frank's move, the dementia-care social worker, key nurse, and specialist physician have all been introduced, mainly to collect advice and history about Frank. Maria has made a mental note to include them

MARIA'S CareMap

6/25/2018

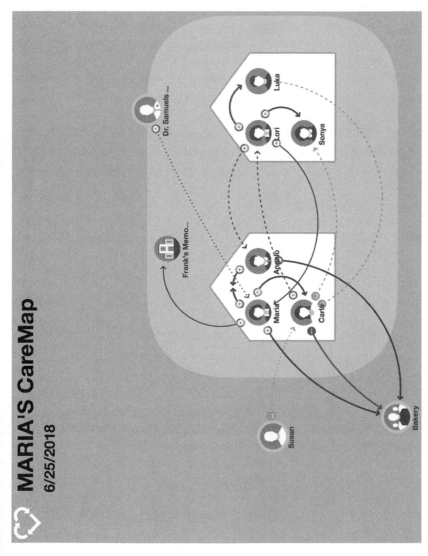

Figure 10.2. Maria's CareMap

Actors

Undefined | Girl | Woman | Woman | Man | Non-binary
Group | Boy | Man | Baby | Health Professional | Woman
Health Pro. Group | Health Professional | Potential Actor | Health Professional
Pet | Dog | Cat | Bird | Horse
Care Facility | Care Service | Outdoors | Sports | Place of Worship | Online Support

Links

Support frequency

—— Frequently
— Daily
···· Weekly
····· Occasionally
–·–· Undefined

Support type

○ Care Coordination
● Financial
● Healthcare Mgmt
● Household Chores
○ Medical Activities
○ Personal Help
● Social / Emotional
● Other
● Undefined
○ Multiple

Location

Household
Near
Less than 6 miles/10km away
Middle
Between 6 miles/10km and 60 miles/100km away
Far
More than 60 miles/100km away

♡ ATLAS CAREMAP

MARIA'S CareMap 6/25/2018

Figure 10.2. *(continued)*

○ Actors Table (1/2)

Actors are the main elements of your CareMap.
They represent the people, pets and places
that are part of your care ecosystem.

Name	Label	Location	Condition	Notes
◌ **Household #1**				
◉ Angelo		Milwaukee, WI, USA	None	
		No Email - No Phone		
◉ Carla		Milwaukee, WI, USA	None	
		No Email - No Phone		
◉ Maria		Milwaukee, WI, USA	None	
		No Email - No Phone		
◌ **Household #2**				
◉ Lori		Milwaukee, WI, USA	None	
		No Email - No Phone		
◉ Luka		Milwaukee, WI, USA	None	
		No Email - No Phone		

Figure 10.2. *(continued)*

○ Actors Table (2/2)

Actors are the main elements of your CareMap.
They represent the people, pets and places
that are part of your care ecosystem.

Name	Label	Location	Condition	Notes
○ Sonya		Milwaukee, WI, USA	None	
		No Email - No Phone		
○ Bakery		Milwaukee, WI, USA	None	
		No Email - No Phone		
○ Dr. Samuels GP		Milwaukee, WI, USA	None	
		No Email - No Phone		
○ Frank's Memory Ca...		Milwaukee, WI, USA	Dementia - Alzheimer's Disease	
		No Email - No Phone		
○ Susan		Milwaukee, WI, USA	None	
		No Email - No Phone		

Figure 10.2. *(continued)*

⊙ Links Table (1/3)

Links represent the support, including type of support and frequency, provided by one Actor to another.

ACTOR A	RELATIONSHIP		ACTOR B	A → B	B → A
Angelo	Husband	- Husband	Maria		
		- Father	Lori		
	Employment-		Bakery		
Bakery		- Employment	Maria		
		- Employment	Angelo		
		- Employment	Carla		
Carla		- Daughter	Maria		
		- Friend	Susan		
	Sister	-	Lori		
	Nephew	-	Luka		
	Employment-		Bakery		
	Niece	-	Sonya		
Dr. Samuels GP	General Pra..		Maria		

♡ ATLAS CAREMAP   MARIA'S CareMap 6/25/2018

Figure 10.2. *(continued)*

⊙ Links Table (2/3)

Links represent the support, including type of support and frequency, provided by one Actor to another.

ACTOR A	RELATIONSHIP		ACTOR B	A → B	B → A
Frank's Memory Ca...	-	Father	Maria		
Lori	Daughter	-	Sonya		
	Mother	-	Maria		
	Mother	-	Luka		
	Father	-	Angelo		
	-	Sister	Carla		
Luka	-	Mother	Lori		
	-	Nephew	Carla		

♡ ATLAS CAREMAP   MARIA'S CareMap 6/25/2018

Figure 10.2. *(continued)*

Links Table (3/3)

Links represent the support, including type of support and frequency, provided by one Actor to another.

ACTOR A	RELATIONSHIP		ACTOR B	A → B	B → A
Maria	Husband	- Husband	Angelo		
	Employment-		Bakery		
	Father	-	Frank's Memory Ca...		
	Daughter	-	Carla		
		- General Pra...	Dr. Samuels GP		
		- Mother	Lori		
Sonya		- Daughter	Lori		
		- Niece	Carla		
Susan	Friend	-	Carla		

ATLAS CAREMAP

MARIA'S CareMap 6/25/2018

Figure 10.2. (continued)

in her next Atlas CareMap as their role expands over the coming months to support Maria and Angelo emotionally.

The power of Atlas CareMaps is revealed when people see their own relational lives reflected back to them. Gaps in support are illuminated, but so are connections of strength, love, and resilience. Maria realized that she is not alone in caring for her family and that Carla is a big help, both in the bakery and to Lori. But she also learned that she wants to find ways to spend more time with her grandchildren and to have other family members help in supporting Frank. Angelo offered to visit Frank on weekends, and Lori suggested that Maria, Angelo, and Carla could come over for dinner sometime to visit with the children and give Maria a break from cooking. Maria shared her Atlas CareMap with her family practitioner and with the staff at her father's new care home. Now, Maria feels hopeful about trying out a new model of sharing care in her family, and she feels grateful for everyone's contributions at home and at the bakery.

How to Draw Your Own Atlas CareMap

Atlas CareMaps can be drawn on paper by hand using a pen or pencil. Or, they can be drawn online.[7] For newcomers to Atlas CareMaps, the easiest way to begin is on paper. Symbols represent people, places, and relationships (whether you see someone several times a week or only occasionally, for example).

KNOW YOUR SYMBOLS

Use simple symbols to represent different people. Although you can make up your own, here are some suggestions:

- stickmen and stickwomen—for yourself and the people in your household as well as male and female family and friends
- triangles—for professional caregivers
- circles—for pets (or draw little animals if you prefer)
- houses—for facilities, such as a day center, clinic, or hospital
- boxes with small stick figures—for clubs or groups, such as online communities or support groups

KNOW YOUR CONNECTIONS

Connect people with differently styled lines to show how frequently care is provided, using arrowheads to indicate who cares for whom. These are the types of line styles we use, when caregiving is:

- Often (many times a day)—Thick line
- Daily—Simple line
- Weekly—Broken (dashed) line
- Occasionally (less than weekly)—Dotted line

IDENTIFY THE PEOPLE

It's helpful to write names under the symbols for the people, places, and services on your map. As you add information, don't worry about trying to make it perfect or complete. There'll be plenty of time to add missing people and make other corrections once you've established the overall structure—and don't forget that you have an eraser (even if you are drawing online).

LOCATION, LOCATION, LOCATION

OK, let's get started.   Begin by drawing yourself right in the middle of the paper, then steadily add other people. As you do this, try to use distance on the paper to represent geographical distance. So if someone lives nearby, draw them close to you on your map. If they're far away, draw them near the edge of the paper.

Group people together if they live:

- in your home
- nearby (less than twenty minutes away)
- in the middle distance (between twenty minutes and two hours away)
- far away (more than two hours away)

Finally, add your name and the date. When your caregiving situation changes, it's time to redraw your map.

How to Read Your Atlas CareMap

Begin by asking yourself and noting what you see on the Atlas CareMap. Who is indispensable? What happens when they cannot be present due to other life commitments or illness? Is there a backup plan to replace them? Is everyone on the map aware of each other's involvement with your family and the role each person plays? What are the responsibilities of everyone on the map? At first, it's natural to think only of medical-care responsibilities, but there may be friends or family members who help with household chores or paperwork or simply provide friendship. These are also valuable forms of support. How is communication and coordination managed among all parties?

Next, consider what you *don't* see on your map. Perhaps you have forgotten someone important (a spouse or a sibling, for example?). Are there family members or friends who could be involved but aren't? Could they become allies if they had a specific task or role to contribute? Are there missing professionals or untapped services? Perhaps there is someone on the map who could help to identify those service gaps. And consider how your map may have changed over time, especially in transitions. Consider how the situation was different sometime in the past. Was it easier before? If so, is there something from the previous situation that could be recreated today?

Also, consider the future. What changes do you anticipate in your future Atlas CareMap? Is there anything you could do now to be better prepared for those transitions?

Finally, do not look at your Atlas CareMap with only a "problem-solving" perspective, looking to fix what's not working well. Look to see what *is* working well, and take a moment to acknowledge and appreciate those aspects of your caring life.

Sharing Your Atlas CareMap

Once you have reflected on your Atlas CareMap and identified both what is working well in your care "eco-system" and where improvements could be made, it is time to consider how to use the Atlas CareMap as a conversation facilitator. Explaining the mapping process to family, friends, and support professionals will help them more deeply understand you and your loved one, including what's going well and where you need extra support.

A NEW WAY OF SEEING AND BEING

Caring for someone who is seriously ill or dependent due to aging and frailty is challenging at the best of times. But without the required skills, knowledge, or experience to manage caring competently, families can feel "adrift," or as if they have "fallen off a cliff." And these intense feelings of performance anxiety are amplified during transitions in care when everything must be learned all over again in order to achieve a sense of calm and competency. An Atlas CareMap is helpful because it enables caregivers to gaze into a nonjudgmental, dispassionate mirror. It reflects back the caring life in a way that makes the very personal possible to examine and evaluate. By looking at their pictured relationships, caregivers are offered a glimpse of control over their lives. The Atlas CareMap makes visible a separation between caregivers and their experiences—this distance allows caregivers to view their own relationships anew. Just as we rely on a map or GPS to guide us when we're lost, Atlas CareMaps tell us where we are so that we can consider where we'd like to be.

Making It Personal

BETTY'S STORY[8]

When Betty drew her Atlas CareMap, she looked at the representation of her caring life and shook her head. "I never realized how overwhelmed I am," she said. "I can't pretend anymore to be super-Betty." At home, Betty spoke with her husband and children, telling them that she needed their help. "Before, I would buy the food, make breakfast, set the table and do the dishes. Now, I ask my husband to buy the food. I make breakfast, but I ask my daughter to set the table and do the dishes." Because the Atlas CareMap helped Betty understand that she needed help, it was easier to ask for and accept help. "Before I did my CareMap," Betty observed, "I thought that asking for help or accepting it would have been an insult to my wifehood. Not anymore!" she laughs. For Betty, the Atlas CareMap was a tool to open up conversations about sharing care in her family. And it was a tool that helped Betty transition from a rigid role of "Super-Betty" into a more relaxed, flexible version of herself.

MAYRA'S STORY[9]

Mayra is a middle-aged mother of teenagers and the caregiver for her mother, who has Alzheimer's disease. At the beginning of the Atlas CareMap Workshop, Mayra thought, "What are all these stick people and bubbles on the paper? They don't mean anything to me. Why am I doing this?" As she slowly began to see her own caring life reflected back to her, Mayra felt alone and overwhelmed. But later, on reflection, the Atlas CareMap helped Mayra to see two realities in her life: that she had a lot of caring responsibilities but that she was not alone. Mayra began to appreciate that her children were very sensitive to their grandmother's needs. If her mother opened her hands, Mayra's son brought his grandmother a bible. If the elderly woman's index finger touched her lips, Mayra's daughter fetched a cup of tea. Mayra's workload didn't change, but she realized by drawing and reflecting on her Atlas CareMap that she had family allies in caring.

SUSAN'S STORY

Susan is the mother of a teenaged son who has Asperger's Syndrome. In a CareMap Workshop, Susan spoke in glowing terms about the strong support network her family had built for her son. Her Atlas CareMap was a powerful testament to the breadth and depth of that support. But on reflection, Susan realized that her son would likely leave home to attend college in a few years, and he would need a new support network. For Susan, the Atlas CareMap enabled her to glimpse the future and plan ahead for her son's transition to college.

Susan, Mayra, and Betty have very different lives, families, and care responsibilities. All of them agree that mapping helped them determine which aspects of their relational lives they would like to change and which they choose to leave alone. And they all report feeling more in control, especially during times of transition.

11

NOT A SOCIAL NETWORK, BUT A *CARE* NETWORK

When my mother was diagnosed with breast cancer, there was one person I thought we could count on for help—my Mom's best friend, Krista. But after Mom's mastectomy and with the start of chemotherapy, Krista was always too busy to call or visit. She knew that we were struggling at home with Mom's ill health, but she used to tell us, "Now if there's anything I can do . . . but I'm sure there's nothing I can do." I knew that Krista was frightened by the scale of what might be required to be helpful—I recalled her saying that she'd been traumatized by her own Mom's serious illness when she was a child. I finally realized that she was probably afraid that I might ask her to change Mom's surgical dressings or even bathe or feed Mom. One day, I was exhausted and needed food in the house. So I picked up the phone and called Krista. "Would you be able to bring over a casserole tonight and maybe some of your cookies that we like?" I asked. "Of course, I would LOVE to bring you dinner!" Krista exclaimed. We accidentally found the right way for Krista to feel comfortable helping us out. For Mom and Krista, it was a tearful reunion. —Sue B., the daughter of a breast cancer survivor

We all have a personal network—a group of people we depend on for friendship and support. At the beginning of a care journey, caregivers often have personal relationships from a past life "before caring." Later, in the thick of caregiving, medical professionals might join the circle of friends and become allies in the task of keeping a loved one safe and secure, whether at home or in a care facility. These friends and associates help us achieve our goals—goals that we would never be able to achieve without the help of others.

But a personal network is not the same as a personal *support* network. In life before caring, our friends and family members stepped up to help us on an infrequent, as-needed basis. A personal-support network is a group that is intentional and coordinated in being helpful to the caregiving family (according to everyone's needs and preferences). Rallying the troops and creating a personal-support network that is truly supportive and collaborative is *possible* because:

- People want to help because they care about you.
- People are motivated to help in areas they know about and to do tasks they are good at.
- People want to contribute in small chunks so that they don't feel overwhelmed.
- People like to feel appreciated and see signs that their caring actions make a positive difference.

A personal-support network is *necessary* because for the most part, our current approach to health and social care is an individual model of care that focuses on the patient's needs and deficiencies. Assessments, diagnoses, prescriptions, and interventions are frequently executed as if the patient lives alone, in isolation. The care and contributions of the family are not considered.

Yet, two realities render the individual model of care (see figure 11.1) a house of cards in today's world: almost one-third of the US population provides over twenty hours of care to a loved one each week,[1] and 40 to 70 percent of family caregivers report experiencing significant symptoms of depression.[2] In other words, families today approach caregiving as a second full-time job—one that can cause extreme levels of stress. Compounding these challenges is the increased longevity of those with complex needs. With the loving care of family at home, individuals with even very high dependency needs are living longer. An ethic of independence and self-reliance has harmed caring families because the simple fact is that we cannot bear this very high burden of care without the coordinated help of others in the community.

Individual Model of Care

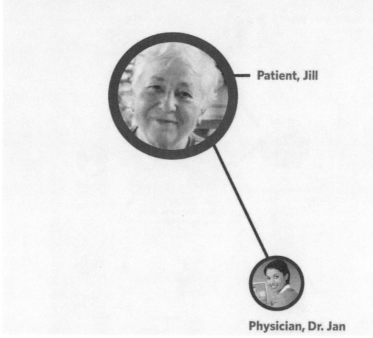

Patient, Jill

Physician, Dr. Jan

Figure 11.1. Individual Model of Care
Source: SE Health Care

THE NETWORK MODEL OF CARE

A network model of care (figure 11.2) acknowledges that people want to care for one another and that our caring relationships keep us healthy and safe. In fact, there is ample research[3] that proves the old adage, "A good friend is the medicine of life." But how is it possible to turn a group of friends and involved medical professionals into a personal support network? How is it possible to persuade all the key players to help out regularly and to communicate effectively with others in the network? How is it possible to persuade all concerned that the collaboration within a personal-support network is an important key to patient and family well-being? Some organizations like the PLAN Institute[4] in

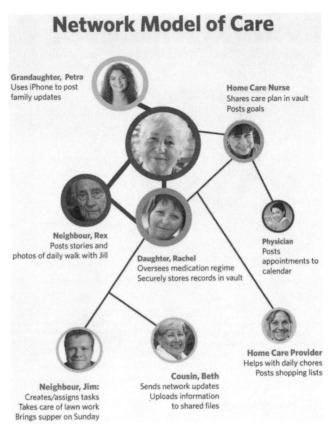

Network Model of Care

Grandaughter, Petra
Uses iPhone to post
family updates

Home Care Nurse
Shares care plan in vault
Posts goals

Neighbour, Rex
Posts stories and
photos of daily walk with Jill

Physician
Posts
appointments to
calendar

Daughter, Rachel
Oversees medication regime
Securely stores records in vault

Home Care Provider
Helps with daily chores
Posts shopping lists

Neighbour, Jim:
Creates/assigns tasks
Takes care of lawn work
Brings supper on Sunday

Cousin, Beth
Sends network updates
Uploads information
to shared files

Figure 11.2.   A network model of care
Source: SE Health Care

Canada (and their international affiliates) train professional facilitators or community connectors to create and maintain personal-support networks for vulnerable individuals and their families. But in the absence of a paid facilitator, it is possible to build a DIY support network.

When Building Your Own Support Network:
Be Clear on Your Goals

Even the most generous and willing friend can't act if they don't know what kind of help to offer. Setting goals—both short term and long term—is the first step in building a personal support network. If you are building a support network for the first time, begin with short-term goals for yourself and possibly for your loved one too such as, "Mom would like to spend more time with friends, and I would like to actually relax when Mom is at the Senior's Center every Tuesday. Right now, all I do are household chores on that day." Stating your goals and those of a loved one helps friends and family understand the challenges that you face in meeting your own needs *and* those of your loved one. Network members will want to help both the patient and the caregiver achieve their personal goals for the good of the whole family.

Next, the Calendar

A shared calendar is the next step in creating a support network. Calendars can be shared online using Google Calendar,[5] any one of the online care-coordination platforms described below, or even just by sharing the week's activities via group email. If managing an online calendar is too complicated for a caregiver who is not tech savvy, this task could be given to a network member for whom such a contribution would be no trouble at all.

Task lists for network members flow naturally from agenda items such as doctor appointments or shopping for a grandchild's birthday present. Transportation must be arranged, notes from the doctor's appointment must be taken and shared as needed, banking may be part of a shopping trip, and birthday presents must be wrapped. Each of these tasks is time limited and can be "claimed" by network members as a one-off. Alternatively, friends or family members who like to cook, for example, can offer contributions on a regular basis, such as a weekly meal delivery or a standing dinner invitation on busy caregiving days. Use the calendar to embed the family's personal goals into claimable tasks for network members. If Mom's goal is to visit friends, add time slots to the agenda for when visits from friends would be welcome. If household maintenance is burdensome, add in specific chores at home that could be claimed by members of the network. Remember to include tasks that a loved one could perform with support—this will have the dual benefit of reducing the household to-do list and enabling purpose and contribution in the life of a loved one.

The Ask

Once goals have been identified and a family caregiving agenda is complete (with appointments, outings, recreation, treatments, shopping, etc.), it's time to invite people to the network. The Atlas CareMap will have revealed those already in supporting roles, and those individuals will have a natural, vested interest in participating in an organized support network. Asking family and friends to be part of a support network might feel awkward and tricky, especially for those who aren't used to asking for help, but it can be stress free with the right introduction:

> I know that you care about us and would like to help us at home. I'm putting together a support network of friends and family—everyone can claim whichever tasks on our list that they like. You can have a look at our agenda and see what's convenient and which activities or skills you'd like to share with us. The network is designed so that everyone will help in a way that feels comfortable, and no one ever feels overwhelmed.

Inviting friends or family members to join the network also gives them a comfortable path to being helpful—one that doesn't have to be navigated without being aware of safe boundaries.

A request for medical professionals to join the network might be more tailored to their particular role. For example, if home-care-agency nurses or personal aides are well known to the family, then having them participate in a support network will be the decision of the agency case manager.

> We would like to coordinate Mom's care by creating a support network so that everyone who cares for and about our family is in the loop. That way, everyone will know each other and important information can be shared efficiently.

Case managers of care providers and physicians will have privacy concerns about participating in a personal support network, especially if communications are shared online. It will be important to address those concerns up front with professional network members. (See HIPAA[6] compliance of online care coordination tools in this chapter.) Once medical professionals are assured that patient privacy will be protected in compliance with the law, they are likely to agree to participate in the network.

Personal networks are possible to coordinate using a combination of pen and paper, emails, shared calendars, and phone calls. But in today's world, there are online caregiving coordination tools that will make the task of working together easier.

Online Network Coordination Tools

There are many personal support network coordination tools available online today. The most significant difference between the two main groups of tools is data security. All are password protected, but many free online network coordination tools are not secure enough to contain highly personal or sensitive documents such as medical records or banking information. Only those with hospital-grade security (HIPAA compliance[7]) are designed for the inclusion of medical professionals. Online platforms such as CareZone,[8] LotsaHelpingHands,[9] and CaringBridge[10] are free, password enabled, easy to navigate, and adaptable for a network of informal care helpers (family members, friends, and neighbors), but they do not offer levels of privacy protection high enough to accommodate the storage and sharing of medical records. All contain a message board, shared calendar, and the means to ask for or offer help. CareZone offers pharmaceutical services such as medication ordering and dispensing. It also has a tracking feature for symptoms, weight, vital signs, and other health-related goals. LotsaHelpingHands features a "help calendar" where caregivers can post activities so that network members can offer transportation to a hospital appointment or meal delivery on a particularly busy day. Volunteers receive reminders before their scheduled activities.

Families that wish to include medical professionals in their online support network will need to explore sites with greater data security. In the United States, one such care-coordination platform is Alska.[11] Alska offers a suite of resources for caregivers and medical professionals who work with caring families in the community. They also have corporate packages for caregiver employees who could benefit from the help of professional patient advocates and care-transition guides. Alska has high data security, enabling network participation by physicians and community nursing-service providers as well as the safe storage of medical records and other sensitive documents. Comparable online tools in Canada are Tyze Personal Networks[12] and CareRelay.[13] While Tyze and CareRelay are currently free for individual users, Alska offers a monthly subscription rate based on the services and resources chosen by the subscriber. Families can examine the costs, possible security risks, and benefits to every online caregiving support platform and decide which is the best fit.

A NEW WAY OF SEEING AND BEING

Sharing responsibility for the well-being of a vulnerable loved one is inevitable in long-term caring, and it requires practice. Part of what makes relinquishing the role of sole caregiver challenging is the stubborn idea that we must be continually vigilant and perpetually competent. And as competency in caring evolves into mastery, it's natural to be afraid that others would fail where we have succeeded. But as aging or disease progresses, exhaustion, stress, and eventually burnout rear their ugly heads. Caregivers who once thought they could "go it alone" finally realize that when a loved one's needs exceed caregiver capacity, the choice is to risk the health of a loved one by skipping care tasks or risk asking others for help. For some, that is when the realization dawns that loving care given over years is best delivered as a team.

The other truth that emerges from embarking on an experience of managing a personal support network is that directing others to care is also a form of caring. Others want to give what they can for the sake of the bonds of affection. The caregiver receives the gifts of friends and family in order to keep giving. These nested dependencies or circles of reciprocity are good for everyone. "I take so that I can give more. I give so that I might also receive."

Sharing power and giving important responsibility to others in caring feels risky at first, but it is in managing a network and witnessing its growth and competency to share care that leadership confidence grows. But what if a caregiver lacks the talent or even energy for tackling a management role? Someone else can be tapped to take the role of "operations director" of a support network, and the caregiver can be freed up to deliver training and support to contributing friends and family members, or take up another role. In a personal support network, there are more than enough roles to go around.

Handy Tip: In a personal support network, more is not better. Invite only the friends and family whom you trust to follow through on their agreed commitments to participate. If someone fails to keep dates and promises in their support role, ask them if they need more reminders or if they would prefer to leave the network. Participation has to be a good fit with members' interests and with their own work and family commitments.

Making It Personal

Our son needs twenty-four-hour care, and we've always had some paid help at home provided by a small cadre of care workers. We've also been blessed with a supportive family and friends who shared our son's keen interest in NHL hockey and English "football." When I first started using an online care-coordination tool to manage our support network, I thought of my leadership role as "just one more thing" in a long to-do list. Like learning any new operating system, I was reluctant to change from my habitual emails, phone calls, and bedside charts, even though my old ways often didn't work well. Quite frequently, important messages failed to get through to everyone on our care team. As I became more adept at using our online care-network-coordination platform, I learned some important lessons:

Online care support networks are purposeful. Like any new and unfamiliar resource, network members may not use a platform to its potential at first. Ensuring that vital information is kept only within the care platform and is not easily accessible in other places such as email will encourage network members to rely on the chosen communication hub. I put home-care staff schedules only on our care platform, so caregivers had to check there to know when they were working. Using our care platform eventually became habit for everyone.

Make your chosen platform the one and only room for communication and information. Putting everyone in one room (our online support network) enabled an ongoing conversation with everyone involved in our son's care. Communication breakdowns can occur when conversations take place among individuals and are not shared with others in the network. Sharing in "one room" ensures that everyone is working with the same information. Photos and stories encourage everyone to participate and help more. Planning for life events, both medical and social, through updates and stories can be turned into task lists. "If we organize an outing for our son to go to a hockey game with his uncle, it's easy to announce this and post a task for the group to problem solve wheelchair transportation for that evening." Actively acknowledging the contribution of others is critical. Saying thank you publicly in the network is a powerful motivator. Having everyone be witness to thanks is team building and more powerful than individual thanks. Finally, here are more ideas that I discovered to strengthen our network:

- I asked everyone to post messages, stories, and photos. If members of the network were going away on holiday, I asked them to post photos of their trip. It's just human nature to love looking at photos, so we were motivated to click on our network site!
- If life got very hectic at home, I would post a list of the things I needed help with as an extra prompt. Asking for help was hard for me, but the more desperate I felt, the easier it became. I reminded myself that people joined the network to pitch in and that it was my job to offer suggestions about how they could succeed in doing that.
- I also asked network members to share a list of things they could do and to consider forward planning to include contributing to our family as they went about their own daily lives. Slowly, network members began to let everyone know if they were planning to go grocery shopping on Saturday and could pick up items for us, for example.
- At first I thought that all I had to do was to start the online network, and something magical would happen to make caregiving easy. But over time, I began to realize that the online platform is there to support what happens offline—it's a tool that helps people coordinate, communicate, and support each other. It's not magic—it's about increasing the face-to-face contact in a circle of care.

12

HOW TO KNOW WHAT
YOU WANT AND GET
WHAT YOU NEED

*If you wish to persuade me, you must think my thoughts,
feel my feelings and speak my words. —Cicero*

Caregivers aren't chosen on the basis of personality type. Anyone can "fall into" a caring role, but every single one will have to advocate, whether they are shy or outgoing. In caregiving, advocacy can mean many things. It can be asking the family physician for a same-day appointment, even though the secretary says there is no availability. Advocacy can be asking the director of a local swimming pool to consider building an accessible changing room. And for many caregivers, advocacy can be negotiating the payment of treatment with insurance or medical providers.

How does anyone convince another to change policy or practice in a way that supports his or her needs? Often, we find ourselves constantly asking for information, support, or simply for people to change their approach in order to accommodate our needs. But if we don't have a plan for asking, we may just encounter a litany of noes. The chances of success in advocacy are greater with a strategic approach and with a "business" model to employ; in which case, our emotions are not as likely to be casualties of the process.

The building blocks of effective advocacy are: *analyzing* what help you already have that is helpful, *identifying* the kind of help you need, *researching* the community for sources of direct help as well as people to help you advocate, *cultivating* a champion within your target organization, and *executing* your request under winning conditions. Professional lobbyists use these techniques to influence government—families can use them, too.[1]

171

ADVOCATING WITH EMPATHY

> If you wish to communicate effectively with someone, you
> must communicate within *their* experience. —Saul Alinsky

Family caregivers who succeed at getting what they need to support their loved ones are usually employing tactics of "solution-based" advocacy. They are not spoiling for a fight every time someone says no. Instead, they seek ways of understanding the various forces at play, and they actively work at building strong relationships so that cocreating solutions (rather than seeking to persuade people based on a zero-sum principle) is possible. They understand that most roadblocks to getting what they need are not black-and-white issues. Rather, the realities of meeting the needs of a rapidly growing population of caregiving families lie in the gray area somewhere between "success" and "failure." They are always civil, polite, and focused on issues, not personalities.

Al Etmanski,[2] an internationally renowned advocate for people with disabilities describes five elements of solution-based advocacy this way:

1. Search for a Heart of Gold
   Look for points of connection regardless of political affiliation. It's not that our differences don't matter, but their potential—what they can be and should be—matters more.
2. Use Strategic Inquiry
   Strategic inquiry is a prelude to more active lobbying. It's based on the premise that the best way to learn about the procedures, language, and priorities of those you're trying to influence is to ask them.
3. Cultivate a Network of Champions
   Solution-based advocacy focuses on relationships. People are more likely to say yes to someone they know and trust. There are allies attached to every system, at every level, who are waiting for a good idea and the right person to come along. It's important to cultivate an informal network of champions that includes service providers, politicians, and public servants, as well as business and community leaders and, potentially, celebrities.

4. Solve Problems Together

Authentic collaboration among sectors is needed. Charities, agencies, and other relevant systems must shift from doing "for" to doing "with." This means that citizens, far from being by-standers, must be meaningfully engaged. Some have labeled this new approach to public policy development and service design as "co-creation." The question a caregiver asks changes from "Will you do this for me?" to "Would you like to work with me to achieve our common goal?"

5. Do It Yourself

To move your issue along, you may have to take the lead and do it yourself. Today, advocates have to do a lot more of the heavy lifting if they want to advance their issues in a timely manner and increase their chances of success. In today's climate of com-petition for resources, advocates have the best chance of success by representing their interests and perspectives in a collaborative and strategic way.[3]

STRATEGIC INQUIRY[4]

Strategic inquiry is the first and potentially the most important building block of advocacy. It is really just a fancy name for information gathering with a purpose. The process involves developing a deep understanding of "who's who" in the community or organization you're advocating to, seeking advice and building a relationship with key players who hold sway with your issue. The purpose of the strategic inquiry is to develop a clear understanding of the support provider's objectives and priorities. Because in asking for support, it is vital to first understand whose job it is to provide that support and whether the person you are asking is in a position to say yes to your request right now.

For example, if you need curbs cut in a sidewalk in your neigh-borhood to accommodate your family member's wheelchair, the city government might be your advocacy target. A cold call to the office of the mayor might not be successful. But an information-gathering appointment with a relevant municipal government official will likely reveal some strategic next steps. An appointment to ask advice could be the first step in cultivating a senior employee to be "your champion" within the target organization—in this case, the city government. He or she will represent your family's interests when budgets are being decided and programming decisions are made.

Strategic inquiry can be used for formal (in organizations or systems, such as with hospital personnel or with an insurance provider) or informal (within groups of family and friends) information gathering as a first step in advocating. Strategic inquiry is:

- about seeking advice (not asking for anything yet);
- a relationship-building tool;
- for gaining insight on the perspective of your advocacy target;
- a key input before you ask for what you need.

If you are conducting a strategic inquiry with an organization, the following steps are recommended to boost your chances of success:

- Identify a few individuals who are involved in your issue.
- Request a half-hour telephone call with each.
- Send a one-to-two-page, point-form briefing note in advance (see instructions for writing a briefing note below).
- During the telephone call, give a brief explanation of your purpose, which is to seek advice and insight.
- After the call, send a thank-you note (email will do).

Questions to ask:

- What do I need to know about this issue or program in order to understand the organization's or agency's approach? What are their current priorities, realities, and pressures?
- Who is involved in decision making on my issue? Look at the organization's Web page for a staff list. Call someone at a management level, and ask who has responsibility for your issue. What are the relevant time frames (e.g., are there funding application deadlines)?
- Whom else should I be speaking with?
- What advice can they offer to assist in achieving my objective?

There are palpable differences between good and poor practice in strategic inquiry. Good practice can be characterized by the following:

- Your inquiries have given you insights about your advocacy target's concerns and objectives.
- You can tell a brief story illustrating your situation.
- You have identified and cultivated a champion or sponsor *within* your target agency/organization.
- You have aligned your request with the objectives of your target agency.
- You keep your advocacy team (if you have one) informed and coordinated.
- You ensure that your communications are always clear and concise.

Whereas chances of success in advocacy will be diminished if you:

- are unfamiliar with the advocacy target organization's priorities and their staff;
- are unprepared for meetings or calls;
- have a request for support that is not aligned with the mission and objectives of the advocacy target;
- engage in wandering and disorganized storytelling;
- are too emotional;
- are demanding or hectoring.

We've all been at a medical clinic when someone begins to complain angrily to the desk clerk about the wait time to see the doctor. Though this response may be authentic, it is an example of poor practice in advocacy. The desk clerk has no responsibility for the doctor's time management or the cases that may be more complex, causing him or her to run late. The conversation is demanding in tone, so the desk clerk becomes defensive. Other people in the waiting room may become annoyed by the angry outburst. The complaining customer is isolated and has not achieved his or her goal of being seen by the doctor more promptly.

On the other hand, a polite, questioning conversation with the desk clerk may shed light on how late the doctor is running, and when the appointment is likely to take place. Although the clerk is not responsible for a physician's time management, she may have the ability to gather key facts about wait times and to alert the doctor to your needs. If there are particular concerns such as a loved one who has pain and is not managing the wait time well, these issues may well have an effect on how the wait can be managed. There may be another person in the waiting room who is willing to swap appointment times in your favor. The clerk might facilitate finding an examination room where your loved one may lie down in the interim. Or it may be better for you and your loved one to come back later or on another day. In this situation, the desk clerk can become an ally within the clinic system because this person is in a position to give relevant information and brainstorm solutions.

When advocating to large organizations, governments, or insurance providers, for example, it's worthwhile to ask questions of anyone who has previously achieved success with your objective. Those individuals represent precedents for your success. Promising places to seek out precedent setters are disease associations and online caregiver support groups. Other caregivers with the same issue or concern will have key information enabling you to learn from their experience of success or failure in advocacy.

ORGANIZE WHAT YOU LEARN
—THE BRIEFING NOTE

The briefing note is a simple one-page, bullet-point document that is shared in advocacy meetings so that everyone has easy access to key information and a place to write notes. The briefing note begins with an introduction to the caregiving family and a simple, general statement of need (such as "to reduce social isolation" or "to improve well-being"). Often, a simple, nonspecific statement of need opens the door to explorative discussion. Next, a list of relevant factors can be added (e.g., family bankruptcy, divorce, recent disease progression). And finally, a list of questions in point form should be included, together with space for note-taking during the meeting. Sample questions might be: "What advice do you have for our family? How have others dealt with similar situations? Who else can I speak with about our request? What can we do for follow-up?" After the meeting, don't forget to send an email to say thank you—in advocacy, a polite expression of gratitude is worth its weight in gold.

Sample Briefing Note Template

- Date, Place, Names, and Affiliations of All Attending Meeting
- Purpose of Meeting
- What You Need and Why You Need It
- What You've Tried So Far and Whom You've Spoken To, if that's relevant (including champions with influence, if you have them)
- Barriers or Challenges You Already Know Of
- Positive Outcomes of Getting What You Need
- Next Steps and Action Items (leave blank to fill in at meeting)

Good practice in advocacy will not guarantee outcomes, but it *will* deliver greater opportunities for success. And that's vital, because going without help at home over the long term is not a healthy future plan for any family. Caring is a complicated enterprise with many moving parts and multiple players. We would never consider managing alone in other endeavors, so it's worth considering why we think it's possible in caring. Caregiving is an activity that is built upon interdependence and an emphasis on teamwork. And for that reason, we need to have strong, loyal allies who act in our interests, even in our absence.

A NEW WAY OF SEEING AND BEING

Our intimate duties and quiet commitment to caring at home transform us into outsiders, adrift in a sea of people who speak a language that we have forgotten—the language of achievement and independence. The shift from being a "normal" loved one to being a caregiver sets us apart from every other person who doesn't understand our daily life. But when we develop a personal vocabulary and understanding of our particular care experience, we begin to comprehend how our past connects to our present and to our future. Our life begins to make sense when our personal vocabulary is conceived of as part of an advocacy story we tell and retell to others.

Stuttering and half-formed sentences cut short our conversations and shut down opportunities for sharing. Becoming fluent in a new language brings with it the confidence to converse with others and understand their experience. When we can talk about our caring life with ease (or with growing coherence), our humanity is made clear to ourselves and to others. Being able to describe and make sense of a care experience positions us as normal within the human race. A personal narrative of caring that is neither heroic nor tragic carries with it a greater acceptance of "this is who I am now." In the absence of a struggle to escape the "now," empathetic listening to others becomes possible.

A deep understanding and acceptance of the caring role together with the language to describe it brings wisdom. Put another way, the caregiver has learned through language that the counterweight to humility and silence is confidence and expression. Some social scientists call this shift toward wellness and narrative integration "posttraumatic growth."[5]

With self-understanding and the language to describe experience comes the confidence to advocate effectively.

Making It Personal

It was the summer of 1993, and our family had moved to London the year before. Our son Nicholas has severe cerebral palsy, and he was five years old at that time. After he was in a full-time therapeutic day school for a year, my husband and I decided it was time to seek out a mainstream, neighborhood school for our boy. I began the search.

Confident of my advocacy skills, I thought it would be easy to convince any principal that my son was an ideal candidate for his or her student body. I was wrong. "I am sure your son's needs would be better met elsewhere," was the constant refrain. Another disability mom told me that her son was a successful pupil at an elementary school down the street from where she lived. That school had an elevator (rare in the older architecture of London!) but was in the adjoining district, not our own. I launched my advocacy campaign to get our son into that school, even though we lived outside the catchment area. When, finally, I received a letter from the principal informing me that her final decision was "No," I was devastated.

I knew that the Victorian-era junior school up the street from our apartment building was not wheelchair friendly in the least, so I hadn't even considered it. As a last resort, I picked up the phone and called. I remember saying to the principal in a dejected tone of voice, "I suppose there's no way you would want my son at your school." "Want him?!" she exclaimed. "He's in!" "Sorry, what did you say?" I stammered, not believing my ears. "He's in! Our school *needs* your son." "But your building isn't wheelchair accessible," I warned. "Architecture . . . it's only architecture, dear," she replied breezily.

That experience taught me powerful lessons in advocacy that would help me get what our family needed over the years for our son and now for my mom, too.

Here are the lessons I learned:

1. What I thought was a good fit and an answer to our need wasn't always accurate.
2. A warm welcome is the first, most important element of a problem-solving partnership.
3. Sometimes potential partners have their own (unknown) reasons for wanting to work with you to address your needs. In this case, the principal wanted her students to learn about disability. For her, Nick addressed this gap in her educational objectives to model an inclusive society.
4. Obstacles and barriers in plain sight are not always barriers to partnerships. Creative solutions can sometimes be found if partners are determined to work in collaboration.

13

POWER AND LOVE
= EMPOWERMENT

Power and love are fundamental elements of caregiving, but we don't always understand how they work to shape our experience. Adam Kahane[1] is an author and designer of social change in arenas of conflict, but he offers a vital message for caregivers in his book *Power and Love.* It's the author's conception of these forces that makes his ideas so pivotal for families. Kahane defines power as "the drive of everything living to realize itself." So power in this sense is the drive to achieve one's purpose, to get one's job done, to grow. Much of our consumer-driven society functions on that operating system. He defines *love* as "the drive towards the unity of the separated."[2] In this sense, love is the impetus to connect and make whole what is fragmented. Imagine what these definitions of power and love mean about our relationships with our loved ones, with members of our extended families, with medical professionals, and even with ourselves in the conversations we have within our own minds. In Kahane's book, the illustration of love is a bonfire with many logs alight. The image of power is a single, lit torch. We want unity with our loved one, good relations with both our families and our medical teams, and perhaps most of all, we want inner peace. Yet, we strive to not lose ourselves in the daily business of caring. No caregiver wants to be forever relegated to being just another log on the inferno. But without other sources of fuel, a single flame will soon be extinguished. In caregiving, the drive toward unity and the drive toward self-realization are in constant tension.

Kahane says that we need *both* love and power if we want to achieve peaceful and balanced relations. Kahane's work is in the sphere of social change, and most often, he mediates peaceful relations between political organizations. But listen to what he says about balancing love

181

and power—caregivers will recognize themselves and their own battles to achieve equilibrium here:

> People who can understand the concerns of others and mix those concerns with their own agenda have access to a power source denied to those who can push only their own interests. In this fuller understanding, power is a verb meaning to give and take, to be reciprocal, to be influenced as well as to influence. To be affected by another in relationship is as true a sign of power as the capacity to affect others. . . . As you become more powerful, so do those in relationship with you. As they become more powerful, so do you. This is power understood as relational, as power "with," not power "over."[3]

Deep change, Kahane maintains, calls for a balance of these two forces because systems based on just one of those forces alone will result in stagnation (as in allowing oneself to be subsumed by another's needs or conversely, dominating a weaker loved one). And both of those scenarios carry the risk of the overall failure to respond to the chaotic changes that are the natural fallout of human dependency relationships. We simply collapse under the strain.

LOVE AND POWER WITH YOUR LOVED ONE

Balancing power is much trickier than just recognizing that it's a worthwhile aspiration. We are all in relationship with some people who have more power than us, and often those people mean to keep it. Disrupting the status quo is often uncomfortable, but it's a little easier when love is part of the equation. Sometimes, in order to achieve a comfortable level of self-realization in a caring relationship, we have to examine the historical power dynamics of our ongoing relationships and intentionally reboot the love-power equation.

Caring for an elderly parent is a case in point. Sometimes "eldercare" is referred to as a role reversal in which the parent becomes the child and vice versa. This is a crude (and some would say inaccurate) manner of describing the changing roles required to meet a parent's dependency needs over time. But it falls far short of encompassing the love and power dynamics of what occurred before the effects of aging took hold and how the nature of reciprocal caring over time determines dignity and decision making in the household.

> My father is a retired army major and he brought up my sister and me as if we were two of his recruits. Dad was very strict and even though we knew he loved us, he didn't talk so much as he barked orders. Mom was just the opposite—she was sweet, quiet and always in a good mood. They kind of balanced each other. Mom died about five years ago and after that, Dad began to go downhill. At first we thought he was just lonely and sad, but then we began to notice more worrying signs. One day, I went over to his place to deliver some home baking. He answered the door wearing just his dressing gown, and there were toast crumbs all down the front. He hadn't shaved and he didn't even seem to notice that he looked terrible. That day frightened my sister and me into actively caring for our Dad. Now, I feel strange doing things for him because I've had a lifetime of him being in charge. Sometimes it's easier because he doesn't seem to recognize me, and that's when I can kind of pretend he's not my Dad. But sometimes his old self shines through and he'll bark out something like, "Shut that door, young lady!" and I'm afraid to offer the help I know he needs to shave or button his shirt. It's so hard and I can't even think about his loss of dignity without crying. It's like I'm not supposed to see it, but I have to because I have to give him the help he needs. —Sue W.

Every family has a unique history of love and power. Adult children are sometimes asked to care for an abusive parent because there is no one else. In other families, sibling discord or rivalries play out when childhood power relationships resurface in unhelpful ways. The conceptual framework of power and love helps to compartmentalize conflicting emotions. The idea that we can understand old triggers for anger and feelings of powerlessness gives us dominion over our emotions and a glimpse of control in the midst of chaos.

Time plays havoc with our notions of superiority and self-determination. As children develop independence and parents age into dependency, adults are forced to let go of childcare roles. A child refuses to cross the street hand in hand. Care becomes watchful and vigilant, rather than physical. Changing dependency roles make us uncomfortable. Witnessing and even enabling the risky vulnerability of our loved ones unleashes our greatest fears. It's not easy to feel at peace when independence is being tested, and outcomes are impossible to predict. And part of what makes the practice of looking away so hard is our stubborn idea that we must be perpetually competent and perpetually vigilant. The logic of "letting go" battles continuously with protective love, tormenting the caregiver with guilt and self-doubt. We may pride ourselves on enabling independence in our loved ones, but each time a child fails or an elderly parent stumbles, the myth of independence is pierced, and our veil of delusory comfort is lifted. We are bullied into a tolerance for risk and ambiguity. Our caring roles may shift or reverse. Giving autonomy to the frail can resemble abandonment. And limiting mobility to prevent wandering can look a lot like imprisonment. The caregiver must walk the balance beam of paternalism and autonomy and often, we get it wrong. When we do, guilt is the result. And every time a child experiments with newfound independence, or the time comes for a frail parent to move into assisted living, what remains between people is the bond of intimacy. That, and the discovery of a new care relationship with a different set of rules.

Loosening the ties that bind can take many forms. But a little distance is critical to allowing some measure of self-realization or power to kindle. Sometimes letting go can include an intentional enabling of risks as an expression of love and dignity. How people feel cared for depends on what caregivers do for them, but sometimes, too, it means what we do *not* do for them. Sometimes, letting a child walk to school unaccompanied for the first time or booking a transatlantic flight for an elderly parent who is determined to travel alone can feel like a terrible but necessary risk.

Every caring relationship has its own history and a future that is unknowable. It's worth remembering in caregiving, though, that there are two people who are in the new terrain of shifting dependency needs; both must write a brand-new relationship script every day.

POWER RELATIONSHIPS
WITH MEDICAL PROFESSIONALS

Home care can be an unnatural model of care and is sometimes fraught with tricky negotiations of power and pecking order. Personal support workers who at first are strangers enter a private home in order to perform highly intimate tasks of personal care. Over time, those aides may become trusted confidantes and even lifelong friends. But when someone new arrives at the door every day, the question of who's in charge must be negotiated constantly.

According to Dr. Sonia Lupien, director of the Center for Studies on Human Stress in Montreal,[4] there are four "threats" that form the key ingredients for stress:

1. Novelty—something new that you have not experienced before
2. Unpredictability—something that you had no way of predicting would occur
3. Threat to the ego—your competence as a person is called into question
4. Sense of control—you feel that you have little or no control over the situation

It's no wonder that caregivers feel stressed—in the face of a loved one's evolving clinical picture, we naturally feel out of control due to the novelty and unpredictability of the situation. But upon meeting a doctor in the clinic or a home-care aide at the front door, we may feel our expertise called into question. We perceive a clear and present threat to our ego—and quite possibly, so do our clinicians.

Consider the perspective of health care providers. After all, they form one-half of our important conversations about health care, so it's important that they feel at ease, too. Physicians and therapists are human, too—they may feel stressed for exactly the same reasons that we do. Neither party is likely to prioritize a need to reassure the other of his or her professionalism or capabilities, especially in the hurried clinic discussions of a loved one's severe illness. Patients, families, and medical professionals getting to know one another is a business fraught with fear of judgment and worry about "missing something" important. In the early days of relationship building within a circle of care, love and power are in a race, and each is in it to win. If equilibrium is not achieved in a manner that facilitates compassionate acting and listening for the good of the patient and family, then new relationships will have to be formed in place of the old.

We ran an ICU-like hospital room in our family home until a few years ago when our son moved into a nearby care home. Our son has always needed someone to stay awake by his bedside overnight to monitor his respiration and seizures. When he was a teenager and my husband and I became exhausted, we received funding from our local health authority to pay for nighttime nursing care. One evening, a new nurse arrived at our door. He greeted me politely but formally. As he handed me his overcoat, I realized that he was wearing a nursing uniform. I smiled and said, "Oh, our son is nervous when staff wear uniforms because he has bad memories of the hospital. Would you mind not wearing your uniform the next time you come?" "Sure, Mom," he answered. I bristled. "Mom" is the word all mothers of sick children in Canada are called in the hospital. It saves doctors the trouble of having to recall names, but after so many in-patient stays, I didn't like it. "Oh, I insist that you call me Donna—you are welcome in our home!" I said warmly (but willing him to understand the meaning of "our home" and the importance of calling me by name). "OK, Mom," he answered. Upstairs, he began rearranging the furniture in our son's room and setting tube-feeding supplies out in a tray on the desk. "I usually keep those in the adjoining bathroom close to the sink," I said, my voice on edge now. "This is the way we do it in the hospital," he responded as he gazed at me from above his bifocals. "Well, this is not the hospital and we will keep our home routine as it is. Thank you." I was angry. Over the years, I've learned to always give everyone a second chance, but the next time, when he showed up wearing a uniform and calling me "Mom" again, I asked the agency to send us someone else. —Donna T.

Balancing love and power among patients, families, and medical professionals has a great deal to do with reciprocal kindness. Because caregivers are on a highly emotional and unpredictable journey with very high stakes, they need medical professionals to use proper names, achieve eye contact, and even hold a trembling hand, if that is appropriate to the situation. In short, caregivers need a human interaction with medical professionals, especially at times of crisis and especially when caring lasts months or years. In situations of very serious illness or the delivery of a difficult prognosis, patients and families want and need a display of power (this is the professional's expertise) and of love (this is his or her compassion). At no time is the imperative for a balance of love and power in conversation more evident than at the time of making a very serious health-care decision.

Family caregivers need medical professionals to operate as consultants would. The collaborative relationship between the interior designer and the family is an apt analogy[5] to reflect on the productive relations families would like to have with their health-care professionals. Before a decorator is able to design a plan that meets with a family's approval, she will need to gather information. She may inquire about the household routine and typical use of space. Any designer will ask what is already working well and which design elements seem to be lacking. Options, costs, risks, and benefits are presented and weighed. Samples are displayed and discussed. There is ample opportunity to ask questions and express concerns. A feasible plan is agreed upon, and its execution begins. The analogy of the decorator is an excellent one because patients and caregivers need their clinicians to understand the medical and social realities of living with illness, and they need options presented for treatment. Patients and caregivers need support before, during, and after taking treatment decisions—the need to balance love and power never stops in relations between patients, families, and their health-care professionals.

If knowledge is power, then health-care professionals are in positions of great power. The patient may want the doctor to be godlike, because then perhaps he or she could be strong enough to fight off the forces of nature—those same forces that cause serious illness. But the doctor's role is as a care partner—to cure sometimes, to heal often, to console always. In relationships of balanced love and power, reciprocal kindness is the operating system.

BALANCING LOVE AND POWER
IN OUR OWN HEADS

The stories we tell ourselves combine with our own knowledge and experience to give us a road map for thinking differently about crafting a future for ourselves as caregivers. What are the forces that have power over us and prevent us from achieving peace of mind? One force is our own inclination to diminish the value of our needs. It's common to believe that our own needs are never worthy as competitors for those of a loved one. And the twin of that belief is that there can be only one person's needs met at any given time.

> When Mom was dying at home, I remember filling out an agency form for home help. An older, more experienced caregiver was sitting beside me at the kitchen table, and she asked how much I was asking for. I replied, "Ten hours a week—they say here that's the maximum they offer." "But that's ridiculous," said my friend. "You need at least thirty hours a week. Write 30 hours." I began to realize that day that the needs in our family were not something imaginary and they certainly did not represent my failure as a caregiver. I was doing the best that any one person could, and I did not need to apologize for the manpower it required to keep my mom alive and happy in her dying days. And if an agency of some sort did not provide me with the help we really needed, well, I would look elsewhere. But that day I decided to proclaim our family's "real" needs. Never again would I apologize for calling and asking for help. Never again would I limit my requests for help to only what was on offer. From that day forward, I decided that I would calmly state the truth of our needs. —Angela L. (palliative caregiver for her mother)

Caregivers have a tendency to be highly self-critical. "Should" is a word that worms its way into every phrase in the caregiver psyche. Ironically, magazines and social media are peppered with lectures on the importance of self-care. It's as if self-care is just one more thing that caregivers should master immediately. If they don't, they have no right to complain about being tired. Yet many of the strategies proposed in popular culture are impossible for most caregivers to implement. A bubble bath may not be an option when a loved one cannot be left alone. Coffee with friends may be just a distant memory for a mother of a child with severe autism. And "just set limits on the amount of care you give" is a ridiculous notion for people who would be faced with catastrophe at home if they walked out the door.

Balancing the imperatives of love and power in the caregiver's mind is similar to self-care, but differs in an important way. Love and power must be claimed and given freely to our loved ones, but we must do the same for ourselves as well. Achieving balance in self-care cannot occur without the recognition of power dynamics within the family. How care duties are shared between siblings for example, will be affected by old power dynamics that inevitably find their way into ongoing care-based discussions. Being aware of these dynamics can make them easier to control.

In a conversation about self-care with a group of caregivers,[6] a series of questions was posed. The first question was, "What does self-care look like for you when you're alone with your loved one?" The answers were revealing: "I paint or draw with my daughter. That is relaxing for us both." Another said, "I get up very early while everyone else is sleeping. That's my quiet time when I can really relax." The second question posed was, "What does self-care look like when you are together with your whole family?" One caregiver replied, "I feel cared for when we visit friends who 'get us'—who don't judge us and who feel comfortable with us." The next query: "What does self-care look like when you are home alone?" One caregiver responded, "I'm never home alone!" Then someone else reflected, "I meditate. My kitchen window overlooks a field and I look out at the open space. That makes me feel relaxed and soothed." When someone suggested that reading fiction and watching movies on television was a way to climb into "someone else's life and story," others agreed that fiction was a powerful form of self-care. Except when it's too much. "I find, though, that if I watch too much TV, I feel worse. Like I've given more of my time than I've received in return. I feel empty after watching too much television." The final question for the group was, "What about self-care in the community? How do you care for yourself outside of home in your neighborhood?" "Walk my dog!" said one. "Go to work and have an intelligent, adult conversation!" said another. "Go outside into the woods. Being in nature feels so good," said a tanned and fit older caregiver.

People giving care over years often discover the internal balance of love and power accidentally. One day, a decision is made to make two cups of tea (one each), rather that "wait till later" to have one's own. Choosing activities that both caregiver and loved one enjoy together, even sitting in silence, takes priority. The realization dawns that there are two people in the caring relationship who need both love and power to give and take what all humans need to survive and even thrive within circumstances of adversity.

POWER AND LOVE IN THE LANGUAGE OF CARE

> When my Mom got older, she wanted to keep her apartment, but with aging, it got harder for her to keep up with cleaning and cooking. She wanted someone else to do the chores, but she didn't want to ask on account of her pride. She worked hard at pretending to be very independent. She would rather die then ask for help! So when we were visiting, she'd begin to sweep the floor and then she'd sigh loudly. That was our cue to jump up and offer to help. She'd say no at first, but then say, "Oh, if you insist!" That saved her dignity and got the job done. But she would never just ask for the help. —Jennifer J.

Offering help can be fraught with the social dangers of embarrassment, potential humiliation, hurt feelings, or even anger and insult. Sometimes, what results from this social anxiety is that all parties stay silent, avert their gazes, and pretend human needs do not exist. Fear of getting "too involved" in a dependency relationship can have the same stifling effect. How to ask and how to offer in ways that are sure to lead to a "clean transaction" of care are very tricky. Most people don't know the secrets of using language to construct a care relationship that feels safe and manageable.

The language of care is sometimes so foreign that expressing needs or the willingness to meet them is akin to speaking a foreign language. Trying to interpret and respond sensibly to a parent's report of symptoms can be as challenging as deciphering the meaning of a radio broadcast with a very weak signal.

> My girlfriend called me in a panic. She said she'd been talking to her father, who said, "Mom's had a spell." When my friend probed, she learned that her mother was face down on the kitchen table and was unresponsive. "A spell" turned out to be a stroke followed by months in a rehabilitation hospital. —Brenda J.

The way we experience illness or caregiving is a result of the experience itself seen through the lens of all our other life experiences. A child finding a parent unresponsive in a diabetic coma could later become unable to cope with the anxiety of her own baby suffering from an infantile seizure brought on by fever. Our vantage point determines everything we see. And the way we express our illness or care experiences will have a lot to do with the way we've experienced love and power throughout our personal and family histories.

A NEW WAY OF SEEING AND BEING

How do we evolve into a personalized and intimate knowledge of another? We may know a loved one, but only in a particular role. We think we can predict our parents' responses until personalities are stripped raw or altered by the onset of dependency needs. Rules and fundamentals of close relationships must be negotiated anew. But the inherent intimacy of care relationships can lead to discovered memories and family histories. In dementia care, the roles of children and parents are blurred and sometimes even turned upside down. Of course, this is painful because there is always loss involved in aging toward mortality, but sometimes the good days can yield expected gifts. The day a parent with Alzheimer's recalls a grandchild's name is cause for celebration in any family. Power and love are essential ingredients of our intimate relationships. But in caregiving, power and love must be intentionally shared with the self, as well. There are two people in a caring relationship, and they are both vulnerable.

Making It Personal

I remember talking to my friend Judy a few years ago. She and her husband Steve had been our neighbors for over twenty years, and our kids played together. One day Judy and I were laughing, talking about our husbands. Judy said, "You want to know how I keep Steve happy? I put some earth in a pot and I put in some seeds. Then I water the earth and put the pot on the windowsill so it gets lots of sun. I take care of it until one day, a beautiful flower blooms. Then I call Steve over to look at it and say, "Hey honey, look what you did! It's so great!" We laughed our heads off at that story. Recently I was thinking of it again, but I'm not laughing anymore. My mom is a lot like Steve, or maybe it's me who's like Judy. Anyway, Mom is the type of person who cannot stand being old. In fact, if I offer to help her out of a chair, she swears at me. Sometimes she hits. I am always on edge trying to figure out how to keep Mom safe without her "noticing" that I'm caring for her. Recently, she asked about buying Christmas presents for everyone in the family. Mom can't afford to spend on presents, but I played along and said I'd get the money out of her bank account and buy generous gifts that would be from her. She seemed pretty happy after that. I used to think that honesty was the best policy, but not anymore. Now I just want life to be easier and less stressful for my mom and for me. I tell her whatever I think will make her happy. —Tracy M.

14

CULTIVATING CONNECTION

Caregiving is not simply about developing close, intense relationships with the person you care for. It also requires a type of opening up, a turning toward others who can help you in ways family and friends may not be able to. More than ever before, caregivers can leverage online opportunities for connection, information, support, understanding, and feedback.[1] Choosing online support and advocacy opportunities, however, doesn't mean neglecting or ignoring face-to-face support.

Instead, caregivers in the twenty-first century must recognize the advantages and disadvantages of all types of support opportunities and know when, and under what circumstances, they might choose one connection possibility rather than the other, or creatively use both. Though you may have had the privilege of choosing one medium of connection over another in your pre-caregiver life, now, as a caregiver, all options must be on the table. No type of interaction is complete, perfect, and total. Rather, empowered caregivers must be able to assess the types of interactions (e.g., face-to-face, online) that will gratify certain informational and support needs, and then be able to effectively access and utilize the particular advantages of that medium.[2] Caregiving isn't just what happens between you and your loved one, it's also about creating new connections so that you can maximize care for your loved one and for yourself.

CONNECTION LITERACY—
FTF AND ONLINE INTERACTIONS

Maybe you believe you are strictly a face-to-face person. This could be a reflection of preferences that characterize your history of interactions with friends, family, and colleagues. Perhaps you are not as confident as you would like when it comes to going online. All of us have prejudices based on what we believe we can accomplish and receive in different interactional contexts. Yet, before you self-select into an either–or approach—*"I only connect with people online"* or *"Real interactions only take place in person"*—it's important to understand that useful and meaningful interactions can be experienced online and face-to-face (FtF). Your connection literacy, or ability to know how to match your needs with appropriate audiences, isn't about whether FtF or online is good or bad. Instead, it's about understanding when, and under what circumstances, you might be able to satisfy specific caregiver and advocacy needs, given the advantages and limitations of each interactional situation.[3]

FtF Interactions

FtF interactions seem natural. No training is believed necessary as we are born into the world using the sound of our voices, facial expressions, touch, and movements (i.e., nonverbal communication) to interact with those nearest to us. We intuitively begin sending, receiving, and making sense of shared meaning with those closest to us. Consequently, FtF communication is often the standard by which all other forms of communication are judged. Experiencing communion with another—or overcoming physiological and individual differences to connect—is associated with sharing a physical presence with those we love and care for in a specific moment, when what is shared can neither be repeated nor fully anticipated. As a caregiver, you know from firsthand experience the comfort and deep reassurance physical presence communicates.

One distinguishing feature of FtF interactions is the amount of streaming stimuli, in any given interaction, available to assess what is happening and what is being experienced between two people. Because of the simultaneous visual, auditory, physical, and environmental cues unfolding in FtF interactions, interpretations are formed in ways that transcend what is being stated. Nonverbal communication in health care is vital to influencing how we interpret and respond to the person in front of us.[4] Separating the *who* from the *what* is so difficult because the "content" of communication is always linked to "how" someone is expressing what they are saying in that particular moment.

We attend not simply to what someone is saying, but to the timber of a voice, the rate at which they speak, and the manner in which they speak. Appearance matters in FtF interactions, too. Does someone turn red when they speak? Do they look you in the eye, or do they look away? What are they wearing? Do they look professional, unprofessional, trendy? Are they tall, small, large, or thin? Are they smiling, or do they look nervous? Is their handshake firm or soft? Are they talking with confidence, or do they look uncomfortable? Do they look like you, or do you perceive them to be different? Amid an ongoing process of interpretation in which raw impressions are transformed into meaning, we can't help but lean on shortcuts and ways of making general impressions to quickly categorize what is transpiring before us.

Judgments are made in the moment about who we believe someone is, as we are experts at imposing "impressions" on people and situations that we then use to make decisions about whether to walk away from or toward another. No one needs to tell us how to assess someone's credibility, likability, attractiveness, or similarity—we just do so, though doing so doesn't mean our perceptions are accurate. Rather, FtF interpersonal judgments rely on visual, social cues to decipher who is perceived as similar or different.[5] A stutter, a rambling sentence, or the color of someone's pants may determine the nature of what is possible in an interaction because the pinpointing of observable difference, as a way of making sense, can be used to quickly sort through unfolding stimuli to determine who and what *isn't* worthy of attention.

When it comes to support and advocacy, audiences can overdetermine meanings based on interpretations that are beyond the control of the sender (e.g., speaker), based on factors such as how fast someone is speaking, whether someone is smiling, length of pauses between words and sentences, and so on. When communicating FtF with another person, you can't control what the other person is paying attention to. Audiences are always making sense of us beyond what we are saying. Where you are interacting, what is going on around you, who else is in the room, your height, weight, skin color, perceived (dis)abilities, and an array of other cues play a significant role in determining what is given attention and understood in any given moment. Attention is placed not where we may want it—focused on what we are saying—but on whatever catches the attention of the person listening to us.

Although no preparation is necessary for FtF interactions, we constantly adjust our communication to match (or diverge from) the person we are communicating with, based on whether we view the person we are communicating with as "in" or "out" of a desired group membership (e.g., caregiver/non-caregiver).[6] When engaged in a conversation, we are constantly scanning for meaning, changing what is said, how something is being presented, and what is revealed and concealed, based on reading the feedback from the other person. Overadjusting to the needs of the audience in a particular moment of interaction, rather than focusing attention on what needs to be said and on the way you need to say it, can take precious energy and focus away from the effort to communicate something difficult and different. Caregivers are always trying to negotiate what they want (and need) to say while also maintaining relationships with loved ones and family members. Ongoing content- and relationship-based negotiations—trying to figure out inoffensive ways to say something or choosing not to ask a question that you know the other is sensitive about—are exhausting because they are full-body, always-on experiences. If you feel as though you want to say more to friends and family but can't, is your frustration revealed in your face? If you feel as though you are saying too much about your experiences and appear needy, is your desperation revealed in your voice? When a friend provides a quick and ready solution that you perceive to be unrealistic, can they see that look of disappointment in your eyes? When a family member tells you all the reasons why he can't help, can he tell that the brevity of your hug says you are full of regret as much as it is a good-bye?

When the stakes of revealing your authentic, in-the-moment FtF feelings are so steep, there is always the temptation to give others what they need by editing out parts of what you most want and need to say—but don't—for concern that it might create embarrassment or awkwardness. The spontaneity of the moment, so vital to FtF connections, can also deceive by luring you into giving voice to a momentary truth—anger, frustration, or just plain venting—that is deeply felt but, if said out loud, can never be taken back because of its irreparable impact not just on that interaction, but on future interactions with that person.

Especially when feeling vulnerable, FtF interactions may be an obstacle when seeking support and advocacy partners. Because caregivers may be hyperaware of how they are different from others, they may be particularly susceptible to focusing too much on other people's needs, rather than on what needs to be communicated. Knowing how to say what you want to say in a way that captures and keeps another's attention centered on what you are talking about can be daunting under the best of circumstances. Questions can be asked and interruptions beyond your control can determine the length, nature, and tenor of the interaction in ways that can't be anticipated, making FtF connections fraught with fragility and unpredictability. Yet support is almost never sought under the best of circumstances. Instead, support is needed when what you are trying to get across may not be familiar, appropriate, or easily understandable to others, especially when you are keenly aware that judgments are constantly being made about you based on what you are (not) saying in any given moment.[7]

Online Connections

Compared to FtF communication, there are far fewer nonverbal cues for assessing the person you are interacting with online. In the absence of nonverbal and environmental cues present in FtF communication,[8] however, greater attention can be directed to what is being communicated than the *who* and *where* of communication. Without the concern of what people look like when sharing, or how they sound when speaking, caregivers can focus their efforts almost entirely on what they want to say, and receivers can devote more attention to making sense of messages than to the "packages" in which the messages are delivered.

In online support groups, caregivers can selectively self-present in ways not possible in audience-centric, in-person interactions.[9] Caregivers, not the audience, can emphasize what they want to communicate, using the exact language they want, and in the specific order desired. Revision is possible. Editing is expected. Not an editing of omission, but a type of editing that encourages thinking about how to begin to voice what is so difficult to express. Since online communication doesn't depend on physical presence, contemplation about what you want to communicate can be constructed over time, rather than articulated and responded to within seconds as is necessary in a FtF interaction. Instead of privileging agility of response, online support can promote depth, detail, and contemplation of experiences not reducible to a sound bite or a witty response so valued in FtF interactions.

Online communication can also provide caregivers the capacity to think about how they want to communicate lived truths, from their perspective, rather than deferring to the way others want or need as so often happens in audience-centric FtF communication. In online support groups, caregivers can create messages that can be separated from them. You and your messages can get distance from one another. You can wait to press *send* when you are ready, not when cajoled by the immediacy of the moment, but by your own timetable of expression. You can read a message and then think, instead of being compelled to respond in that particular moment. Because online interactions are mediated, caregivers are granted the opportunity to *not* be present when someone interprets what you have written or shared.

This distance between you and what you communicate may be particularly empowering. Even when you are concerned that others might think differently or less of you because of what you are communicating—*"I don't know if I can do this anymore"*—you may still express yourself online because you won't have to witness an audience's initial reaction.[10] Separating you from your message means a temporary reprieve from the overreading, always-adjusting (giving audiences what you think they want) temptations so commonplace in FtF interactions. You won't be there when the message is read and interpreted. You and your message can become freed from each other, always interdependent but not so dependent that *you* can't be divorced from it.

Temporarily Escaping the Tyranny of the Now

The nature of responses in online support groups can be experienced differently from that of FtF responses. The convenience of online communication provides an opportunity to reclaim caregiver control by connecting with others when it best fits your schedule. The convenience of online support groups can overcome transportation challenges, timing, and the logistical challenges of shared presence.[11] Given unpredictable hours, caregivers can communicate when it is best for them, rather than having to wait, not only for others' availability but for others' readiness to deeply listen to what you are saying in the way your disclosures deserve.

Online interactions can empower types of interaction not often experienced in FtF settings, wresting control from the pressures of the "now" that is so important when communicating emotionally inspired, difficult truths in person. For example, tears in public spaces can clear rooms quickly. People flee, ever so subtly, because tears are deemed inappropriate in public spaces. Frustration and anger, as emotional responses to challenging situations, have also been deemed taboo in the company of others. As a result, FtF interactions can discourage intimate, emotional-laden sharing because of the implicit rules about what is appropriate and inappropriate to discuss at work, with supervisors, in new relationships, or with people that you know well but don't want to burden with possibly alarming or unsettling responses. Online, however, you can begin mindfully expressing the full range of your experiences, including the parts of your experiences most difficult to express, helping not only to make sense of what is happening, but also rendering some semblance of control over thoughts and experiences.[12]

The convenience of anytime, online support also means that the people you disclose experiences and feelings to have time to process, think through, and respond accordingly to what you are saying without the pressure of having to convince you to stop crying immediately, calm down, or conceal genuine expression because it might not be "appropriate." The situational, in-person qualifiers that can too often inhibit disclosure—"*I can't talk now*" or *"I'm in the middle of something, can we talk later?"* or *"This isn't the right time or place"*—can be circumvented online because audiences can respond when they are ready, rather than relying on the magic of the moment that is romanticized in movies, but often counterproductive when trying to make sense of emotionally layered disclosures.

When interacting FtF, responses can be limited because exchanging messages occurs in real time. This possibility encourages quick responses to acknowledge what was heard rather than creating space to craft a well-thought-out, personalized response.[13] FtF responses can be unrefined and depersonalized because the need to respond immediately is considered more pressing than the need to respond thoughtfully. Online, however, when responses don't have to be immediate, the gap between what is communicated and a response can encourage more thoughtful and nuanced expressions. The immediacy of FtF may mean someone is comforted because they are instantaneously heard, but being immediately heard isn't always synonymous with being deeply understood.

Letting "Outsiders" In

Since sharing physical space is not necessary in online interactions, disclosure may be encouraged because what a caregiver shares can be safeguarded from already existing networks of family and friends. Access to people not in your everyday networks means you won't necessarily see these people at work, at church, or at the next family holiday. This foreknowledge of network protection lowers the stakes of seeking and receiving support. Sometimes, sharing with people who won't take what you are saying personally inspires further sharing and allows what is created together to be the beginning of understanding that goes well beyond personalities and relationship history.

Accessing a diverse network of people online is beneficial, not because you know them or have a shared history, but because of a desire to create new realities, given common challenges.[14] Though anonymity means someone can be deceptive (e.g., scamming), it also makes it possible for you to communicate (without the risk of rejection by family and friends) with people who don't know who you are.[15] Anonymity also means communicating with people who are not invested in what they believe you *should* communicate based on who you are and how what you are sharing impacts them.

One enduring rule of communication patterns is that in our everyday FtF interactions, we tend to interact with people who are similar to us.[16] Networks matching who we are (or who we believe we are) may work for us when things are going well. When life is upended and we find ourselves engaged in situations, relationships, and roles unlike anything experienced before, networks of similarity can become counterproductive because good intentions can be no substitute for firsthand experiences. In the midst of new and foreign experiences, caregivers need the insight, feedback, and objectivity of those who are also responding to common challenges. Instead of relying on the mere chance of finding someone in an existing network who may have similar care experiences and challenges, online support can be forged based on a desired commonality—caregiving.

Once again, online, control is possible in ways it is not in FtF networks because caregivers can actively search, find, access, and interact with narrow and specific types of audiences, given their preferences and needs, instead of being constrained by habit and mere proximity.[17] Finding the right group you most want to connect with, based on type of caregiver relationship (e.g., spouse, parent, child) or the type of condition your loved one has (e.g., Crohn's, COPD, Huntington's disease, Alzheimer's, stroke, dementia, leukemia, cancer, paralysis, PTSD, chronic pain, MS, trigeminal neuralgia, etc.) means caregivers get to choose the specific type(s) of audiences best suited for them and their needs.

Connecting with audiences based on shared needs is also essential when ensuring accuracy while comparing yourself to others. Social comparisons are inevitable and a necessary means of assessing how we are (not) doing by comparing ourselves to others who we believe are doing "better" than we are and vice versa.[18] If FtF networks are your only types of connection, you risk making comparisons that may not be accurate, appropriate, or useful. If the people and situations you are comparing yourself to are misaligned with you, you expose yourself to resentments that may stunt your ability to give yourself permission for the type of self-compassion you need and deserve.

Online support groups can be helpful in providing guidance, advice, resources, and venting because support is about engaging in safe networks (people who have no power over you and who have a common need, not a common neighborhood) whose insights and (re)assurances aren't based on goodwill, but on commonality. Instead of discounting what a neighbor says to you about what you are experiencing—*"How do you know if what I'm feeing is normal; you've never been in my situation?"*—you may be more open to absorbing feedback from people who demonstrate ways of being a caregiver that reflect growth and possibility[19] because the feedback is coming from someone on a similar path to yours, and they may have been on this path longer than you could ever imagine. Reaching out to respected peers—caregivers—can become the bridge to connection, receptivity to others, and self-respect.[20]

EXPANDING PARTICIPATION
AND CREATING COMMUNITY

In online contexts, support can be enacted in much more nuanced ways than in FtF settings. When communicating in person, physical presence is clearly observable. Physical presence is one of the most endearing features of FtF interactions, but it can also keep people from connecting because physical presence can't go unnoticed. Online, however, you can engage with others incrementally and often without notice. You don't need to explain why you are in a particular chat room or support group. You don't need to justify your presence. If you are nervous or embarrassed, or even unsure, you can test the waters in ways not possible in FtF interactions where presence is reducible to being present or absent. Online, there are gradations of engagement and presence. You can read others' comments. You can peruse their bios. You can find comfort in knowing you are not alone by being present with and among others with similar experiences, without being noticed in the ways you can't avoid in FtF settings. And you can make comments, share your own experiences, and provide feedback to others. Seeking support beyond existing networks doesn't just benefit the people sharing; it also can empower listeners, creating a freedom to participate in ways not possible when you are concerned about how what you are hearing will impact existing relationships.

Non-caregivers may seek to find themselves by emphasizing how they are different and distinct from others. Caregivers, on the other hand, can begin to find themselves when surrounded by others having shared experiences. When communicating with people who don't have shared experiences, understanding must be constantly constructed—from scratch. With each new interaction, explaining means reconstructing everything you've been through and are experiencing that family and friends can't know or may never fully be able to appreciate, no matter how articulate and detailed your explanations. Even if you did articulate your experiences with such detail and vividness every time you interacted with someone, there is no guarantee that they would be able to understand, as they may be looking at your world and your experiences from a radically different vantage point—from a perspective of concern, of course, but from afar, looking onto your existence, rather than seeing what you see within your frame of reference. This distinction in perspective, from looking *at* to living *in*, can be exhausting to try to bridge because it requires so much energy on your part and incredible openness from the person you are interacting with.

When engaged in an online support community, this inescapable schism can dissolve. Assumptions can be made, perhaps for the first time. Constructing shared reference points doesn't have to be laborious, one steel beam at a time. Those in similar situations to yours already see and appreciate the foundation. In this process, something also happens to you. When surrounded by those you know and respect because they understand your situation, you change. Without even being aware of it, you are likely to become more open because you don't have to protect yourself as you do in a network of relationships that makes you more vulnerable to accidental, but stinging, barbs cloaked in well wishes. When you know you are communicating with someone who "gets it,"[21] you can begin to open yourself up, knowing that what you say or don't say won't be used against you. And the more you open yourself up to others, the more likely you are to share. Just knowing you are interacting with people who understand the invisible forces at play in your situation means you are more likely to be receptive to what others communicate and, in the process, find additional areas of commonality and identification more important and meaningful than any other differences that might exist.[22]

Unlike a habituated cycle of difference, so commonplace in FtF interactions, online interactions may be enhanced by a feedback loop of commonality, perceived understanding, openness, and intimacy. Not only may you feel less alone, but you may also be buoyed by a sense of togetherness that reshapes the value you gain from others' support as your experiences become a source of connection. Perhaps for the first time, your challenges become an invitation to others. Your insights are appreciated and valued. Questions may no longer be yours alone. Answers may no longer be yours alone. In this shift, you and your experiences aren't interpreted as a burden, but as an asset, as reciprocity becomes the bridge between you and others, forging a community *because* of your caregiver experiences, not in spite of them.

A NEW WAY OF SEEING AND BEING

It's not about *either* going online to find and solicit support *or* exclusively relying on FtF networks. The opportunities and challenges of caregiving are too significant, ongoing, and dynamic to reduce your connection and advocacy opportunities to any one medium. Rather, the goal is to learn to artfully find connections in whatever forms best suit you, your situation, and your and your loved ones' well-being.

Leveraging online and FtF audiences can give you permission to tell multiple stories, to multiple audiences, about your experiences. Caregiver experiences are too multifaceted to be one dimensional. There is not just *one* story or way of accounting for your ongoing experiences. Nor does each audience need to be engaged in the same way. The stories and experiences you share can, and should, work together to create coherence, but not unanimity. For example, online support may make it possible for you to reengage friends and family in ways that you couldn't before. Connecting with online caregiver audiences about the details of your care experiences may also allow you to rethink how you connect with your FtF networks. Knowing you can access audiences that can understand what you are experiencing may allow you to reorient yourself to family and friends. Instead of approaching them through a deficit orientation, or only recognizing what they cannot provide or understand, you may be able to more fully accept those nearest to you for what they can provide. If some of your emotional needs are met by online support groups, family and friends can be recast as a complementary audience, rather than an audience complete in itself, and thus better appreciated for what it can provide that no one else can: in-person comfort, the sharing of a quick phone call just to say hello and hear another person's voice, the peace of mind knowing that they may be only miles away if you need them in an instant, or the sustaining knowledge that no matter what happens, they will be in your life throughout.

This kind of connection literacy means knowing what your audience(s) may or may not be able to provide and create, with you. Asking the impossible of people leads to frustration for all involved, decreasing the likelihood of sharing and of what can be experienced together in future interactions. Integrating your audiences as your situation and needs evolve is the ultimate type of empowerment. It doesn't depend on waiting for others to change or become something other than what they are as much as it asks you to (re)think who the people you engage with are and how they may be able to simultaneously participate at every turning point in your care experiences.

Making It Personal

We asked caregivers at Caregiving.com and The Caregiver Space how they feel about online support.

HOW ARE ONLINE SUPPORT
FORUMS HELPFUL TO YOU?

"There are two things I value most. The first is being able to say the things that you are not supposed to say, but have to get out, in a safe environment. The second helpful aspect is that caregiving is so overwhelming at times and just reading the experiences of others helps me to gain perspective." —Lori J.

"Listening and being able to see what others do in each situation is a great help. Also, it helps to know there are others out there going through exactly what you yourself are going through. If they can make it through this, then I know I can too." —Becky G. C.

"I really thought I was alone until I discovered these support groups. I value that there are some folks out there who are in 'shoes' very much like mine. I met one woman who has a very similar situation to me: older husband and children near the same age as mine. We are Facebook friends now and she's a great soul to be buddies with. I'm very grateful." —Aspen M.

"When one of our fellow caregivers ultimately loses their loved one, the group gathers round and conveys love and support. It is not just a 'moment,' such as at a wake or funeral, but rather ongoing support. After the death of a loved one, the caregiver may continue to participate in this group and feel supported, needed and valued until they are ready to move on." —Sharon K. W. H.

HOW DO ONLINE SUPPORT GROUPS
HELP CAREGIVERS IN WAYS THAT
FACE-TO-FACE SUPPORTS COULD NOT?

"When my dad started dialysis I had a safe and trusted place to get the information I needed. I could rely on others' experience and get immediate support, even at 3 a.m." —Lori J.

"When I'm talking face to face with family or friends, I feel like I appear ungrateful and needy talking about my life, like I should be focused on them without the burden of my own pain." —Sherri C.

"Even though I'm a retired Registered Nurse, using caregiver online forums was the only place I felt I could talk about things and be truly understood. I found that people who have never been a caregiver really didn't get it. My professional experience did not prepare me for the emotional rollercoaster of caring for my own family member." —Connie B.

WHAT IS THE GREATEST BENEFIT YOU HAVE EXPERIENCED USING ONLINE FORUMS?

"I struggle to find a word that can adequately describe the value of the support I get through this group. It's vital to my sanity, and that's no exaggeration. Every time I leave the house, I'm worried that my grandmother will find the step stool and decide to de-clutter a top shelf. Or I'm worried about my grandfather going outside to garden and becoming too weak to stand up when he gets hot. So the fact that I get this safe place of support without leaving my home is a Godsend. We laugh here, we share ideas and information, we vent, we cry. It's AMAZING. I don't think I could keep my sanity without the encouragement afforded by this group. Just today, when my grandfather had trampled all over my last nerve, I was able to vent a bit, right from the doctor office exam room! And within minutes, there were words of encouragement, empathy, and even a bit of laughter. It's a blessing to have this at my fingertips." —Jennifer B. V.

"If it were not for my friends on this site encouraging me with words of kindness and prayers, I don't know if I would have survived taking care of my husband at home with absolutely no help. He died over 3 years ago and I still visit this site to see if I can help someone too." —Sandy O.

CONCLUSION

A New Way of Seeing and Being

You may not accept the title of caregiver. Regardless, you have cared for another, enduring ongoing uncertainty and self-doubt, amid evolving and unwanted relationship changes, and changing networks. It has become a part of you. To deny this aspect of your life is to deny you. You discovered these things about yourself not because you are a caregiver, but because you found parts of yourself *in* caregiving.

Your pre-caregiver life may now feel oddly unfamiliar, like looking in family albums at a person that resembles you but also feels like a stranger.[1] When you began this journey, you may have convinced yourself that it was only temporary. Care would be enacted while you could, until someone else stepped up. Or when life returned to normal. Here you are, weeks, months, or years later. Though you didn't want to go on this journey, what you have seen and what you are continuing to experience cannot be denied. The day-to-day realities of being with another in ways you had never experienced or even conceived of is now indelibly part of how you see yourself. It's part of how you talk about yourself. It's now part of how others view you.[2]

This transformation is an accomplishment—not an accident. Along the way, you have had to reconcile why you've felt disappointed by those closest to you. You've felt isolated and alone, excluded and offended by the beliefs and values others take for granted. You've been hurt by others' (non)reactions to you and your situation. But you've also developed your own voice. This kind of authenticity is deceptive because it makes it appear as if it has existed for all times. But it hasn't. It was earned.

At some point, waiting and deferring was replaced by a desire to begin making sense of your experiences even as you may have had no idea what tomorrow would bring. You still listen to others' voices. Doctors. Nurses. Specialists. Pharmacists. Rehabilitation specialists. Family members. But now, you don't *just* listen. And you don't *just* defer. You have developed your own voice, your own story. In the process, you have begun to discover that your experiences and insights are of equal value to others' perspectives.[3] No one can speak for you. You too are an expert—an expert without an official title, but you are armed with a story that needs to be heard and shared. Storytelling is a process of discovery, and your story, from your distinct perspective, is valuable because it emphasizes what other stories simply cannot represent.

Newfound beliefs and values did not come to you, they were earned in the hours and nights alone, confused, angry, and overwhelmed. But you persisted—yes, you can persist even if you feel you have no choice in the matter—by beginning to reclaim how you think about your experiences. You have enhanced your connection literacy by realizing that not any one audience nor any one medium can suffice. By recognizing your limitations, needs, and capacities, *and* others' limitations, capacities, and networks, you have begun to change how you see yourself and the situations facing you and your loved one. Forging options around and through challenges, rather than being trapped into an either/or approach, you can more fully leverage your ability to create understanding, enact and monitor care, question, advocate, and create pathways to navigate services and needs with providers and family.[4] Sometimes this means facilitating, respectfully disagreeing, and even pursuing care in ways that may differ from well-intentioned providers and family.[5] Leveraging family and caregivers, friends next door, and a growing community defined not simply by geographical proximity, but commonality, highlights how you are reclaiming value in your day-to-day experiences.

Along the way, your voice has changed. Not in how you sound, per se, as much as in the sound of your convictions. You know something and have learned something that others cannot (or choose not to) know when it comes to being with another. You don't *talk* about resilience—you have *shown* what resilience looks like when you don't have the luxury of time and distance to pause and figure out what your experiences mean in the past tense. You have begun to make meaning out of your experiences while care continues.

People may seek you out because you have done something—and are doing something—that they are just now entering. They may want your advice. They may seek your counsel. *"Where can I go to find someone who is in a situation like mine?" "How do I negotiate for more services in my community?" "How did you become such a compelling advocate for you and your loved one?" "How do you persuasively articulate your care situation to your supervisor at work?" "What online networks should I check out?" "What help may be available to me in my community?"*

People ask these questions not because you have all the answers but because they know something about you that may be difficult for you to acknowledge. Yes, you have gained something in this process. You have gained parts of yourself that were called into action out of necessity. And care. And determination. And because you wanted to make space for a better life for you *and* your loved one. In the trenches, your care was a response to what needed to be done. But it also reflects a willingness to reclaim *you* in your situation.

You have cultivated a new way of seeing and being.[6] What you think is possible, or what you believe you are capable of doing, has changed along with you.[7] You may ask questions you wouldn't have asked before. You may question authority in ways you wouldn't have wanted to before. You may have learned to appreciate the perspectives of people who have let you down or with whom you disagree. You may have increased your digital skills in ways that you had once overlooked. You may have found ways to comfort yourself in ways you never would have allowed yourself to when you began this journey. You may have communicated the need for your family—not just you—to become stakeholders in your loved one's care in ways you would have dismissed when this all began. You may be leveraging your neighborhood, city, state, local, and national organizations, and online networks, to find new information, deepen your advocacy efforts, and create spaces for change in ways that, before caregiving, you would have believed too difficult or too much to overcome. And you may be supporting someone who is lost and confused in the midst of their care experiences. You may be someone's inspiration. You may be the guide of what is possible, not because you are perfect or you handle everything with grace, but because your struggles, not your perfection, are the source of connection.[8] Yes, you are in the process of realizing that what you are capable of is always under construction no matter what circumstances you find yourself in.

WHAT STAYS WITH YOU . . .

Just as there is no clear "beginning" to the caregiver role, there is no clear "ending" point.[9] It can't be marked by the end of caregiver responsibilities. That would be like saying parenthood ends when your children go away to college. Or that your love for your spouse or partner immediately stops after their death. There are no clear ending points when love and care and you—your sense of who you are and what you have become—are involved.

Even if your everyday care tasks and responsibilities may have "ended," they are likely still working on you in ways that you could never have predicted because they have become a part of you. Others may believe that caregiving ends when your loved one moves into a nursing home or assisted living facility or when a loved one dies. With this noticeable shift, you are expected to seamlessly return to your previous life. But this expectation doesn't often fit with how you see yourself. Too much focus is on what you *did* in the care role, and not enough attention is given to who you became throughout the process. The disparity between what you thought you would feel (one step closer to your old self with each passing day) and how you actually feel (a revisiting of unease with each passing day) can't help but create more confusion and feelings of inauthenticity.

Even after Caregiving "Ends"

"*Life can now return to normal,*" others proclaim. But what others consider normal may no longer be what you consider normal. "*Now you can start over,*" you are told. Start over? Doesn't that mean denying that you were living while you were caregiving? "*Now you can get your self back again,*" you are reminded. But what if your new self is stronger, more reflective, and more insightful?

Although family, friends, and colleagues may sincerely believe that life can return to normal when caregiving "ends," you know that's not really possible. Caregiving may have radically interrupted your previous life, but somewhere along the way, it became a guide to living. You are not who you once were. Your understanding of normal has been irrevocably changed. The clarity of your caregiver role has been replaced by an overwhelming sense of ambiguity. The emptiness of not knowing what to do in response to your role change can overwhelm in ways you couldn't have predicted. The exhaustion of care is replaced by a different kind of exhaustion: *"How do I explain to others that the values that I developed in my caregiver role are still with me?"*

The clarity of knowing what was expected of you as a caregiver, however challenging, is gone. Now, the uncertainty of what you are to do without a clear and overriding purpose of care can't help but make you doubt who you are and what you should be doing. When you were a caregiver, every day was clear in its purpose, as the routines of care were the ultimate guide. Unending exhaustion was part of your everyday role, but now you find yourself exhausted by the apparent purposelessness of the everyday, not marked by life and death, pain and suffering, love and connection, but by trivialities that no longer make any sense.

How do you explain that you miss parts of yourself as a caregiver, or at least the parts of your role that made clear what you were supposed to be doing and how you were supposed to act? Care doesn't stop when caregiving ends. Others may no longer call you a "caregiver," but the impact of your experiences doesn't just evaporate the moment your caregiver role is omitted from how others label you. Just when family and friends believe your caregiving role is over, you may begin thinking about your experiences in ways that might have been too difficult to comprehend when you were so deeply in the experience. Care isn't something you can turn off immediately, or even slow down, when the caregiving role changes. Though others may no longer refer to you as a caregiver, the care that made you a caregiver has no shelf life.

When it comes to roles that shape how we think about ourselves, there is no clear ending point. Caregiving doesn't end even though the responsibilities that once characterized that role may cease. Caregiving isn't just a set of actions you perform, it's something you become. You don't "recover" from being a caregiver because the experience has become such a vital part of who you are that to let go of that part of yourself would also mean relinquishing everything you learned in the process of caring for someone you love.

You know something that those new to the role will soon learn. Care requires two seemingly incongruous orientations. Yes, it requires a laser-like focus on the needs of another. But the part that others too often forget, but you know intimately, is that care also requires a radical opening-up to others, a willingness to connect with those you know are suffering and in the midst of struggle. We can't help but know that care doesn't end but is always a source of connection that can never be extinguished. This awareness can be the beginning of a new way of seeing and being ourselves, together.

NOTES

FOREWORD BY JUDY WOODRUFF

1. Broadcast journalist Judy Woodruff is the anchor and managing editor of the *PBS NewsHour*. She has covered politics and other news for more than four decades at NBC, CNN, and PBS. https://www.pbs.org/newshour/author/judy-woodruff.

2. Gail Gibson and Susan Reinhard. *2015 Report: Caregiving in the U.S.* AARP and National Alliance for Caregiving (2015), under "Prevalence of Caregiving," https://www.aarp.org/content/dam/aarp/ppi/2015/caregiving-in-the-united-states-2015-report-revised.pdf.

INTRODUCTION

1. The authors recognize that the terms "caregiver" and "loved one" are inadequate descriptors for many people participating in care relationships. We have used these terms for the sake of simplicity and brevity.

CHAPTER 1: I'M (NOT) A CAREGIVER

1. Lisa Sparks and Melinda Villagran, *Patient and Provider Interaction: A Global Health Communication Perspective* (Cambridge, UK: Polity, 2010), 111-13.

2. Clare Ansberry, "America Is Running Out of Family Caregivers, Just When It Needs Them Most," *Wall Street Journal*, July 20, 2018, https://www.wsj.com/articles/america-is-running-out-of-family-caregivers-just-when-it-needs-them-most-1532094538.

3. Gail Gibson and Susan Reinhard. *2015 Report: Caregiving in the U.S.* AARP and National Alliance for Caregiving (2015), under "Caregiving Activities and

Burden of Care," https://www.aarp.org/content/dam/aarp/ppi/2015/caregiving-in-the-united-states-2015-report-revised.pdf.

4. Jennifer Willyard, Katherine Miller, Martha Shoemaker, and Penny Addison, "Making Sense of Sibling Responsibility for Family Caregiving," *Qualitative Health Research 18*, no. 12 (2008): 1678.

5. Kevin Wright and Ahlam Muhtaseb, "Personal Relationships and Computer-Mediated Support Groups," in *Computer-Mediated Communication in Personal Relationships*, ed. Kevin Wright and Lynne Webb (New York: Peter Lang, 2011), 146.

6. Sparks and Villagran, *Patient and Provider Interaction*, 117.

7. People under the age of seventy-five are just as likely as people over seventy-five to serve as an unpaid caregiver. Gretchen Livingston, "Adult Caregiving Often Seen as Very Meaningful by Those Who Do It," *Pew Research Center: FactTank: News in the Numbers,* November 8, 2018, http://www.pewresearch.org/fact-tank/2018/11/08/adult-caregiving-often-seen-as-very-meaningful-by-those-who-do-it/.

8. Ansberry, "America Is Running Out of Family Caregivers."

9. Livingston, "Adult Caregiving Often Seen as Very Meaningful by Those Who Do It," http://www.pewresearch.org/fact-tank/2018/11/08/adult-caregiving-often-seen-as-very-meaningful-by-those-who-do-it/.

10. Dan Witters, "Caregiving Costs U.S. Economy $25.2 Billion in Lost Productivity," *Gallup*, July 27, 2011, https://news.gallup.com/poll/148670/caregiving-costs-economy-%20billion-lost-productivity.aspx.

PREFACE TO CHAPTERS 2–6: DISORIENTATION: FROM LOVED ONE TO CAREGIVER

1. *Merriam-Webster*, "disorient," accessed November 25, 2018, https://www.merriam-webster.com/dictionary/disorient.

CHAPTER 2: LIVING IN BETWEEN SCRIPTS

1. Howard Brody, *Stories of Sickness*, 2nd ed. (Oxford: Oxford University Press, 2003), 73.

2. Michael Bury, "Chronic Illness as Biographical Disruption," *Sociology of Health and Illness 4*, no. 2 (July 1982): 169.

3. The metaphor of a "script" is being used as synonymous with schema and narrative. See Pamela Rutledge, "The Psychological Power of Storytelling,"

Psychology Today, accessed September 1, 2018, https://www.psychologytoday.com/us/blog/positively-media/201101/the-psychological-power-storytelling.

4. Kevin Wright, Lisa Sparks, and H. Dan O'Hair, *Health Communication in the 21st Century* (Malden, MA: Wiley-Blackwell, 2013), 27.

5. Arthur Frank, *The Wounded Storyteller: Body, Illness & Ethics*, 2nd ed. (Chicago: University of Chicago Press, 2013), e-book, chap. 3.

6. Brody, *Stories of Sickness*, 118–20.

7. Frank, *The Wounded Storyteller*, chap. 3.

8. Ibid.

9. Brody, *Stories of Sickness*, 49.

10. *Merriam-Webster*, "nostalgia," accessed November 1, 2018, https://www.merriamwebster.com/dictionary/nostalgia.

11. This is also referred to as anticipatory grieving.

12. Juliet Corbin and Anselm Strauss, "Accompaniments of Chronic Illness: Changes in Body, Self, Biography, and Biographical Time," *Research in the Sociology of Health Care* 6 (1987): 254.

13. Frank, *The Wounded Storyteller*, chap. 5. Frank refers to this as a type of "chaos" narrative.

14. Ibid., chap. 5. Living in between "scripts" can create a perceived absence of a coherent "voice."

CHAPTER 3: A HYPER-INTOLERANCE OF OTHERS

1. Kathy Charmaz, "The Body, Identity, and Self: Adapting to Impairment," *The Sociological Quarterly 36*, no. 4 (1995): 660.

2. Austin Babrow, Chris Kasch, and Leigh Ford, "The Many Meanings of Uncertainty in Illness: Toward a Systematic Accounting," *Health Communication 10*, no. 1 (1998): 1.

3. Walid Afifi and Masaki Matsunaga, "Uncertainty Management Theories: Three Approaches to a Multifarious Process," in *Engaging Theories in Interpersonal Communication,* ed. Leslie Baxter and Dawn Braithwaite (Thousand Oaks, CA: Sage, 2008), 122–23.

4. Katherine Miller, Martha Shoemaker, Jennifer Willyard, and Penny Addison, "Providing Care for Elderly Parents: A Structurational Approach to Family Caregiving Identity," *Journal of Family Communication 8*, no. 1 (January 2008): 31.

5. Ibid., 37–38. See also Jennifer Willyard, Katherine Miller, Martha Shoemaker, and Penny Addison, "Making Sense of Sibling Responsibility for Family Caregiving," *Qualitative Health Research, 18*, no. 12 (November 2008): 1679.

6. Michael Bury, "Chronic Illness as Biographical Disruption," *Sociology of Health and Illness 4*, no. 2 (July 1982): 169.

7. Amy Zhang and Laura Siminoff, "Silence and Cancer: Why Do Families and Patients Fail to Communicate?" *Health Communication 14*, no. 4 (February 2003): 426–27.

8. Blake Ashforth and Glen Kreiner, "'How Can You Do It?': Dirty Work and the Challenge of Constructing a Positive Identity," *Academy of Management Review 24*, no. 3 (1999): 415. See also Julia Lawton, "Contemporary Hospice Care: The Sequestration of the Unbounded Body and 'Dirty Dying,'" *Sociology of Health & Illness 20*, no. 2 (March 2008): 134. http://journals.sagepub.com/doi/abs/10.1177/0893318917696991.

9. Zachary White and Cristina Gilstrap, "'People Just Don't Understand': Challenges Communicating Home Hospice Volunteer Role Experiences to Organizational Outsiders," *Management Communication Quarterly 31*, no. 4 (March 2017), under "We're not Special—We're Special," http://journals.sagepub.com/doi/abs/10.1177/0893318917696991.

10. Olga Khazan, "How Loneliness Begets Loneliness," *The Atlantic*, April 6, 2017, https://www.theatlantic.com/health/archive/2017/04/how-loneliness-begets-loneliness/521841/.

CHAPTER 4: AUDIENCE BETRAYAL

1. Howard Brody, *Stories of Sickness*, 2nd ed. (Oxford: Oxford University Press, 2003), 47–49.

2. Kathleen Galvin, Dawn Braithwaite, and Carma Bylund, *Family Communication: Cohesion and Change*, 9th ed. (New York: Routledge, 2015), 30.

3. Erving Goffman, *The Presentation of Self in Everyday Life*, Monograph no. 2 (Edinburgh: University of Edinburgh Social Sciences Research Centre, 1956), 22–23.

4. Juliet Corbin and Anselm Strauss, "Accompaniments of Chronic Illness: Changes in Body, Self, Biography, and Biographical Time," *Research in the Sociology of Health Care 6*, (1987): 257–60.

5. Zachary White and Cristina Gilstrap, "'People Just Don't Understand': Challenges Communicating Home Hospice Volunteer Role Experiences to Organizational Outsiders," *Management Communication Quarterly 31*, no. 4 (2017), under "We're Not Special—We're Special," http://journals.sagepub.com/doi/abs/10.1177/0893318917696991.

6. In many ways, this is similar to Arthur Frank's conception of the "mirroring body" and "disciplined body." Arthur Frank, *The Wounded Storyteller: Body, Illness and Ethics*, 2nd ed. (Chicago: University of Chicago Press, 2013), Kindle e-book, chap. 2.

7. In many ways, this is similar to Frank's conception of the "disciplined body." Frank, *The Wounded Storyteller*, chap. 2.

8. Sarah Green, Christine Davis, Elana Karshmer, Pete Marsh, and Benjamin Straight, "Living Stigma: The Impact of Labeling, Stereotyping, Separation, Status Loss, and Discrimination in the Lives of Individuals with Disabilities and Their Families," *Sociological Inquiry 75*, no. 2 (March 2005), 197–98.

9. Corbin and Strauss, "Accompaniments of Chronic Illness," 257–60.

10. Rebecca Meisenbach, "Stigma Management Communication: A Theory and Agenda for Applied Research on How Individuals Manage Moments of Stigmatized Identity, *Journal of Applied Communication Research 38*, no. 3 (August 2010): 271.

11. Terrance Albrecht and Mara Adelman, *Communicating Social Support* (Thousand Oaks, CA: Sage, 1987), 24. See also Kevin Wright and Stephen Rains, "Weak-Tie Support Network Preference, Health-Related Stigma, and Health Outcomes in Computer-Mediated Support Groups," *Journal of Applied Communication Research 41*, no. 3 (August 2013): 309–12.

12. Andrew High and Denise Solomon, "Locating Computer-Mediated Social Support within Online Communication Environments," in *Computer-Mediated Communication in Personal Relationships*, ed. Kevin Wright and Lynne Webb (New York: Peter Lang, 2011), 120–21.

13. Kevin Wright, Lisa Sparks, and Dan O'Hair. *Health Communication in the 21st Century* (Malden, MA: Wiley-Blackwell, 2013), 105.

14. Julie Harris, Deborah Bowen, Hoda Badr, Peggy Hannon, Jennifer Hay, and Katherine Regan Sterba, "Family Communication during the Cancer Experience," *Journal of Health Communication 14*, no. 1 (2009): 79.

15. John Caughlin, Sylvia Mikucki-Enyart, Ashley Middleton, Anne Stone, and Laura Brown, "Being Open without Talking about It: A Rhetorical/Normative Approach to Understanding Topic Avoidance in Families after a Lung Cancer Diagnosis," *Communication Monographs 78*, no. 4 (2011): 425–26, 429.

16. Elaine Wittenberg-Lyles, Karla Washington, George Demiris, Debra Parker Oliver, and Sara Shaunfield, "Understanding Social Support Burden among Family Caregivers," *Health Communication 29*, no. 9 (2014): 909–10.

17. Albrecht and Adelman, *Communicating Social Support*, 245–47.

18. Kevin Wright and Stephen Rains, "Weak-Tie Support Network Preference, Health-Related Stigma, and Health Outcomes in Computer-Mediated Support Groups," *Journal of Applied Communication Research 41*, 3 (August 2013): 311–12.

19. Paul Mongeau and Mary Lynne Miller Henningsen, "Stage Theories of Relationship Development: Charting the Course of Interpersonal Communication," in *Engaging Theories in Interpersonal Communication*, ed. Leslie Baxter and Dawn Braithwaite (Los Angeles: Sage, 2008), 366.

20. Ibid., 367–68.

21. Kevin Wright and Claude Miller, "A Measure of Weak-Tie/Strong-Tie Support Network Preference," *Communication Monographs* 77, no. 4 (December 2010): 501.

22. Wittenberg-Lyles, Washington, Demiris, Oliver, and Shaunfield, "Understanding Social Support Burden among Family Caregivers," 907–8.

23. Yaacov Bachner and Sara Carmel, "Open Communication between Caregivers and Terminally Ill Cancer Patients: The Role of Caregivers' Characteristics and Situational Variables," *Health Communication* 24, no. 6 (2009): 530.

24. Blake Ashforth and Glen Kreiner, "'How Can You Do It?': Dirty Work and the Challenge of Constructing a Positive Identity," *Academy of Management Review* 24, no. 3 (1999): 414–16.

25. Kevin Wright and Ahlam Muhtaseb, "Personal Relationships and Computer-Mediated Support Groups," in *Computer-Mediated Communication in Personal Relationships*, ed. Kevin Wright and Lynne Webb (New York: Peter Lang, 2011), 146.

26. Ibid.,147.

27. Zachary White and Jeremiah Wills, "Communicating about Chronic Caregiving in the Workplace: Employees' Disclosure Preferences, Intentions, and Behaviors," *Communication Research Reports 33*, no. 1 (2016): 37.

28. Mongeau and Henningsen, "Stage Theories," 367.

29. Sandra Petronio, *Boundaries of Privacy: Dialectics of Disclosure* (Albany: State University of New York Press, 2002), 50–54.

30. Amy Zhang and Laura Siminoff, "Silence and Cancer: Why Do Families and Patients Fail to Communicate?" *Health Communication 15*, no. 4 (February 2003): 422–23.

31. Leslie Baxter and Dawn Braithwaite, "Relational Dialectics Theory: Crafting Meaning from Competing Discourses," in *Engaging Theories in Interpersonal Communication: Multiple Perspectives*, ed. Leslie Baxter and Dawn Braithwaite (Los Angeles: Sage, 2008), 351.

32. Albrecht and Adelman, *Communicating Social Support*, 251–52.

33. Wright, Sparks, and O'Hair, *Health Communication in the 21st Century*, 105.

34. Ibid.

CHAPTER 5: WHO AM I BECOMING AND WHY AM I SO HARD ON MYSELF?

1. Ann Crouter, "Spillover from Family to Work: The Neglected Side of the Work-Family Interface," *Human Relations 37*, no. 6 (June 1984): 425–41.

2. Blake Ashforth, Glen Kreiner, and Mel Fugate, "All in a Day's Work: Boundaries and Micro Role Transitions," *Academy of Management Review 25*, no. 3 (July 2000): 474–75.

3. Julie Apker, Kathleen Propp, and Wendy Ford, "Negotiating Status and Identity Tensions in Healthcare Team Interactions: An Exploration of Nurse Role Dialectics," *Journal of Applied Communication Research 33*, no. 2 (2005): 95–97.

4. Barbara Simpson and Brigid Carroll, "Re-viewing 'Role' in Processes of Identity Construction," *Organization 15*, no. 1 (2008): 43–44.

5. Sue Clark, "Work/Family Border Theory: A New Theory of Work/Family Balance," *Human Relations 53*, no. 6 (2000): 748.

6. Ibid., 756.

7. John McArthur, *Digital Proxemics: How Technology Shapes the Way We Move* (New York: Peter Lang, 2016), 25.

8. *Mister Rogers' Neighborhood* television program began in 1968 and ended in 2001.

9. Ashforth, Kreiner, and Fugate, "All in a Day's Work," 474.

10. Susan Gregory, "Living with Chronic Illness in the Family Setting," *Sociology of Health & Illness 27*, no. 3 (April 2005): 374.

11. Caryn Medved, "The Everyday Accomplishment of Work and Family: Exploring Practical Actions in Daily Routines," *Communication Studies 55*, no. 1 (Spring 2004): 142.

12. Zachary White, Cristina Gilstrap, and Jennifer Hull. "Me Against the World': Parental Uncertainty Management at Home Following Neonatal Intensive Care Unit Discharge," *Journal of Family Communication, 17*, no. 2 (October 2016), under "Caring through Equipment," https://www.tandfonline.com/doi/abs/10.1080/15267431.2016.1233105?journalCode=hjfc20.

13. Julia Lawton, "Contemporary Hospice Care: The Sequestration of the Unbounded Body and 'Dirty Dying,'" *Sociology of Health & Illness 20*, no. 2 (December 2001): 132–35.

14. Sandra Petronio, *Boundaries of Privacy: Dialectics of Disclosure*, monograph no. 2 (Albany: State University of New York, 2002), 26.

15. Erving Goffman, *The Presentation of Self in Everyday Life* (Edinburgh: University of Edinburgh Social Sciences Research Centre, 1956), 69–72.

16. Simpson and Carroll, "Re-viewing 'Role' in Processes of Identity Construction," 41.

17. *Burnout* typically denotes "professional" caregiver experiences, but analogous language can be used to characterize informal caregiver challenges.

18. For the dimensions of burnout as experienced by hospice employees, see Deborah Way and Sarah Tracy, "Conceptualizing Compassion as Recognizing,

Relating, and (Re)acting: A Qualitative Study of Compassionate Communication at Hospice," *Communication Monographs 79*, no. 3 (September 2012): 294–97.

19. Zachary White and Cristina Gilstrap, "Inside Patients' Homes: A Metaphorical Analysis of Home Hospice Nurses' Experiences Working with Dying Patients," *OMEGA—Journal of Dying and Death 72*, no. 4 (2016): 307–8.

20. Zachary White and Cristina Gilstrap, "'People Just Don't Understand': Challenges Communicating Home Hospice Volunteer Role Experiences to Organizational Outsiders," *Management Communication Quarterly 31*, no. 4 (March 2017), under "We're Not Special—We're Special," http://journals.sagepub.com/doi/abs/10.1177/0893318917696991.

21. Marianne Dainton and Elaine Zelley, "Social Exchange Theories: Interdependence and Equity," in *Engaging Theories in Family Communication: Multiple Perspectives*, ed. Dawn Braithwaite and Leslie Baxter (Los Angeles: Sage, 2006), 249–50.

22. "Absolutism" has been found to be a "possible cognitive vulnerability" factor for certain populations. See Mohammed Al-Mosaiwi and Tom Johnstone, "In an Absolute State: Elevated Use of Absolutist Words Is a Marker Specific to Anxiety, Depression, and Suicidal Ideation," *Clinical Psychological Science 6*, no. 4 (2018): 539.

23. Kristin Neff, "The Development and Validation of a Scale to Measure Self-Compassion," *Self and Identity 2*, no. 3 (July 2003): 224.

24. Ibid., 225.

25. Ibid., 226.

26. Mark Leary, Eleanor Tate, Claire Adams, Ashley Allen, and Jessica Hancock, "Self-Compassion and Reactions to Unpleasant Self-Relevant Events: The Implications of Treating Oneself Kindly," *Journal of Personality and Social Psychology 92*, no. 5 (May 2007): 901.

27. Neff, "The Development," 224.

28. Ibid., 231–32.

29. Ibid.

30. Ibid.

CHAPTER 6: WHEN "GETTING THROUGH" ISN'T GOOD ENOUGH

1. Juliet Corbin and Anselm Strauss, "Accompaniments of Chronic Illness: Changes in Body, Self, Biography, and Biographical Time," *Research in the Sociology of Health Care: The Experience and Management of Chronic Illness 6* (1987): 273.

2. Laura Strafford, "Social Exchange Theories: Calculating the Rewards and Costs of Personal Relationships," in *Engaging Theories in Interpersonal Communication: Multiple Perspectives*, 2nd ed., ed. Dawn Braithwaite and Paul Schrodt (Los Angeles: Sage, 2015), 404–7.

3. See Graham Bodie and Susanne Jones, "The Nature of Supportive Listening and the Role of Verbal Person Centeredness and Nonverbal Immediacy," *Western Journal of Communication 76*, no. 3 (2012).

4. Avinoam Nowogrodski, "Why Listening Might Be the Most Important Skill to Hire For," *Fast Company*, February 23, 2015, https://www.fastcompany.com/3042688/why-listening-might-be-the-most-important-skill-to-hire-for.

5. Douglas Stone, Bruce Patton, and Sheila Heen, "Difficult Conversations: How to Discuss What Matters Most," in *Making Connections: Readings in Relational Communication*, 5th ed., ed. Kathleen Galvin (New York: Oxford University Press, 2010), 224–25.

6. See John McArthur, *Digital Proxemics: How Technology Shapes the Way We Move* (New York: Peter Lang, 2016), 19–20. Categories of space are based on Edward Hall's discussion of proxemics in *The Hidden Dimension*.

7. Corbin and Strauss, "Accompaniments of Chronic Illness," 256–60.

8. Ibid., 250–51.

9. Kathy Charmaz, "The Body, Identity, and Self: Adapting to Impairment," *The Sociological Quarterly 36*, no. 4 (September 1995): 672.

10. Sandra Petronio, *Boundaries of Privacy: Dialectics of Disclosure* (Albany: State University of New York Press, 2002), 26.

PREFACE TO CHAPTERS 7–14: REORIENTATION AND ADVOCACY

1. *Merriam-Webster*, "wisdom," accessed November 10, 2018, https://www.merriam-webster.com/dictionary/wisdom.

CHAPTER 7: MAKING MEANING THAT MATTERS NOW

1. "A First Look at Communication Theory," transcript of Em Griffin's Interview with Barnett Pearce, creator of Coordinated Management of Meaning, accessed August 1, 2018, https://www.afirstlook.com/docs/video-transcript-4.pdf.

2. Walter Fisher, *Human Communication as Narration: Toward a Philosophy of Reason, Value, and Action* (Columbia: University of South Carolina Press, 1987), 47.

3. Howard Brody, *Stories of Sickness* (New York: Oxford University Press, 2003), 29.

4. Richard Tedeschi and Lawrence Calhoun, "Posttraumatic Growth: Conceptual Foundations and Empirical Evidence," *Psychological Inquiry 15*, no. 1 (2004): 12.

5. Ibid., 4.

6. Ibid., 5–7.

7. Juliet Corbin and Anselm Strauss, "Accompaniments of Chronic Illness: Changes in Body, Self, Biography, and Biographical Time," *Research in the Sociology of Health Care: The Experience and Management of Chronic Illness 6* (1987): 261.

8. Barbara Sharf and Marsha Vanderford, "Illness Narratives and the Social Construction of Health," in *Handbook of Health Communication*, ed. Teresa Thompson, Alicia Dorsey, Roxanne Parrott, and Katherine Miller (New York: Routledge), 17.

9. Zachary White and Cristina Gilstrap, "'People Just Don't Understand': Challenges Communicating Home Hospice Volunteer Role Experiences to Organizational Outsiders," *Management Communication Quarterly 31*, no. 4 (March 2017), under "Discussion," http://journals.sagepub.com/doi/abs/10.1177/0893318917696991.

10. Sarah Tracy and Clifton Scott, "Sexuality, Masculinity, and Taint Management among Firefighters and Correctional Officers," *Management Communication Quarterly 20*, no. 1 (August 2006): 29.

11. Lucas Biettie, Ottilie Tilston, and Adrian Bangerter, "Storytelling as Adaptive Collective Sensemaking," *Topics in Cognitive Science* (2018): 11–12, https://onlinelibrary.wiley.com/doi/full/10.1111/tops.12358.

12. Brody, *Stories of Sickness*, 39.

13. Kevin Wright and Ahlam Muhtaseb, "Personal Relationships and Computer-Mediated Support Groups," in *Computer-Mediated Communication in Personal Relationships*, ed. Kevin Wright and Lynne Webb (New York: Peter Lang, 2011), 146.

14. Tedeschi and Calhoun, "Posttraumatic Growth," 11–12.

15. *60 Minutes*, "Helping Ease Childhood Trauma," March 11, 2018, https://www.cbs.com/shows/60_minutes/video/vm02T0fGuBx6X3KK_YPO5Kse6UBHxad8/treating-childhood-trauma/. Dr. Perry is an expert in treating childhood trauma.

16. Kevin Wright and Claude Miller, "A Measure of Weak-Tie/Strong-Tie Support Network Preference, *Communication Monographs 77*, no. 4 (2010): 501.

17. Wright and Muhtaseb, "Personal Relationships," 145–47.

18. Corbin and Strauss, "Accompaniments of Chronic Illness," 279.

19. Wright and Muthaseb, "Personal Relationships," 146.

20. Ibid.,147.

21. Dan O'Hair, Melinda Villagran, Elaine Wittenberg, Kenneth Brown, Monica Ferguson, Harry Hall, and Timothy Doty, "Cancer Survivorship and Agency Model: Implications for Patient Choice, Decision Making, and Influence," *Health Communication 15*, no. 2 (2003): 196–98.

22. James Pennebaker and Janel Seagal, "Forming a Story: The Health Benefits of Narrative," *Journal of Clinical Psychology 55*, no. 10 (1999): 1251.

23. This is similar to what Corbin and Strauss ("Accompaniments of Chronic Illness," 251) call "biographical accommodation."

24. White and Gilstrap, "'People Just Don't Understand,' under 'It's Enjoyable—It's Depressing,'" http://journals.sagepub.com/doi/abs/10.1177/0893318917696991.

25. Ibid.

26. Cristina Gilstrap and Zachary White, "'Like Nothing Else I've Ever Experienced': Examining the Metaphors of Residential Hospice Volunteers," in *Volunteering and Communication: Studies from Multiple Contexts*, ed. Michael Kramer, Laurie Lewis, and Loril Gossett (New York: Peter Lang, 2013), 163–65.

27. Brody, *Stories of Sickness,* 26.

28. White and Gilstrap, "People Just Don't Understand," under "Presence Is Significant—Presence Is Insignificant."

29. Corbin and Strauss, "Accompaniments of Chronic Illness," 273.

30. Arthur Frank, *The Wounded Storyteller: Body, Illness & Ethics*, 2nd ed. (Chicago: University of Chicago Press, 2013), Kindle e-book, chap. 6.

31. Corbin and Strauss, "Accompaniments of Chronic Illness," 273–75.

32. Brian Richardson and Laura Maninger. "'We Were All in the Same Boat': An Exploratory Study of Communal Coping in Disaster Recovery," *Southern Communication Journal 81*, no. 2 (2016): 117.

CHAPTER 8: BEGIN WITH THE BASICS: WHAT IS MY ROLE AT HOME, WHAT DO I *WANT* IT TO BE?

1. Kim Parker and Eileen Patten. "The Sandwich Generation," Pew Research Center, accessed June 14, 2018, http://www.pewsocialtrends.org/2013/01/30/the-sandwich-generation/.

2. "Caring across Generations," accessed June 14, 2018, https://caringacross.org/why-care/.

3. Chris Farrell, "The Shortage of Home Care Workers: Worse Than You Think," *Forbes.com*, accessed June 14, 2018, https://www.forbes.com/sites/

nextavenue/2018/04/18/the-shortage-of-home-care-workers-worse-than-you
-think/#1193ad9c3ddd.

4. National Alliance for Caregiving and AARP, "Research," accessed June 14, 2018, http://www.caregiving.org/research/general-caregiving/.

5. According to the Canadian Medical Protective Association, the "circle of care" is the group of health care providers treating one patient who need information to provide that care.

6. National Alliance for Caregiving and AARP, "Research: General Caregiving."

7. Ibid.

8. Ibid.

9. Ibid.

10. Ibid.

11. David Brooks, "What Suffering Does," *New York Times*, April 7, 2014, accessed June 14, 2018, https://www.nytimes.com/2014/04/08/opinion/brooks-what-suffering-does.html.

12. Posttraumatic Research Group, UNC Charlotte, "What Is PTG?," accessed June 14, 2018, https://ptgi.uncc.edu/what-is-ptg/.

CHAPTER 9: IT TAKES A VILLAGE: REVEALING HIDDEN ASSETS IN THE NEIGHBORHOOD

1. "Resources," Asset Based Community Development Institute, DePaul University, accessed June 13, 2018, https://resources.depaul.edu/abcd-institute/Pages/default.aspx.

2. Brett Iverson, "Richland Together Let's Connect," YouTube, accessed June 13, 2018, https://www.youtube.com/watch?v=ObYBnG245S8.

3. The Aging and Disability Resource Center of Southwest Wisconsin, "Home Page," accessed June 13, 2018. https://adrcswwi.org/.

4. Active Aging Research Center, Center for Health Enhancement Studies (CHESS), University of Wisconsin, accessed June 13, 2018, https://center.chess.wisc.edu/research-projects/view/active-aging-research-center.

5. Ibid.

6. https://www.meetup.com.

7. "Asperger Syndrome: Partners & Family of Adults with ASD (Portland, OR)," Meetup, accessed July 12, 2018, https://www.meetup.com/Asperger-Syndrome-Partners-Family-of-Adults-with-ASD/.

8. "Veteran Stories—The Memory Project," Home—The Memory Project, accessed July 12, 2018, http://www.thememoryproject.com/stories.

9. "Best Buddies International—Best Buddies Is a Non-profit 501(c)(3) Organization Dedicated to Establishing a Global Volunteer Movement That Creates Opportunities for One-to-one Friendships, Integrated Employment, and Leadership Development for People with Intellectual and Developmental Disabilities (IDD)," Best Buddies International, accessed July 12, 2018, http://www.bestbuddies.org/.

10. "Brazilian Teens Learn English by Video Chatting with American Nursing Home Residents," People.com, accessed July 12, 2018, https://people.com/celebrity/fcb-brazils-speaking-exchange-pairs-brazilian-teens-with-elderly-americans/.

11. "FIAO Brooklyn," accessed July 12, 2018, http://www.fiaobrooklyn.org/community_services/social_services/.

12. "Choir Singing Improves Health, Happiness—and Is the Perfect Icebreaker," University of Oxford, accessed October 8, 2018, http://www.ox.ac.uk/research/choir-singing-improves-health-happiness-—-and-perfect-icebreaker.

13. "Men's Shed," Wikipedia, July 3, 2018, accessed July 12, 2018, https://en.wikipedia.org/wiki/Men's_shed.

14. Bernhard Schmidt-Hertha, Sabina Jelenc-Krašovec, and Marvin Formosa, *Learning across Generations in Europe: Contemporary Issues in Older Adult Education* (Rotterdam: Sense Publishers, 2014).

15. Barry Golding, "Men Learning through Life (and Men's Sheds)," *Adult Learning 26*, no. 4 (2015): 170–72, doi:10.1177/1045159515594152.

16. "What Is a Community Kitchen?" Community Kitchens, accessed July 12, 2018, http://communitykitchens.org.au/what-is-a-community-kitchen/.

17. Patrick J. Skerrett, "Pets Can Help Their Humans Create Friendships, Find Social Support," Harvard Health Blog, October 30, 2015, accessed July 12, 2018, https://www.health.harvard.edu/blog/pets-can-help-their-humans-create-friendships-find-social-support-201505067981.

18. "Pet Partners," Pet Partners.org. "Therapy Pets & Animal Assisted Activities," Pet Partners.org, accessed July 12, 2018, http://www.petpartners.org/.

CHAPTER 10: NAVIGATING THE ROUGH WATERS OF TRANSITION

1. Ann Malley and Carole Kenner, "Transitions in Care: A Critical Review of Measurement," *Journal of Perioperative & Critical Intensive Care Nursing 2,* no. 4 (December 2016), https://www.ncbi.nlm.nih.gov/pmc/articles/PMC5656252/ (accessed June 25, 2018).

2. Next Step in Care, accessed June 25, 2018, https://www.nextstepincare .org/.

3. Vicki R. Strang, Priscilla M. Koop, Suzanne Dupuis-Blanchard, Marlene Nordstrom, and Betty Thompson, "Family Caregivers and Transition to Long-Term Care," *Clinical Nursing Research* 15, no. 1 (2006): 27–45, doi:10.1177/1054773805282356.

4. "About Atlas CareMaps," Atlas of Caregiving, accessed October 8, 2018, https://atlasofcaregiving.com/caremap/.

5. Ibid.

6. Ibid.

7. Ibid.

8. "Entrevista Con Beatriz Angeles—El Impacto Del CareMap," Vimeo, October 4, 2018, accessed October 8, 2018, https://vimeo.com/256813229.

9. "Entrevista Con Mayra Perez—El Impacto Del CareMap," Vimeo, July 9, 2018, accessed October 8, 2018, https://vimeo.com/256813224.

CHAPTER 11: NOT A SOCIAL NETWORK, BUT A *CARE* NETWORK

1. "Caregiver Statistics," Caregiver Action Network, accessed July 4, 2018, http://caregiveraction.org/resources/caregiver-statistics.

2. Ibid.

3. Debra Umberson and Jennifer Karas Montez, "Social Relationships and Health: A Flashpoint for Health Policy," *Journal of Health and Social Behavior 51*, no. 1 (2010).

4. "Working to Improve the Lives of People with Disabilities," PLAN Institute, accessed July 10, 2018, http://planinstitute.ca.

5. Google Calendar, accessed July 10, 2018, https://calendar.google.com.

6. Health Information Privacy, US Department of Health and Human Services, accessed July 7, 2018, https://www.hhs.gov/hipaa/index.html.

7. Ibid.

8. "CareZone—Easily Manage Multiple Medications and Health Information in One Place," accessed July 10, 2018, https://carezone.come/home.

9. "Care Calendar Website, Lotsa Helping Hands," accessed July 10, 2018, http://lotsahelpinghands.com.

10. "Personal Health Journals for Recovery, Cancer & More," Caring Bridge, accessed July 10, 2018, https://www.caringbridge.org/.

11. "Alska Connected Caregiving," accessed September 7, 2018, http://alska.com/; "Alska Is Caregiver Software That Simplifies Caregiving.—Start Your Free Trial," Alska, accessed July 10, 2018, http://alska.com/.

12. "Tyze Personal Networks," accessed September 7, 2018, http://www.tyze.com.

13. "CareRelay the Caregiver Portal," CareRelay, accessed September 7, 2018, http://carerelay.com.

CHAPTER 12: HOW TO KNOW WHAT YOU WANT AND GET WHAT YOU NEED

1. "Section 7. Lobbying Decisionmakers," Chapter 33. Community Tool Box, accessed November 25, 2018, https://ctb.ku.edu/en/table-of-contents/advocacy/direct-action/lobby-decisionmakers/main.

2. "About," Al Etmanski, accessed July 14, 2018, http://aletmanski.com/about/#bio.

3. "Solution-Based Advocacy: Advocating with Empathy," Planned Lifetime Advocacy Network, March 24, 2016, accessed November 13, 2018, http://plan.ca/2016/03/24/solution-based-advocacy-advocating-with-empathy/.

4. Jacqueline Stavros, David Cooperrider, and D. Lynn Kelley, "Strategic Inquiry with Appreciative Intent: Inspiration to SOAR!," *AI Practitioner: International Journal of Appreciative Inquiry 5* (2003): 10–17.

5. See Richard Tedeschi and Lawrence Calhoun, "Posttraumatic Growth: Conceptual Foundations and Empirical Evidence," *Psychological Inquiry 15*, no. 1 (2004).

CHAPTER 13: POWER AND LOVE = EMPOWERMENT

1. "Adam Kahane," Reos Partners, accessed July 25, 2018, https://reospartners.com/reos-management/adam-kahane/.

2. Adam Kahane, *Power and Love: A Theory and Practice of Social Change* (Oakland, CA: Berrett-Koehler), 2009. For definitions, see also "Power and Love," Adam Kahane at TEDxNavigli, accessed November 15, 2018, https://www.youtube.com/watch?v=1nPfpepxEuE.

3. Ibid., 104.

4. Sonia Lupien, "Trouble Obsessionnel Compulsif," accessed July 25, 2018, http://www.iusmm.ca/research/researchers/researchers/sonia-lupien.html.

5. The caregiver activist Vickie Cammack first used this analogy in conversation with Donna Thomson, https://www.donnathomson.com/2015/11/what-do-caregivers-need-from-health.html.

6. Donna Thomson, "Self Care? You Have to Be Kidding," accessed July 29, 2018, https://www.donnathomson.com/2017/12/self-care-you-have-to-be-kidding.html.

CHAPTER 14: CULTIVATING CONNECTION

1. Susannah Fox, Maeve Duggan, and Kristen Purcell, "Family Caregivers Are Wired for Health," *Pew Research Center: Internet & Technology*, June 30, 2013, http://www.pewinternet.org/2013/06/20/family-caregivers-are-wired-for-health/.

2. Kevin Wright and Stephen Rains, "Weak-Tie Support Network Preference, Health-Related Stigma, and Health Outcomes in Computer-Mediated Support Groups," *Journal of Applied Communication Research 41*, no. 3 (2013): 311.

3. Matching the particular support needs of those seeking support with the capacities of support providers is referred to as the Optimal Matching Model. Wright and Rains, "Weak-Tie Support," 311.

4. Thomas D'Agostino and Carma Bylund, "Nonverbal Accommodation in Healthcare Communication," *Health Communication 29*, no. 6 (2014), under "Nonverbal Communication in Healthcare Interactions," https://www.ncbi.nlm.nih.gov/pmc/articles/PMC4939478/.

5. Kevin Wright and Ahlam Muhtaseb, "Personal Relationships and Computer-Mediated Support Groups," in *Computer-Mediated Communication in Personal Relationships*, ed. Kevin Wright and Lynne Webb (New York: Peter Lang, 2011), 141.

6. D'Agostino and Bylund, "Nonverbal Accommodation in Healthcare Communication," under "Communication Accommodation Theory."

7. Wright and Rains, "Weak-Tie Support Network Preference," 319.

8. Joseph Walther, "Theories of Computer-Mediated Communication and Interpersonal Relations," in *The Sage Handbook of Interpersonal Communication*, 4th ed., ed. Mark Knapp and John Daly (Thousand Oaks, CA: Sage, 2011), 460.

9. Ibid., 461.

10. Wright and Rains, "Weak-Tie Support Network Preference," 319.

11. Walther, "Theories of Computer-Mediated Communication," 461–62.

12. James Pennebaker and Janel Seagal, "Forming a Story: The Health Benefits of Narrative," *Journal of Clinical Psychology 55*, no. 10 (1999): 1243.

13. Andrew High and Denise Solomon, "Locating Computer-Mediated Social Support within Online Communication Environments," in *Computer-Mediated Communication in Personal Relationships*, ed. Kevin Wright and Lynne Webb (New York: Peter Lang, 2011), 120–24.

14. Wright and Rains, "Weak-Tie Support Network Preference," 320.

15. Ibid., 319.

16. Miller McPherson, Lynn Smith-Lovin, and James Cook, "Birds of a Feather: Homophily in Social Networks," *Annual Review of Sociology 27* (2001): 415.

17. High and Solomon, "Locating Computer-Mediated Social Support," 124–32.

18. Lisa Sparks and Melinda Villagran, *Patient and Provider Interaction: A Global Health Communication Perspective* (Cambridge, UK: Polity, 2010), 120–21.

19. Sanghee Chun and Youngkhill Lee, "The Experience of Posttraumatic Growth for People with Spinal Cord Injury," *Qualitative Health Research 18*, no. 7 (August 2008): 887.

20. Howard Brody, *Stories of Sickness*, 2nd ed. (Oxford: Oxford University Press, 2003), 75.

21. Brody, *Stories of Sickness*, 76–78.

22. Walther, "Theories of Computer-Mediated Communication," 463–64.

CONCLUSION: A NEW WAY OF SEEING AND BEING

1. Kathy Charmaz, "The Body, Identity, and Self: Adapting to Impairment," *Sociological Quarterly 36*, no. 4 (1995): 672.

2. Juliet Corbin and Anselm Strauss, "Accompaniments of Chronic Illness: Changes in Body, Self, Biography, and Biographical Time," *Research in the Sociology of Health Care 6* (1987): 251, 276–78.

3. Arthur Frank, *The Wounded Storyteller: Body, Illness & Ethics*, 2nd ed. (Chicago: University of Chicago Press, 2013), Kindle e-book, chap. 7.

4. Kris Pizur-Barnekow, Amy Darragh, and Mark Johnston, "'I Cried Because I Didn't Know If I Could Take Care of Him': Toward a Taxonomy of Interactive and Critical Health Literacy as Portrayed by Caregivers of Children with Special Health Care Needs," *Journal of Health Communication 16* (2011), 211–14.

5. Ibid., 216–17.

6. Caregivers rated approximately half (47 percent) of their care experiences as "very meaningful." Gretchen Livingston, "Adult Caregiving Often Seen

as Very Meaningful by Those Who Do It," *Pew Research Center: FactTank: News in the Numbers,* November 8, 2018, http://www.pewresearch.org/fact-tank/2018/11/08/adult-caregiving-often-seen-as-very-meaningful-by-those-who-do-it/.

7. Yaacov Bachner and Sara Carmel, "Open Communication between Caregivers and Terminally Ill Cancer Patients: The Role of Caregivers' Characteristics and Situational Variables," *Health Communication 24,* no. 6 (2009): 530.

8. Frank, *The Wounded Storyteller,* Kindle e-book, chap. 7.

9. Michael Bury, "Chronic Illness as Biographical Disruption," *Sociology of Health and Illness, 4,* no. 2 (July 1982): 170. See also Charmaz, "Stories and Silences: Disclosures and Self in Chronic Illness," *Qualitative Inquiry 8,* no. 3 (2002): 314.

BIBLIOGRAPHY

"About." Al Emanski. Accessed July 14, 2018. http://aletmanski.com/about/#bio.

Active Aging Research Center. Center for Health Enhancement Studies (CHESS), University of Wisconsin. Accessed June 13, 2018. https://center.chess.wisc.edu/research-projects/view/active-aging-research-center.

"Adam Kahane," Reos Partners. Accessed July 25, 2018. https://reospartners.com/reos-management/adam-kahane.

Afifi, Walid, and Masaki Matsunaga. "Uncertainty Management Theories: Three Approaches to a Multifarious Process." In *Engaging Theories in Interpersonal Communication,* edited by Leslie Baxter and Dawn Braithwaite, 117–32. Thousand Oaks, CA: Sage, 2008.

The Aging and Disability Resource Center of Southwest Wisconsin. "Home Page." Accessed June 13, 2018. https://adrcswwi.org/.

Albrecht, Terrance, and Mara Adelman. *Communicating Social Support.* Thousand Oaks, CA: Sage, 1987.

Al-Mosaiwi, Mohammed, and Tom Johnstone. "In an Absolute State: Elevated Use of Absolutist Words Is a Marker Specific to Anxiety, Depression, and Suicidal Ideation." *Clinical Psychological Science 6*, no. 4 (2018): 119–24.

"Alska Connected Caregiving." Accessed September 7, 2018. http://alska.com/.

Ansberry, Clare. "America Is Running Out of Family Caregivers, Just When It Needs Them Most." *Wall Street Journal*, July 20, 2018. https://www.wsj.com/articles/america-is-running-out-of-family-caregivers-just-when-it-needs-them-most-1532094538.

Apker, Julie, Kathleen Propp, and Wendy Ford. "Negotiating Status and Identity Tensions in Healthcare Team Interactions: An Exploration of Nurse Role Dialectics." *Journal of Applied Communication Research 33*, no. 2 (2005): 93–115.

Ashforth, Blake, and Glen Kreiner. "'How Can You Do It?': Dirty Work and the Challenge of Constructing a Positive Identity." *Academy of Management Review 24*, no. 3 (1999): 413–34.

Ashforth, Blake, Glen Kreiner, and Mel Fugate. "All in a Day's Work: Boundaries and Micro Role Transitions." *Academy of Management Review 25*, no. 3 (July 2000): 472–91.

"Asperger Syndrome: Partners & Family of Adults with ASD (Portland, OR)." Meetup. Accessed July 12, 2018. https://www.meetup/Asperger-Syndrome -Partners-Family-of-Adults-with-ASD/.

"Atlas of Caregiving: CareMap Tutorial." Accessed June 25, 2018. https:// atlasofcaregiving.com/caremap-tutorial-2/

"Atlas of Caregiving: Digital CareMaps—How to Draw." Accessed June 25, 2018. https://vimeo.com/261399102.

"Atlas of Caregiving." Accessed June 25, 2018. https://atlasofcaregiving.com/.

Babrow, Austin, Chris Kasch, and Leigh Ford. "The Many Meanings of *Uncertainty* in Illness: Toward a Systematic Accounting." *Health Communication 10*, no. 1 (1998): 1–23.

Bachner, Yaacov, and Sara Carmel. "Open Communication between Caregivers and Terminally Ill Cancer Patients: The Role of Caregivers' Characteristics and Situational Variables." *Health Communication 24*, no. 6 (2009): 524–31.

Baxter, Leslie, and Dawn Braithwaite. "Relational Dialectics Theory: Crafting Meaning from Competing Discourses." In *Engaging Theories in Interpersonal Communication: Multiple Perspectives*, edited by Leslie Baxter and Dawn Braithwaite, 349–61. Los Angeles: Sage, 2008.

"Best Buddies International." Best Buddies International. Accessed July 12, 2018. http://www.bestbuddies.org/.

Biettie, Lucas, Ottilie Tilston, and Adrian Bangerter. "Storytelling as Adaptive Collective Sensemaking." *Topics in Cognitive Science* (2018), https:// onlinelibrary.wiley.com/doi/full/10.1111/tops.12358.

Bodie, Graham, and Susanne Jones. "The Nature of Supportive Listening II: The Role of Verbal Person Centeredness and Nonverbal Immediacy." *Western Journal of Communication 76*, no. 3 (2012): 250–69.

Brody, Howard. *Stories of Sickness*, 2nd ed. Oxford: Oxford University Press, 2003.

Brooks, David. "What Suffering Does." *New York Times*, April 7, 2014. https:// www.nytimes.com/2014/04/08/opinion/brooks-what-suffering-does.html.

Bury, Michael. "Chronic Illness as Biographical Disruption." *Sociology of Health and Illness 4*, no. 2 (July 1982): 167–82.

"Care Calendar Website," Lotsa Helping Hands. Accessed July 10, 2018. http://lotsahelpinghands.com/.

"Caregiver Statistics." Caregiver Action Network. Accessed July 4, 2018. http://caregiveraction.org/resources/caregiver-statistics.

"CareRelay the Caregiver Portal." CareRelay. Accessed September 7, 2018. http://carerelay.com.

"CareZone—Easily Manage Multiple Medications and Health Information in One Place." Accessed July 10, 2018. https://carezone.come/home.

"Caring across Generations." Accessed June 14, 2018. https://caringacross.org/why-care/.

Caughlin, John, Sylvia Mikucki-Enyart, Ashley Middleton, Anne Stone, and Laura Brown. "Being Open without Talking about It: A Rhetorical/Normative Approach to Understanding Topic Avoidance in Families after a Lung Cancer Diagnosis." *Communication Monographs 78*, no. 4 (2011): 409–36.

Charmaz, Kathy. "Stories and Silences: Disclosures and Self in Chronic Illness." *Qualitative Inquiry 8*, no. 3 (2002): 302–28.

———. "The Body, Identity, and Self: Adapting to Impairment." *The Sociological Quarterly 36*, no. 4 (1995): 657–80.

Chun, Sanghee, and Youngkhill Lee. "The Experience of Posttraumatic Growth for People with Spinal Cord Injury." *Qualitative Health Research 18*, no. 7 (August 2008): 877–90.

Clark, Sue. "Work/Family Border Theory: A New Theory of Work/Family Balance." *Human Relations 53*, no. 6 (2000): 747–70.

Corbin, Juliet, and Anselm Strauss. "Accompaniments of Chronic Illness: Changes in Body, Self, Biography, and Biographical Time." *Research in the Sociology of Health Care 6* (1987): 249–81.

Crouter, Ann. "Spillover from Family to Work: The Neglected Side of the Work-Family Interface." *Human Relations 37*, no. 6 (June 1984): 425–41.

D'Agostino, Thomas, and Carma Bylund. "Nonverbal Accommodation in Healthcare Communication." *Health Communication 29*, no. 6 (2014): 563–73. https://www.ncbi.nlm.nih.gov/pmc/articles/PMC4939478/.

Dainton, Marianne, and Elaine Zelley. "Social Exchange Theories: Interdependence and Equity." In *Engaging Theories in Family Communication: Multiple Perspectives*, edited by Dawn Braithwaite and Leslie Baxter, 243–59. Los Angeles: Sage, 2006.

"Entrevista Con Beatriz Angeles—El Impacto Del CareMap," Atlas of Caregiving. Accessed October 8, 2018, https://vimeo.com/256813229.

Farrell, Chris. "The Shortage of Home Care Workers: Worse Than You Think." *Forbes.com.* April 18, 2018. Accessed June 14, 2018. https://www.forbes.com/sites/nextavenue/2018/04/18/the-shortage-of-home-care-workers-worse-than-you-think/#1193ad9c3ddd.

"FIAO Brooklyn." Accessed July 12, 2018. http://www.fiaobrooklyn.org/community_services/social_services/.

"A First Look at Communication Theory." Transcript of Em Griffin's interview with Barnett Pearce, Creator of Coordinated Management of Meaning. Accessed August 1, 2018. https://www.afirstlook.com/docs/video-transcript-4.pdf.

Fisher, Walter. *Human Communication as Narration: Toward a Philosophy of Reason, Value, and Action.* Columbia: University of South Carolina Press, 1987.

Fox, Susannah, Maeve Duggan, and Kristen Purcell. "Family Caregivers Are Wired for Health." *Pew Research Center: Internet & Technology.* June 30, 2013. http://www.pewinternet.org/2013/06/20/family-caregivers-are-wired-for-health/.

Frank, Arthur. *The Wounded Storyteller: Body, Illness & Ethics*, 2nd ed. Chicago: University of Chicago Press, 2013. Kindle e-book.

Galvin, Kathleen, Dawn Braithwaite, and Carma Bylund. *Family Communication: Cohesion and Change*, 9th ed. New York: Routledge, 2015.

Gibson, Gail, and Susan Reinhard. *2015 Report: Caregiving in the U.S.* AARP and National Alliance for Caregiving (2015). https://www.aarp.org/content/dam/aarp/ppi/2015/caregiving-in-the-united-states-2015-report-revised.pdf.

Gilstrap, Cristina, and Zachary White. "'Like Nothing Else I've Ever Experienced': Examining the Metaphors of Residential Hospice Volunteers." In *Volunteering and Communication: Studies from Multiple Contexts*, edited by Michael Kramer, Laurie Lewis, and Loril Gossett, 149–68. New York: Peter Lang, 2013.

Goffman, Erving. *The Presentation of Self in Everyday Life*, monograph no. 2. Edinburgh: University of Edinburgh Social Sciences Research Centre, 1956.

Golding, Barry. "Men Learning through Life (and Men's Sheds)." *Adult Learning* 26, no. 4 (2015): 170–72.

Google Calendar. Accessed July 10, 2018. https://calendar.google.com/.

Green, Sarah, Christine Davis, Elana Karshmer, Pete Marsh, and Benjamin Straight. "Living Stigma: The Impact of Labeling, Stereotyping, Separation, Status Loss, and Discrimination in the Lives of Individuals with Disabilities and their Families." *Sociological Inquiry* 75, no. 2 (March 2005): 197–215.

Gregory, Susan. "Living with Chronic Illness in the Family Setting." *Sociology of Health & Illness* 27, no. 3 (April 2005): 372–92.

Harris, Julie, Deborah Bowen, Hoda Badr, Peggy Hannon, Jennifer Hay, and Katherine Regan Sterba. "Family Communication during the Cancer Experience." *Journal of Health Communication* 14, no. 1 (2009): 76–84.

Health Information Privacy. US Department of Health and Human Services. Accessed July 7, 2018. https://www.hhs.gov/hipaa/index.html.

High, Andrew, and Denise Solomon. "Locating Computer-Mediated Social Support within Online Communication Environments." In *Computer-*

Mediated Communication in Personal Relationships, edited by Kevin Wright and Lynne Webb, 119–55. New York: Peter Lang, 2011.

Iverson, Brett. "Richland Together Let's Connect." YouTube.com. Accessed June 13, 2018. https://www.youtube.com/watch?v=ObYBnG245S8.

Kahane, Adam. *Power and Love: A Theory and Practice of Social Change*. Oakland, CA: Berrett-Koehler Publishers, 2009.

Khazan, Olga. "How Loneliness Begets Loneliness." *The Atlantic,* April 6, 2017. https://www.theatlantic.com/health/archive/2017/04/how-loneliness-begets-loneliness/521841/.

Lawton, Julia. "Contemporary Hospice Care: The Sequestration of the Unbounded Body and 'Dirty Dying.'" *Sociology of Health & Illness 20*, no. 2 (March 2008): 121–43.

Leary, Mark, Eleanor Tate, Claire Adams, Ashley Allen, and Jessica Hancock. "Self-Compassion and Reactions to Unpleasant Self-Relevant Events: The Implications of Treating Oneself Kindly." *Journal of Personality and Social Psychology 92*, no. 5 (May 2007): 887–904.

Livingston, Gretchen. "Adult Caregiving Often Seen as Very Meaningful by Those Who Do It." *Pew Research Center: FactTank: News in the Numbers,* November 8, 2018. http://www.pewresearch.org/fact-tank/2018/11/08/adult-caregiving-often-seen-as-very-meaningful-by-those-who-do-it/.

Lupien, Sonia. "Trouble Obsessionnel Compulsif." Accessed July 25, 2018. http://www.iusmm.ca/recherche/chercheurs/lupien-sonia/publications-sonia-lupien.html

Malley, Ann, and Carole Kenner. "Transitions in Care: A Critical Review of Measurement." *Journal of Perioperative & Critical Intensive Care Nursing 2*, no. 4 (December 2016). https://www.ncbi.nlm.nih.gov/pmc/articles/PMC5656252/. Accessed June 25, 2018.

McArthur, John. *Digital Proxemics: How Technology Shapes the Way We Move*. New York: Peter Lang, 2016.

McPherson, Miller, Lynn Smith-Lovin, and James Cook. "Birds of a Feather: Homophily in Social Networks." *Annual Review of Sociology 27* (2001): 415–44.

Medved, Caryn. "The Everyday Accomplishment of Work and Family: Exploring Practical Actions in Daily Routines." *Communication Studies 55*, no. 1 (Spring 2004): 128–45.

Meisenbach, Rebecca. "Stigma Management Communication: A Theory and Agenda for Applied Research on How Individuals Manage Moments of Stigmatized Identity." *Journal of Applied Communication Research 38*, no. 3 (August 2010): 268–92.

"Men's Shed." Wikipedia. Accessed July 12, 2018. https://en.wikipedia.org/wiki/Men's_shed.

Miller, Katherine, Martha Shoemaker, Jennifer Willyard, and Penny Addison. "Providing Care for Elderly Parents: A Structurational Approach to Family Caregiving Identity." *Journal of Family Communication 8*, no. 1 (January 2008): 19–43.

Mongeau, Paul, and Mary Lynne Miller Henningsen. "Stage Theories of Relationship Development: Charting the Course of Interpersonal Communication." In *Engaging Theories in Interpersonal Communication*, edited by Leslie Baxter and Dawn Braithwaite, 363–76. Los Angeles: Sage, 2008.

National Alliance for Caregiving and AARP. "Research." Accessed June 14, 2018. http://www.caregiving.org/research/general-caregiving/.

Neff, Kristin. "The Development and Validation of a Scale to Measure Self-Compassion." *Self and Identity 2*, no. 3 (July 2003): 223–50.

Next Step in Care. Accessed June 25, 2018. https://www.nextstepincare.org/.

Nowogrodski, Avinoam. "Why Listening Might Be the Most Important Skill to Hire For." *Fast Company*. February 23, 2015. https://www.fastcompany.com/3042688/why-listening-might-be-the-most-important-skill-to-hire-for.

O'Hair, Dan, Melinda Villagran, Elaine Wittenberg, Kenneth Brown, Monica Ferguson, Harry Hall, and Timothy Doty. "Cancer Survivorship and Agency Model: Implications for Patient Choice, Decision Making, and Influence." *Health Communication 15*, no. 2 (2003): 193–202.

Parker, Kim, and Eileen Patten. "The Sandwich Generation." Pew Research Center, January 30, 2013. http://www.pewsocialtrends.org/2013/01/30/the-sandwich-generation/. Accessed June 14, 2018.

Pennebaker, James, and Janel Seagal. "Forming a Story: The Health Benefits of Narrative." *Journal of Clinical Psychology 55*, no. 10 (1999): 1243–54.

"Personal Health Journals for Recovery, Cancer & More." CaringBridge. Accessed July 10, 2018. https://www.caringbridge.org/.

"Pet Partners." Pet Partners.org. "Therapy Pets & Animal Assisted Activities." Accessed July 12, 2018. http://www.petpartners.org/.

Petronio, Sandra. *Boundaries of Privacy: Dialectics of Disclosure*. Albany: State University of New York Press, 2002.

Pizur-Barnekow, Kris, Amy Darragh, and Mark Johnston. "'I Cried Because I Didn't Know If I Could Take Care of Him': Toward a Taxonomy of Interactive and Critical Health Literacy as Portrayed by Caregivers of Children with Special Health Care Needs." *Journal of Health Communication 16* (2011): 205–21.

Posttraumatic Research Group, UNC Charlotte. "What Is PTG?" Accessed June 14, 2018. https://ptgi.uncc.edu/what-is-ptg/.

"Power and Love," Adam Kahane at TEDxNavigli. Accessed November 15, 2018, https://www.youtube.com/watch?v=1nPfpepxEuE.

"Resources." Asset Based Community Development Institute, DePaul University. Accessed June 13, 2018. https://resources.depaul.edu/abcd-institute/Pages/default.aspx.

Richardson, Brian, and Laura Maninger. "'We Were All in the Same Boat': An Exploratory Study of Communal Coping in Disaster Recovery." *Southern Communication Journal 81*, no. 2 (2016): 107–22.

Rutledge, Pamela. "The Psychological Power of Storytelling," *Psychology Today* (January 16, 2011). Accessed November 15, 2018. https://www.psychologytoday.com/us/blog/positively-media/201101/the-psychological-power-storytelling.

Schmidt-Hertha, Bernhard, Sabina Jelenc-Krašovec, and Marvin Formosa, *Learning across Generations in Europe: Contemporary Issues in Older Adult Education*. Rotterdam: Sense Publishers, 2014.

Sharf, Barbara, and Marsha Vanderford. "Illness Narratives and the Social Construction of Health." In *Handbook of Health Communication*, edited by Teresa Thompson, Alicia Dorsey, Roxanne Parrott, and Katherine Miller, 9–34. New York: Routledge, 2003.

Simpson, Barbara, and Brigid Carroll. "Re-viewing 'Role' in Processes of Identity Construction." *Organization 15*, no. 1 (2008): 29–50.

60 Minutes. "Helping Ease Childhood Trauma." March 11, 2018. https://www.cbs.com/shows/60_minutes/video/vm02T0fGuBx6X3KK_YPO5Kse6UBHxad8/treating-childhood-trauma/.

Skerrett, Patrick J. "Pets Can Help Their Humans Create Friendships, Find Social Support." Harvard Health Blog. October 30, 2015. Accessed July 12, 2018. https://www.health.harvard.edu/blog/pets-can-help-their-humans-create-friendships-find-social-support-201505067981.

"Solution-Based Advocacy: Advocating with Empathy." Planned Lifetime Advocacy Network. March 24, 2016. Accessed November 13, 2018. http://plan.ca/2016/03/24/solution-based-advocacy-advocating-with-empathy/.

Sparks, Lisa, and Melinda Villagran. *Patient and Provider Interaction: A Global Health Communication Perspective*. Cambridge, UK: Polity, 2010.

Stavros, Jacqueline, David Cooperrider, and D. Lynn Kelley. "Strategic Inquiry with Appreciative Intent: Inspiration to SOAR." *AI Practitioner: International Journal of Appreciative Inquiry 5* (2003): 10–17.

Stone, Douglas, Bruce Patton, and Sheila Heen. "Difficult Conversations: How to Discuss What Matters Most." In *Making Connections: Readings in Relational Communication*, 5th ed., edited by Kathleen Galvin, 223–31. New York: Oxford University Press, 2010.

Strafford, Laura. "Social Exchange Theories: Calculating the Rewards and Costs of Personal Relationships." In *Engaging Theories in Interpersonal Communication:*

Multiple Perspectives, edited by Dawn Braithwaite and Paul Schrodt, 403–15. Los Angeles: Sage, 2015.

Strang, Vicki R., Priscilla M. Koop, Suzanne Dupuis-Blanchard, Marlene Nordstrom, and Betty Thompson. "Family Caregivers and Transition to Long-Term Care." *Clinical Nursing Research 15*, no. 1 (2006): 27–45.

Tedeschi, Richard, and Lawrence Calhoun. "Posttraumatic Growth: Conceptual Foundations and Empirical Evidence." *Psychological Inquiry 15*, no. 1 (2004): 1–18.

Thomson, Donna. "Self Care? You Have to Be Kidding." The Caregivers' Living Room. Accessed July 29, 2018. https://www.donnathomson .com/2017/12/self-care-you-have-to-be-kidding.html.

Thorson, Allison, Christine Rittenour, Judy Koenig Kellas, and April R. Trees. "Quality Interactions and Family Storytelling." *Communication Reports 26*, no. 2 (2013): 88–100.

Tracy, Sarah, and Clifton Scott. "Sexuality, Masculinity, and Taint Management among Firefighters and Correctional Officers." *Management Communication Quarterly 20*, no. 1 (August 2006): 6–38.

"Trioova Home Page." Trioova. Accessed September 7, 2018. https://trioova.ca.

"Tyze Personal Networks." Tyze Personal Networks. Accessed September 7, 2018. http://www.tyze.com.

Umberson, Debra, and Jennifer Karas Montez. "Social Relationships and Health: A Flashpoint for Health Policy." *Journal of Health and Social Behavior 51*, no. 1 (2010): 254–66.

"Veteran Stories—The Memory Project." The Memory Project. Accessed July 12, 2018. http://www.thememoryproject.com/stories.

Walther, Joseph. "Theories of Computer-Mediated Communication and Interpersonal Relations." In *The Sage Handbook of Interpersonal Communication*, 4th ed., edited by Mark Knapp and John Daly, 443–79. Thousand Oaks, CA: Sage, 2011.

Way, Deborah, and Sarah Tracy. "Conceptualizing Compassion as Recognizing, Relating, and (Re)acting: A Qualitative Study of Compassionate Communication at Hospice." *Communication Monographs 79*, no. 3 (September 2012): 292–315.

"What Is a Community Kitchen?" Community Kitchens. Accessed July 12, 2018. http://communitykitchens.org.au/what-is-a-community-kitchen/.

White, Zachary, and Cristina Gilstrap. "Inside Patients' Homes: A Metaphorical Analysis of Home Hospice Nurses' Experiences Working with Dying Patients." *OMEGA—Journal of Dying and Death 72*, no. 4 (2016): 302–15.

White, Zachary, Cristina Gilstrap, and Jennifer Hull. "'Me against the World': Parental Uncertainty Management at Home Following Neonatal Intensive

Care Unit Discharge." *Journal of Family Communication* 17, no. 2 (October 2016): 105–16.

White, Zachary, and Cristina Gilstrap. "'People Just Don't Understand': Challenges Communicating Home Hospice Volunteer Role Experiences to Organizational Outsiders." *Management Communication Quarterly 31*, no. 4 (March 2017). http://journals.sagepub.com/doi/abs/10.1177/0893318917696991.

White, Zachary, and Jeremiah Wills. "Communicating about Chronic Caregiving in the Workplace: Employees' Disclosure Preferences, Intentions, and Behaviors." *Communication Research Reports 33*, no. 1 (2016): 32–39.

Willyard, Jennifer, Katherine Miller, Martha Shoemaker, and Penny Addison. "Making Sense of Sibling Responsibility for Family Caregiving," *Qualitative Health Research 18*, no. 12 (November 2008): 1673–86.

Wittenberg-Lyles, Elaine, Karla Washington, George Demiris, Debra Parker Oliver, and Sara Shaunfield. "Understanding Social Support Burden among Family Caregivers." *Health Communication 29*, no. 9 (2014): 901–10. https://www.ncbi.nlm.nih.gov/pmc/articles/PMC4029862/.

Witters, Dan, "Caregiving Costs U.S. Economy $25.2 Billion in Lost Productivity." *Gallup*. July 27, 2011. https://news.gallup.com/poll/148670/caregiving-costs-economy-%20billion-lost-productivity.aspx.

"Working to Improve the Lives of People with Disabilities." PLAN Institute. Accessed July 10, 2018. http://planinstitute.ca/.

Wright, Kevin, and Claude Miller. "A Measure of Weak-Tie/Strong-Tie Support Network Preference." *Communication Monographs 77*, no. 4 (December 2010): 500–517.

Wright, Kevin, and Ahlam Muhtaseb. "Personal Relationships and Computer-Mediated Support Groups." In *Computer-Mediated Communication in Personal Relationships*, edited by Kevin Wright and Lynne Webb, 137–55. New York: Peter Lang, 2011.

Wright, Kevin, and Stephen Rains. "Weak-Tie Support Network Preference, Health-Related Stigma, and Health Outcomes in Computer-Mediated Support Groups." *Journal of Applied Communication Research 41*, no. 3 (August 2013): 309–24.

Wright, Kevin, Lisa Sparks, and H. Dan O'Hair. *Health Communication in the 21st Century*. Malden, MA: Wiley-Blackwell, 2013.

Zhang, Amy, and Laura Siminoff. "Silence and Cancer: Why Do Families and Patients Fail to Communicate?" *Health Communication 14*, no. 4 (February 2003): 415–29.

INDEX